M000305708

Published by Innova1st Publishing 2018
Copyright © May 2018 Erich R. Bühler
Second Edition May 2019

en.innova1st.com

All rights reserved. No part of this publication may be reproduced, stored in a retrieval system, or transmitted in any form or by any means, electronic, mechanical, photocopying, recording or otherwise, without the prior written permission from the publisher.

Disclaimer
Every effort has been made to ensure that this book is free from error or omissions. Information provided is of general nature only and should not be considered legal or financial advice. The intent is to offer a variety of information to the reader. However, the author, publisher, editor or their agents or representatives shall not accept responsibility for any loss or inconvenience caused to a person or organization relying on this information.

Copyediting for English-language edition performed by James Gallagher, Castle Walls Editing LLC (www. castlewallsediting.com)
Copyediting for Spanish-language edition performed by Carol Libenson (Carol.libenson@gmail.com)
Spanish-English translation by Michelle Masella (masella.translation@gmail.com)
Book cover design and formatting services by Victor Marcos

ISBN: 978-1527222083 (pbk)

LEADING EXPONENTIAL CHANGE

Second Edition

ERICH R. BÜHLER

Contents

Acknowledgments

The initial drafts of this book, in both Spanish and English, have passed through multiple hands and undergone several revisions. Each revision provided me with invaluable feedback from the following collaborators. Their contributions enabled me to include additional concepts, refine ideas, increase my focus, and add clarity.

Without their support, this work wouldn't have evolved into the book you are now reading.

Stefan Sohnchen (New Zealand), Business Agile consultant. I thank Stefan for his keenly critical eye on every word written in this book. His questions about the ideas shared in this book, along with his professional insight and recommendations, led to many improvements.

Carol Libenson (Venezuela), proofreader and editor. Carol worked on the Spanish version, making it easier to read. She also provided excellent suggestions and ideas for enhancing the content.

Michelle Masella (USA), Spanish–English translator. In addition to putting together the initial English draft, Michelle offered suggestions that helped improve both versions of the book.

Adeyinka Adesanya (New Zealand). Thank you, Yinka, for fine-tuning the work.

Victor Marcos (Philippines), book cover designer and typesetter. I thank Victor for his dedication and the time spent away from his family to ensure this book was ready in record time.

James Gallagher (USA), copy editor. James worked on the final draft of the English version, polishing the manuscript and helping to connect readers with the author's vision.

My thanks, as well, to those who contributed their real stories: **Carlton Nettleton** (USA), **Claudia Patricia Salas** (Spain), **Sebastian Vetter** (Germany), **Stefan Sohnchen** (New Zealand).

Last but not least, thank you, **Amparo Sánchez**, for your unconditional support during the year I invested in making this achievement a reality.

Introduction

Why did I choose NOT to write a book about Agile, Lean, or Scrum and choose instead to write about the rules that govern change—and about how these rules can be used for the transition to better, more flexible companies?

Historically, we have thought that evolution is linear and cumulative, that one idea leads to another, and that this next idea will lead to a new discovery. Following this pattern, advances are predictable, and people have time to adapt.

Current technology, though, has changed how evolution takes place, and we are now witnessing *exponential change*. Companies are facing markets in an accelerated process of change. There is more information available. Consumers are connecting with each other via technology and developing ever more advanced ideas. Computers are increasing in capacity and artificial intelligence. All of this results in greater innovation, but also, in a future that isn't as easy to anticipate as it once was.

Products, especially software, have altered day-to-day activities and changed consumer habits, even in people's private lives. If you look around, you'll notice that many of these products were provided by companies that did not exist a few years ago. Although they may seem to have appeared from out of nowhere, these new companies have succeeded by offering exceptional ideas and services while employing innovative methods for managing employees.

You might think that these companies got lucky, that they were "*in the right place, at the right time,*" or that they simply hired some very smart people. But even if all this was true, it would only account for a minor fraction of their success.

These new companies have taken advantage of new market opportunities. They have made use of new technologies, and they've helped their people feel more comfortable working collaboratively in places with highly varying tasks.

Many of the leaders I've helped have been paying special attention to these organizations. These leaders realize that change is now a mandatory requirement for facing new challenges.

Just as cloud computing, artificial intelligence and Big Data are essential components in the digital company, so are new ways of thinking, methodologies and frameworks.

Lean, Agile, Scrum, SAFe, LeSS, and Scrum at Scale have helped organizations to grow and improve more quickly, increasing learning and giving clients new possibilities.

With the exception of Lean, these techniques, or mindsets, have been created to improve the development of software products. They are, therefore, difficult to adapt when we want to transform an entire company.

It is no longer enough to understand framework functionalities, principles, or techniques, or new ways to manage people. We must also understand deeper factors of organizational change and learn how these can help entire companies to improve.

Most consultants and leaders agree that changing an organization is an emotional roller coaster. There's sheer satisfaction when individuals learn and believe the trip was worthwhile, but conflict arises when individuals or teams do not want to change.

On many occasions, people stop supporting the business-transformation initiative, or it loses traction for no apparent reason, making the plan more complex. This happens because human beings are not biologically prepared for constant change. In fact, having to adapt quickly to highly volatile environments increases a person's resistance to change.

Knowing why this happens and having the tricks and techniques to accelerate transformation without a substantial loss of traction—or putting your company's stability at risk—is part of what I will convey in this book.

In the following pages, I provide the fundamentals for understanding what happens in highly volatile environments. Relying on psychology and neuroscience applied to organizational change, I have included ideas, techniques, and activities for accelerating your company's transformation.

You will find innovative techniques for coping with resistance to change, recommendations on how to make difficult decisions, and effective ways to prepare the organization for exponential growth.

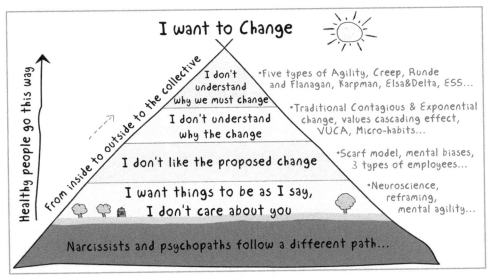

FIGURE 1: Five mindsets and the techniques you'll learn here (c) Erich R. Bühler

I also explain how to help teams with low motivation levels, and I describe the differences between traditional, contagious, and exponential change, so that you can distinguish between them and implement your ideas more easily.

I've tried to make this book enjoyable and useful for any executive, manager, change agent, business consultant, Agile Coach, Scrum Master, or anyone else wanting to reinvent their company.

Throughout the book, you will find real stories by consultants from different countries and cultures, and these stories will allow you to gain a wide variety of perspectives.

How to Use This Book?

I recommend reading Chapters 1 through 6 in order, but if you wish to jump ahead, reading Chapter 1 will give you the background for understanding Chapters 7 and 8 (Enterprise Social Systems).

The first two chapters explain the situation in which companies currently find themselves. These chapters describe an exponential company, what differentiates it from traditional organizations, and why it's necessary to have an exponential company.

Chapters 3 and 4 expand on the techniques of business transformation and show how the brain acts in each case. I also present activities for facing resistance to change and offer suggestions on how to work with teams that have lost motivation.

Chapters 5 and 6 present methods for accelerating the transformation of the company and offer suggestions so that any change is easy to scale.

Finally, Chapters 7 and 8 focus on Enterprise Social Systems, providing solid foundations for creating new processes and frameworks that support the rapid evolution of your company.

Chapter 8, in particular, explains the ELSA and DeLTA change frameworks. While the first framework can be used when the company's leaders actively support the transformation of the company, the second can be used when they are not yet involved.

As you progress, you will see that I have tried to stay away from subjects for which there is already plenty of information, such as Agile, Scrum, Lean, or

Lean Startup. This has been a challenge, because there's a close link between these and many of the points in this book.

I believe a good balance has been achieved, though, and references for additional information are indicated by the following icons:

Additional information on a specific topic.

Recommendations for specific, ready-to-use techniques or activities.

At the end of each chapter, you will find a summary and guided self-reflection questions to help confirm and strengthen your learning.

I also refer to other authors and research for digging deeper. My belief is that this book will provide you with the knowledge to accelerate the transformation of your company. Good luck!

Erich R. Bühler

From Zero to a Million in Two Seconds

CHAPTER 1

> "It is a mistake to think that moving fast is the same as actually going somewhere."

Steve Goodier, Writer

How is it possible that no more than a few electoral polls correctly predicted the presidency of Donald Trump? Why did Brexit take so many by surprise?

For many, these surprises came like a bolt from the blue. Some may have recognized the possibility of such events, but they were *remote* possibilities, and even the most established prediction techniques showed them to be unlikely.

I would never have imagined that a simple search engine like Google would dominate the world of information, that we would stop using SMS, or that Apple would resurface as an industry front-runner. The world is more complex than ever before, moving and changing at an incredible rate. No one is immune, not even the most successful leaders of today's best-known companies.

Shocking events and surprises are part of daily life. We can access more information in a week than a president two decades ago could access during an entire term in office. Unfortunately, all this input makes it harder to foresee and adapt to what's coming next.

Thanks to social media, information travels instantly, without borders. People from different cultures and corners of the world can collaborate using software tools, and they can reach conclusions that are more thought-out and elaborate than previously possible. Watching the world premiere of a film while sitting comfortably on your sofa is no longer a problem. You can play video games online with someone on the other side of the planet or acquire specific, high-quality knowledge without having to attend university. And yet, when it comes to knowing what's going to happen in the next few weeks, we're at a loss, and it's only getting worse. But foreseeing the near future is something companies need to do to establish effective change and adaptation tactics that will position them strategically within the market.

Perhaps, like me, you lived through the nineties, when creating a new product meant using well-established practices and methods. Everything was standardized. It was a culture of cumulative progress. Innovation occurred naturally, following processes that involved sharing opinions on known and controlled subjects. You had an idea, I built on it, someone else built on my idea, and so on in a linear and predictable way. Back then, we knew what our next product updates would look like. We could even create prototypes that gave us a rough idea of where we were heading in the next five years. The future seemed relatively stable. Taking firm steps to create a new service and run with it was something that required only well-known business skills. Knowing our client base and following the steps laid down by standard methodologies helped solve most day-to-day problems.

It was always the same story: There was an initial idea. The product was created and produced as cheaply as possible. Finally, the product was launched through distribution channels or intermediaries. At its core, the process involved hiring a large number of employees and accessing extensive space to develop the idea.

Distributors were a key part of the equation, because they got our products to the people who'd buy them. Success and return on investment were virtually guaranteed—as long as the competition didn't get ahead of us. Then we'd begin working on the next version, and the cycle would repeat, over and over again.

As you've probably noticed, the evolution of the Internet has changed the story dramatically. A company with a couple of employees can now create a service or product that alters the rules of the market—and can be delivered in a matter of weeks.

Today, it's possible for a world-class business to suddenly dissolve for no apparent reason. It isn't just the relationship between the size of a company and its impact that has changed. Artificial intelligence, augmented reality, and robotics are also affecting companies, the speed with which they need to adapt, and their methods for obtaining and analyzing market feedback.

We no longer think in terms of copying the competition. It's now innovation that moves markets in new directions. We no longer build a business as a group of individuals following a plan or list of repetitive tasks. Rather, we provide an environment in which employees feel motivated, learn, and have the freedom to modernize and evolve the way they work. No longer do we tell employees how to do their jobs. We encourage them to self-organize around the problems they face and to discover new habits that will enable them to find collective solutions.

Society is also advancing astronomically thanks to technologies that are changing the way companies are structured, and this is part of the new challenge leaders are facing.

The Decade of Moore's Law

In 1965, Gordon Moore predicted that the number of transistors in a processor would double approximately every two years, and that this trend would continue for decades. His assertion is an example of cumulative growth. If we want to understand why companies are changing so rapidly, Moore's law seems like a good place to start. Keep in mind, though, that this will be only part of the answer.

Let me guess. Your iPhone or equivalent smart device isn't farther away than arm's length, perhaps in your pocket as you're reading this. If so, you probably realize the huge processing power contained within those few square inches. The most sophisticated phones today can process at a rate around 600 gigaflops.

The Gigaflop is a measuring unit for calculating the speed of a microprocessor. 1 Gigaflop equals 1 billion floating-point operations per second.

At the time this book was published, the iPhone X was selling in the United States for about $1,000. It offers the same processing power that would have cost you $12 million in 1997, or $15 trillion in 1984. These devices are incredibly powerful, and more people in the world have access to a smartphone than to drinking water. Realizing this is the first step to understanding how technology is accelerating change and why businesses must find new ways to operate and develop new frameworks to adapt.

The Era of Accelerating Returns

In 1999, Raymond Kurzweil, recognized futurist and the director of engineering at Google, proposed the *law of accelerating returns*. According to Kurzweil, the rate of change in a wide variety of evolutionary systems tends to increase exponentially when their systems are converted into *digital information*.

Take, for example, the processing power of your phone or other easily purchased electronic device. That processing power will multiply in a year, regardless of whether it doubles its circuits. This is because everyday discoveries are made that affect the speed of processors. Speed multiplies because devices and people interconnect. Think of domestic appliances that use the web to obtain information, or the possibilities the Internet offers in connecting individuals and ideas. That's why you must take into account the habits of modern-day society and the impact of computers on the network of people (including smart gadgets, electronics, and software). Every day, tens of millions of people are accessing ever-cheaper technologies with power that will multiply in the next twelve months.

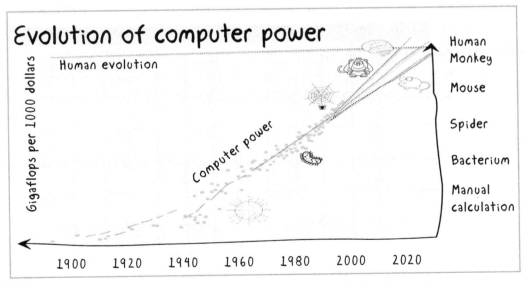

FIGURE 1.1: Kurzweil's exponential acceleration of results, based on Raymond Kurzweil

In 2023, according to Kurzweil, people will have phones capable of processing the same amount of information as the human brain—and by 2050, of all the brains on the planet combined. This prediction applies not only to phones but to any technological device, including the software a business uses to discover, create, or improve products or services.

Even if you still think Kurzweil's exponential acceleration is no more than an optimistic prediction, it is clear that the way products evolve is accelerating enormously.

The curve in Figure 1.1 is exponential, even though the line is relatively flat in its early stages. Each increment represents an increase in power between 10 and 100 times. Had we drawn the line cumulatively, it would easily reach Mars from your home.

The previously manual processes in many markets have been transferred to a microprocessor. Take photo processing. Around 1850, it would take weeks or even months to get your wedding photos. The tedious chemical process, done manually, required precise knowledge of the steps and chemical reactions involved. By 1950, the process had been simplified by advances in developing equipment and solutions. This reduced the processing time from weeks to days and required less expertise. But in the 1990s, a momentous event occurred, and photography entered the mainstream consumer's price range. Photography had changed forever. *Can you guess what happened?*

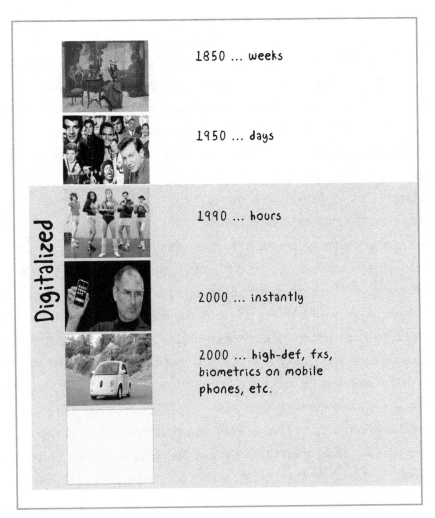

1850 ... weeks

1950 ... days

1990 ... hours

2000 ... instantly

2000 ... high-def, fxs, biometrics on mobile phones, etc.

Digitalized

FIGURE 1.2: Exponential evolution of photography

In the nineties, processes were digitalized, and cameras became sufficiently powerful at an affordable price. Photographs were transferred from a physical to a virtual form (computerized), becoming ones and zeros. From that moment on, there was an exponential acceleration in development similar to the curve on the Kurzweil graph. At this point, not only was it possible to instantly obtain photographs, but an extremely rapid evolution of the product had been sparked.

Kodak's first digital camera weighed 3.5 kilos (7.7 pounds) and had a whopping 0.01 megapixels. Today, we carry 17-megapixel cameras in our pockets. We can add special effects, crop images, and retouch photos. We can even make biometric evaluations in a matter of seconds. I will explain later how and why Kodak's digital-innovation strategy failed.

Every time manual processes pass from physical to digital (that is, composed of ones and zeros), there follows an evolution pattern that involves exponential acceleration. This is why future innovation is difficult to predict, leaving businesses open to constant surprises.

Before we move on, allow me to further illustrate what's happening to help you better understand why it's so difficult to predict the near future.

Imagine you and I are on a path, heading to a town on the outskirts of your city, and I ask you to take thirty steps in any direction. I could easily predict where you'd end up, assuming each step is about 80 cm, or 31 inches, long. If I told you that each step had to be 20% longer than the previous, you'd end up much farther away, but I'd still be able to guess where you'd end up, because the results are clearly cumulative.

The real challenge comes when I tell you that the length of each step must be exponentially greater than the previous. The first five or six steps would be easy to predict. We could even confuse those first couple of steps with a linear progression, since they'd be quite small. But as you go on, making a prediction would become increasingly more difficult, bearing in mind that the distance between steps 29 and 30 would be about twenty-six times the earth's orbit! Big jumps like this make it very difficult to guess where you'd be after each step, and it only gets harder. I could predict that step 29 would be large, but I'd have no idea where you'd land.

This is how exponential acceleration impacts on products, and this shift requires that companies adapt faster than ever. Business leaders who rely only on traditional techniques and methods will find it difficult to create an organization that can adapt quickly enough to the current market.

In the early stages of an exponential process, you can use tried-and-tested ways of working, because at this point the process is still linear and cumulative. But once it starts to accelerate, everything changes, and you'll have to find a new approach if you want your company to succeed.

Digital-product innovation follows an exponential pattern of development. This makes it difficult to know where your product or company will stand in its next version and to predict the direction your competition will take in the coming months. When a process or task is digitalized, its speed goes from zero to a million in a matter of weeks—instead of decades, as we were once accustomed to.

So the problems we face can change at any time, and expectations are altered. This exponential pattern of development impacts on how we interact, and ultimately it influences society as a whole.

Unfortunately, exponential technological growth is counterintuitive to the way our brain perceives the world. We are biologically programmed for life in an environment where events follow each other sequentially, and where evolution is cumulative. Because of this, all too many current business practices make it hard for employees to adapt. So how can you lead business transformation if common practices are becoming obsolete? What direction do you take if the future is so uncertain?

Change requires that we modify the foundation of our company, reason differently, and develop habits that enable us to acquire new skills in record time. But we must first understand why human beings cannot adapt to change so rapidly, and what tricks can be employed to overcome some of the obstacles. There are also social patterns we must examine—patterns derived from how we relate to one another in highly hierarchical organizations and patterns that prevent things from moving faster.

If all this isn't reason enough to see reality through a different lens, business leaders, consultants, and coaches face a further challenge: technology is constantly learning.

When a Tesla car collided with another vehicle, the company run an update to make sure it wouldn't happen again in the same way. The change affected not only that one vehicle but all the cars of the same model. The result was rapid, uniform technological "learning."

But humans learn differently. We have to wait months, or even generations, to pass on learning and ensure that a group of people do not repeat the same mistake. This is why we need techniques that enable us to incorporate and apply learning more rapidly.

Change in the Era of Exponential Acceleration

You probably bought this book in part to learn how to make a change in your business and create a remarkable organization that offers superior products and services. But perhaps you're not sure whether your company has products that will accelerate exponentially, or you might be unsure how to identify the current stage of your products. If this is what you're thinking, you're not alone.

You're probably familiar with the Kodak company and even have childhood memories involving film that had to be developed. You might remember how it felt when we discovered what good (or bad) photographers we were. Kodak was huge back then. By the late seventies, it had 140,000 employees and a 28-billion-dollar market. It was practically a monopoly, and apart from Fujifilm, few companies dared, or had the strength, to take it on. In the United States, Kodak controlled 90 percent of the cinematographic market and 85 percent of the still-camera market. But only decades later, the company was bankrupt.

Kodak started out producing and selling photography development equipment, gradually moving into cameras for end consumers. In 1975, Steven Sasson, a twenty-four-year-old engineer, fresh out of university, demonstrated the first digital camera. It was bulky and took twenty-four seconds to take a black-and-white photo. Kodak's management asked Sasson if he could calculate how long it would take for the digital camera to displace the paper-based industry. He came up with an estimate based on Moore's law, and that's when the problems began. The existing camera had 0.01 megapixels, and if this number doubled every two years, as Moore predicted, it would take ten to twelve years to reach the two megapixels required for acceptable image resolution. So managers who thought the new digital camera would undermine their chemical and photographic paper business decided to bury the idea.

What these managers failed to realize was that the leap the digital camera would undertake was exponential rather than cumulative, as Moore suggested, and they surely couldn't have imagined the social impact this would have. Remember the example of the thirty steps? Well, doubling in the digital world is unusually deceptive, and we are not ready for it. Sasson was right in that there would be a disruption of the paper-based photography market, but the impact was to be much greater than he had imagined.

That's when we learned that digital products, regardless of market niche or technology, accelerate after an initial stage of absolute calm. This means that companies must be ready to adapt ever more rapidly. For some companies, this will entail growing their development teams. For others, it will mean an increase in the list of things to do or shifts in their internal structures to better respond to their markets. The adaptation process might reveal that resources within the organization are scarce. Digital products accelerate exponentially, learn uniformly, and force businesses to be increasingly more flexible each day.

During its initial stages, a digital product evolves slowly, which can mislead people into believing that it will grow in a linear fashion. Although it's true that at first you can use traditional techniques to manage products, as soon as the evolution curve accelerates, everything changes, and this will catch you off guard if you're not ready.

Steven Kotler and Peter H. Diamandis, authors of Abundance: The Future Is Better Than You Think, point out that the six Ds of Exponentials have to be considered to identify the stage of acceleration a product has reached. The six Ds are a chain reaction that enable us to recognize what comes next. The following six Ds thereby help us make better, more informed decisions. These six Ds are:

1. **Digitalization**
2. **Deception**
3. **Disruption**
4. **Demonetization**
5. **Dematerialization**
6. **Democratization**

The first step for something to accelerate exponentially, and possibly surprise us, is for its process to go **Digital**. Once this happens, it can propagate at the speed of light—or at least the speed of the Internet—and become free to reproduce and share. This propagation follows a consistent pattern: an evolution or growth curve that is exponential (although it looks linear in the early stages). In the case of Kodak, once film changed from a physical to a digital medium, its rate of growth turned totally unpredictable.

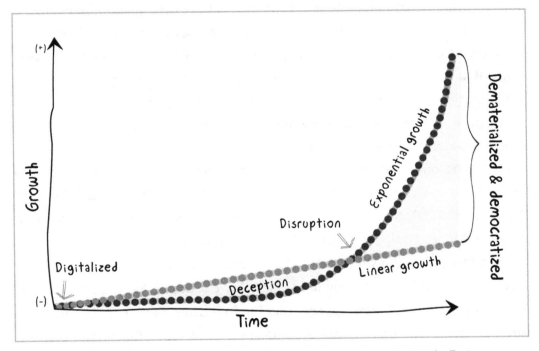

FIGURE 1.3: The impact of exponential growth and the six Ds

This is followed by the Deceptive growth phase. The first 0.01 megapixel Kodak camera went unnoticed for a long time. It grew from 0.01 to 0.02, 0.04, and 0.08 megapixels, and this certainly seemed linear enough. Again, remember that the first steps in an exponential curve produce small changes and are consequently confused with a linear process, tempting many to use traditional methods to manage growth. No one would want a 0.04 or even a 0.16 megapixel camera. The industry carried on looking the other way, and leadership continued thinking that the product would have no short-term impact.

What comes next is deceptive early growth, or so-called market Disruption. Think back to the steps illustration again. From steps 15 or 20 onward, growth turned unimaginable. As it relates to a specific product, this means that the market is left perplexed. Competing companies won't know how it was possible that something, in such early stages, could grow so quickly, and they will struggle in deciding how to respond. The first camera was 0.01 megapixels. Then, all of a sudden, it was ten megapixels—and you have to compete with them. Surprise!

You won't see much change in the early stages of a product. It's only in later stages that the line begins to curve upward. This is simply the nature of exponential multiplication—things happen slowly before accelerating abruptly.

Because photographs are now bits (Demonetization & Dematerialization), cameras become smaller and begin to be integrated into other devices. At this point, you no longer have a camera. You have a mobile phone with the functionality of a camera, as well as music, and a long list of added functionalities. Think of all the luxury technologies of the eighties that have been dematerialized and are now incorporated into a single device at the same, or much lower, price.

The last phase is Democratization. Technology makes it possible to take pictures without having to buy film, much less develop it. Everything is digital. You can download editing applications for free or at a low cost ($1 to $3 in any app store). The possibilities are endlessly more accessible and affordable. Mobile phones are a classic example of democratization. In the eighties, they were considered luxury technology, products we'd only see on programs such as Miami Vice. But today, just about anyone can buy one.

The six Ds cycle repeats itself with any product or process that goes digital. If you try to use work methods that do not account for this concept, your method may work reasonably well—until you reach the third stage, Disruption. This will be deceptive at first, because standard metrics will give you the illusion that everything is under control.

Managers and employees may be happy for a few months, drawing up their long-term plans and predictions. However, the situation will turn chaotic as soon as growth of the competing product starts to multiply—exponentially. And that's when the team will get nervous, and management will mistakenly want to exercise more control to get the results they are hoping for. But more control will not give way to rapid adaptation.

Focusing on a Healthy Organization

If markets are stable and the evolution of innovation is predictable, you could use rigid processes to ensure everything is under control. Problems arise when threats to success cannot be controlled, are mostly unpredictable, and accelerate over time. And we must add the deceptive initial stages, which falsely lead us to believe that a linear evolution is involved. Under this insecurity, you'll have to look for solutions to enable your business to adapt and thrive.

For several decades, the mantra of successful organizations was to maintain a strategy that aligned people around long-term objectives and well-structured plans. But this promotes neither development nor constant adaptation, and I'll explain this further in later chapters.

Innovation is constrained by deep-rooted beliefs such as micromanaging people and results to increase performance and production. Whereas a single idea can change the course of history, a hundred can go unnoticed in a micromanaged business. Therefore, a different approach is needed to handle employees' habits, their coordination and motivation, the way their minds reason and resolve problems, the power distribution within the company, and the objectives that are shared when creating a product. We also need to consider the best ways to lay out the physical environment and the best ways to tackle conflict when exponential acceleration causes a market change.

> Today, competitive advantage doesn't go to the company with the best widget. It goes to the organization that can reinvent itself and defend itself from attackers—wherever they may come from—better than anyone else.
>
> Colin Price, Senior Business Consultant.

We've only recently begun facing the exponential growth challenge with new project management options like Scrum, Kanban, eXtreme Programming, Lean Startup, and new mindsets such as Six Sigma, Lean, and Agile. These developments have been extremely positive, and they've enabled businesses to develop better products and deliver them more rapidly. Thanks to these options, businesses are now able to do the following:

▶ Give added importance to the company's values and principles when creating services and products.
▶ Focus on what really impacts clients.
▶ Use smaller teams and give added importance to their interactions.
▶ Work in short work cycles that permit the rapid creation of products or services and greater interaction with the client, which in turn increases mutual learning.
▶ Increase transparency in the organization to reduce the complexity of processes and activities.
▶ Devote time to reflect on what hasn't turned out as well and establish action plans for continuous improvement.
▶ Evolve products through experimentation.

Still, trained business-transformation consultants are often stumped when they work with companies that employ seemingly irrational behavior. They teach employees modern working habits, but all too often these don't have the desired impact. More is needed than understanding and using a new business framework or process. The present challenge requires other advanced skills:

▶ Mastering organizational social patterns.
▶ Making positive mental states go viral.
▶ Understanding how the brain works (neuroscience) and using this in our favor to create better business strategies.

▶ Turning individual tasks into collaborative efforts.
▶ Using experimentation techniques in all areas of the business, not solely within software-development departments.

When the speed of change defies comprehension, employees must be able to arrive at ideas and consensus through collaboration. But confronting exponential acceleration is difficult if we don't first build an organization with healthy habits. Achieving this is what I explain in this book.

A healthy business is one in which people feel confident, where there are fewer political decisions and greater collaborative effort, where conflict is used as a tool for continuous improvement, and where individuals can find and use techniques to overcome human limitations when facing constant change. Companies unable to create this kind of environment will fail at becoming exponential. Their dysfunctions will grow and bar them from adapting quickly.

You could work in a vast, conventionally hierarchical, monopoly organization awash with money, fantastic TV ads, and end consumers who have little option but to use its services. But this company will never succeed in the era of exponential acceleration. Companies like this are unable to produce high-impact innovation and are destined to copy others. They find it hard to understand, or implement, the ingredients to build a healthy company that's capable of adapting to market surprises.

When companies are organizationally healthy, they adapt better to new situations and their strategy is sustainable over time. This requires changing habits and beliefs and having technology in areas where resources are scarce.

Over the span of five years, Workplace Dynamics LLC, a consulting firm specializing in human resources, conducted hundreds of interviews with employees in the United States.

They found the following connections between healthy businesses and success:

- A desire to create a clear path for the future.
- A culture of high performance and a sense of execution.
- A strong connection between employees and the company's culture.
- A clear purpose for the company's activities.
- An appreciation for the work.

Workplace Dynamics also evaluated the performance of organizations that were considered healthy. To the surprise of many, they outperformed the Standard & Poor's 500 index by 48 percent, generating an equivalent to an average of 12.5 percent in additional revenue annually.

The consulting firm McKinsey & Company also carried out a survey of hundreds of companies, adding an additional perspective to understanding why initiatives for change often fail. Fewer than 30 percent of the participating companies said it was because of inadequate resources, poor planning, bad ideas, or unexpected market events. Surprisingly, 70 percent pinned the problem on employee reluctance to change or unproductive management behavior.

To change an organization, we must improve the way individuals connect, the way they resolve conflict, and the way they solve problems in areas with scarce resources.

Allow me to pause here for a moment. Exponential acceleration clearly places a lot of pressure on how people work, think, and share knowledge, which would increase conflict in any organization. Runde and Flanagan's conflict resolution model could help you determine where your company stands. *Is your company ready for massive change, or only for some habit adjustments?*

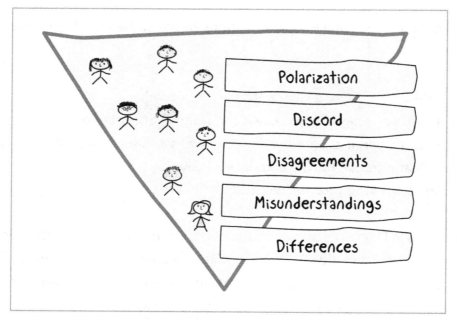

FIGURE 1.4: Runde and Flanagan's conflict framework

At the first level, **Differences**, people or teams see a problem from different points of view, different mindsets, and varying interests. But they are aware of this. This happens every day at the companies I help. There are arguments, but in the end everyone cooperates, and then they go and have a beer together. Differences are seen as something positive.

The second level, **Misunderstandings**, involves one of the most common problems in traditional organizations: interpreting a situation differently because of a lack of transparency, an inability to know what the other person expects, or not being "*on the same page*" regarding the business. The solution may lie in making expectations clear, speaking openly and clearly, and increasing face-to-face communication. At this level, it's still relatively easy to get employees to use new working habits and kick-start exponential growth in your product and market.

Level 3, **Disagreements**, occurs when people see a situation differently and (however well they understand the other person's position) remain upset that the person disagrees with them. This situation could be the result of a company without a clear definition of the business value for a single product or a company that has conflicting goals. The company might use methodologies with processes incompatible with the company's principles or make decisions based on assumptions versus experimentation. This level of conflict can be extremely productive if it is taken as an opportunity for improvement and change. Part of the solution here is to thrash out explicit working agreements that reinforce transparency, increase experimentation, engage people in common goals, and provide the necessary time for reflection at the end of each work cycle. In this case, you'll have to focus efforts on acquiring such habits before adding new processes or working structures that will tackle exponential growth.

The fourth level, **Discord**, marks a break from the first three, as it is here that we begin to see adverse effects on interpersonal relations. You can tell this level has been reached when individuals criticize each other, avoid each other, and block colleagues' initiatives. The conflict is then very likely to escalate to the next level, **Polarization**. At this point, opponents try to recruit allies to their cause and the tactical objective is exclusively to win the battle—with no regard to how it benefits the company.

The first three levels can be extremely productive in the creation of an outstanding business, but the last two are dysfunctional and lead to a loss of trust, focus, and sense of execution. So before taking a step toward change, analyze the level of conflict at your company. Exponential acceleration of results could aggravate problems, so you should have the right environment before setting out.

Empirical Learning

Just about everyone has heard of Louis Pasteur (1822–1895), the person who made your morning milk safe to drink. This is probably his greatest contribution to society, but he's responsible for much more than *pasteurization*. During Pasteur's time, doctors believed there were four different body fluids (blood, phlegm, yellow bile, and black bile) and that these were behind most diseases. When all four fluids were in harmony, a person was healthy. If the fluids weren't in harmony, a person would fall ill.

This theory was known as humorism, and doctors based all their practices on it, even though they had no idea why imbalances occurred. Almost everyone followed the theory, and because of this, many patients died because doctors misunderstood the cause of the illnesses.

The key to Pasteur's success wasn't simply his research explaining what made people ill, but rather that he based his work on an idea called the germ theory of diseases, proposed by Girolamo Fracastoro in 1546. Pasteur and Robert Koch worked to prove that germs were transmitted through a process in which microorganisms, which live everywhere, invade and reproduce inside hosts, making them ill.

As you can see, theories help us ask the right questions and provide us with a powerful lens to study problems from different perspectives. Just as Pasteur did not conform to the common thought process of his time, it's imperative that we also recognize potentially flawed mechanisms and adopt new ways of working.

Changing existing mechanisms and adopting new ways of working are key to solving problems, but attempting to do so is futile if you do not have the right conditions. You must understand organizational patterns to make progress in your company, because, by default, your ideas compete against established behaviors and shortcuts that have been in the company for years.

Your teams should have real experiences and establish a working style that proves it's possible to advance in a different direction. Closer observation and overcoming the temptation of deep-rooted habits, as well as constantly developing the processes you find yourself immersed in, are part of the solution to the exponential acceleration problem.

Some companies want to take a great leap in the dark without having first established essential habits. Take the software industry. In the nineties, managers thought that strictly controlling processes and people was the best way to create a product (Prince2, Waterfall, etc.). The assumption was that every step in the creation of a software application should be clearly set and defined, thereby reducing uncertainty. Development would be managed and controlled, step by step, through rigid structures. The thought followed that the creation process would be easy to repeat and require little or no variation. The underlying principle was something like, "*Do what you've always done, and you'll always get the same results.*" But today, we know there's a great deal we don't know about the future of a product, and that there are sociological and organizational patterns a leader needs to account for.

Uncertainty in markets is inevitable, and we are dealing with complex processes requiring research, creativity, patience, and experimentation. Creating innovative products requires not only the transfer of explicit knowledge between people or teams (items we can document or verbalize) but also an understanding of how they reach conclusions that help them solve problems. This last point is the hardest to grasp, but it's essential if you intend to create new processes to confront exponential acceleration.

If events are uncertain or unpredictable, *does it mean you can't control them?* Not necessarily. But you will have to change how you think and create new habits.

Empiricism—the theory that knowledge comes from working experience—could be a good start to improving whatever you do. It sets a foundational work style that commits us to trying things first to determine whether we're on the right track, and then learning and reflecting on what we've experienced.

From this theory, every idea or plan is merely a hypothesis until we are certain our team can do it properly and that those who will use the product like the final implementation. Many companies imagine that clients will love a service or feature because it solves a problem. They also figure that if a process was previously performed with one group of people, then performing the same with other groups will yield the same result. This is not correct.

Next time you hear the phrase "*product requirement*" or "*product feature*" used about something the company is trying to implement, try replacing the word "*requirement/ feature*" with "*hypothesis*." This will enable those around you to understand that the success of any new idea is mere speculation until it makes contact with the end user.

Until we get the product or new feature to the market, success will only be a hypothesis or speculation—and as a general rule for diminishing risk, hypotheses should be kept small to prove on a controllable scale that an initial assumption is correct.

You can download the latest Scrum guide from here: *en.innova1st.com/10A*

The Scrum framework, initially used for software development but now extended to other industries, is based on empiricism.

Its foundation consists of three pillars that reinforce positive habits:

1. **Transparency**

   Every aspect of a company's process must be visible and known to everyone involved (including both managers and those who report to them). This entails a common language shared by all participants, inside and outside the company, so that clients understand the difficulties involved in product development and become part of the solution.

2. **Inspection**

   Processes must be inspected or reviewed by members of the teams frequently enough to detect variations or surprises. It is expected that those doing the work will have conversations on how to improve the process and its interactions. This also calls for thinking explicitly about the next steps and ensuring these are sustainable over time. The Scrum framework uses retrospective meetings, which have had a positive effect on how organizations evolve.

3. **Adaptation**

   Adaptation requires that after inspection, improvements are made in the processes, interactions between people, or anything else that gets in the way of a bigger positive impact.

Because transparency, inspection, and adaptation become part of the day-to-day mental attitude, the group regularly starts asking itself, "Why are we doing things this way?" Challenging existing processes and beliefs is an important step for organizations starting to cement a proper foundation.

From the Linear to the Exponential Mindset

Once your company is capable of working empirically, you need to start reflecting on the differences between the linear and the exponential mindset and its possible effect on products.

Remember that the incremental way of thinking is represented as a straight line from present to future: one thing follows another and each cause leads to its effect. An incremental business plan allows you to see exactly how you will get from here to there. However, an exponential path is not a straight line. It's like a curve in the road that prevents you from seeing around the corner. The strategy could change at any moment, and you could even hit the brakes before making a substantial leap forward. You need a different approach that will enable you to create more business value in a world where the rules have changed. That approach requires different habits and ways of reasoning that allow people to change constantly and with less resistance.

Business value is the result of an action that supports healthy and sustainable habits in the organization, providing the protection of, or increase in, the company's income, increasing customer satisfaction, and avoiding or reducing costs. In this book, customer means clients, companies, business units, product and services, marketing and sales, portfolios, compliance, etc.

A few months before this book was published, I was visiting Auckland, New Zealand, on business. While there, I rented a minivan to visit towns outside the capital. At first, I found the van difficult to park because of its size. But after a few days, I got the hang of it, because it was a purely mechanical process. The real challenge, however, was that people drove on the left side of the road, unlike in Spain and Latin America. But driving on the left wasn't my *main issue*. My main issue was **NOT** driving on the right.

With any distraction, I would involuntarily drift over to the other side of the road. It's hard to stop old habits, because you have to *"unlearn"* behavior accumulated over years. Doing so requires that you understand how the brain works and adopt techniques to face the challenge (we'll learn more about this in Chapter 4). We generally stick to old mental models until new ways of thinking appear. During the change process, however, we tend to see the new only through the old lens.

> In formal logic, a contradiction is the signal of defeat, but in the evolution of real knowledge it marks the first step in progress toward a victory.

Alfred North Whitehead, Mathematician and Philosopher.

When the first motorized vehicles were built in the nineteenth century, cars looked more like carriages than automobiles. This was because people imagined them as an extension of horse-drawn transport. New ideas, concepts, and words were introduced, but old ways of thinking continued to be used to analyze and solve problems (Figure 1.5). It's possible that the same thing is happening today in companies trying to use the Lean or Agile mindset.

FIGURE 1.5: Cars were an extension of the carriage mindset

With the exponential mindset, you can understand that the future is uncertain while still creating a vision that helps others understand which way to go. Look at Amazon or Netflix. The first began selling books and the second renting mail-order films. They had a vision that motivated people to keep going, that gave them confidence, and that evolved as the way forward became clearer.

The multiplying effect also occurs because products that used to be independent are now interconnected, offering an enhanced experience. Think of Google, which is no longer just a search engine but is now a solution that makes it possible to link a range of experiences, thereby multiplying knowledge creation and usefulness.

When things go exponential, you must know how organizational social patterns and soft skills work. Patience and the ability to reframe problems are two necessary qualities here.

Imagine you have a product in the early stages of exponential growth. Progress will seem slow, almost coming to a halt, before making the leap. How would you align the expectations of those around you so that they understand they are in a lift-off phase that could last weeks or months?

I remember a time when it seemed that the main goal of mobile phone manufacturers was to keep making them smaller. Can you imagine what would have happened if you'd been the visionary (betting all your friends' money) who said that in four years' time the industry would be focused on making them more intelligent, and that size would no longer matter? You would have needed great communication skills and patience to help those around you understand the behavior of exponential products. Your friends would probably have resisted the thought, using unsuitable metrics from the linear world to measure only the size of the gadgets.

The Exponential Company

In the era of exponential growth, companies and strategies need to be built on the idea that there will be a high degree of uncertainty. When traditional organizations find themselves in this situation, they tend to place emphasis on increasing alignment and coordination. But this limits the ability of teams and people to self-organize. This is true because traditional companies use linear processes and forms (in contrast to exponential) to implement change and to manage its resources.

If the company goes to the other extreme, reducing coordination, each team will choose its own course and this, when added to constant market changes, will lead to chaos. At this point, a company in the era of exponential acceleration needs to have specific habits:

▶ Have organizational structures that can regularly evolve by consensus (collaboratively).
▶ Have clients that are co-creators of products and not just consumers.
▶ Encourage learning and decision-making under consensus.
▶ Use artificial intelligence or robotics in areas where the human element cannot multiply exponentially.
▶ Use different ways of measuring progress.
▶ Use tactics that constantly reduce complexity and bureaucracy in the company.
▶ Understand how people's brains work when faced with change and the need to use techniques that overcome these difficulties.
▶ Understand how to manage conflict in times of turbulence.

Whereas linear organizations are necessarily constrained by limited resources, exponential organizations are governed by an assumption of abundance. As you can see, the digital era also requires making tasks collaborative from the outset. People must be able to provide feedback and ask for a change of direction in the product, and clients have to start being cocreators of the service.

If you are using Scrum framework, discover how using the integration theory can help you multiply the results of your existing products. Learn more at *en.innova1st.com/11B*

The strategy also requires turning every process into an exercise in learning and reflection, which may include these tasks:

▶ Review of common objectives (what we intend to do together).
▶ Definition of joint commitments (the commitments we make to others).
▶ Use of shared resources (self-organization around scarce resources).
▶ Overall evaluation of risks
▶ Working in pairs as much as possible, with the aid of artificial intelligence when appropriate.

But the strongest focus must remain on the human factor and making it easier for each person to change more quickly and adapt to the new situation. This requires techniques such as *reframing*, understanding how to create a plan for change that can adapt to exponential growth, being familiar with organizational patterns, understanding how the human brain works, having techniques for dealing with conflict, and knowing why the problems we face are now complex.

How to Rally Organizational Health by Changing Just One Habit

By: Carlton Nettleton, *President of Look Forward Consulting and Certified Scrum Trainer™*

Bad meetings are a sign of poor organizational health and conflict. This is a fairly common problem with many of my clients—a lot of bad meetings that eat up valuable time, break organizational focus and kill employee engagement.

Contrary to what we all have experienced and seen in our careers, meetings do not have to be so awful. Meetings are bad because people make them bad. Yet, in my experience, nobody thinks to themselves, *"Today I am going to make the next design review meeting simply unbearable for myself and everyone else in the room."* Rather, people adopt a default set of behaviors and expectations about a meeting based on how they think the ideal meeting is structured and act accordingly. In consulting-speak, we call this a *"mental model."* Unfortunately, the mental model most people use for meetings when an enterprise is experiencing exponential growth is wrong.

Mental models are useful approximations of the world created by the brain to rapidly interpret everything we experience so that we can quickly identify the relevant facts, make decisions and solve problems.

For instance, imagine we walk into an auditorium on a college campus during the middle of the day. As we walk into the auditorium, multiple college-aged students pass by carrying books and backpacks while a woman in front of multiple whiteboards attaches a lapel microphone to her jacket. *What is going to happen next?* If you are like most people, your brain is anticipating a lecture from a college professor. That anticipation of a *"lecture from a college professor"* is an example of your brain making an interpretation based upon some simple facts that have been matched against a pre-existing mental model you have about what to expect in a university environment.

Ideally, mental models are accurate. However, as long as they are mostly correct, the brain will use a flawed mental model until there is a very good reason to change them.

For example, Newton's Laws of Motion are a simple set of mental models that describe how moving objects interact with one another. Newton's Laws work flawlessly to describe objects at the macro scale (cannonballs, comets, planets, etc.), but when scientists in the late 19th and early 20th Centuries applied the same mental model to subatomic particles, the found some problems with Newton's Laws.

To accurately describe the behavior of protons, neutrons and electrons, early 20th Century scientists needed a new mental model— quantum mechanics.

For people, the common mental model about how a meeting is supposed to work is little something like this: a new idea is introduced to a meeting and it flows smoothly from one person to the next until, at last, we arrive at a rational resolution of the topic that has the unanimous agreement and support of the entire group.

Yet, as anyone who has spent any amount trying to discuss a new, complex problem in a group knows this mental model of a smoothly flowing, linear conversation that stays mostly on track is simply not accurate.

Like our example of Newton's Laws of Motion, this simple mental model only works for topics that are business as usual or for discussions about problems that have obvious solutions. The type of things discussed when the enterprise is experiencing linear growth.

So, *what is a more accurate mental model for a meeting?* It is simple - in order for an enterprise to develop sustainable solutions for complex problems associated with exponential growth, business teams need to go through three stages. A phase of divergent thinking followed by a phase of integration, to develop shared understanding, followed by a phase of convergent thinking.

Only after convergent thinking has been completed can the enterprise achieve closure on the topic and commit to a sustainable solution that has the enthusiastic and unanimous support of the all the key stakeholders.

The key difference between this mental model and the simplistic mental model from earlier would the addition of a facilitator. Without a facilitator, most groups will not able to overcome the interpersonal tensions associated with divergent thinking, integration and convergent thinking. Consequently, business teams within the enterprise will revert to familiar ideas and solutions that more-or-less worked during periods of linear growth but are ineffective solutions now that the business is experiencing *exponential growth*.

When people complain there are too many meetings in your organization, what they are really complaining about is that there are dysfunctionalities and bad organizational health in your company.

So how is a facilitator any different from a typical manager running a meeting?

A facilitator is any substantially neutral person whose have been given the authority to help a group increase their effectiveness by improving its process and structure. A facilitator understands the stages of group decision-making—divergent thinking, integration, convergent thinking and closure—and shares this knowledge with meeting participants so they can develop shared understanding. Managers use meetings to get the information they need to drive a project to completion. Meetings are a tool that managers use to extract knowledge and information from meeting participants so that they can deliver on their own personal goals and objectives.

What does a facilitator bring to a discussion that your typical manager does not? Facilitators are well-versed in multiple, facilitative listening techniques to apply at each stage of group decision-making and make use of them to support the group in their best thinking as they work to achieve a sustainable solution.

Unlike managers, who have a stake in the final outcome, facilitators seek to understand how the people and the work intersect with one another.

A facilitator watches what happens in the negative space between meetings to identify recurring patterns of behavior, spot missed opportunities for collaboration and suggest ways a group can advance the quality of their work and their interpersonal relationships.

Facilitators are patient knowing that eventually, the group will discover a sustainable solution which has the enthusiastic support of all the keys players within the enterprise.

So apart from not having to personally endure another awful meeting, *why do business leaders care about fixing the problem of bad meetings?* Because fixing issues around bad meetings are one of the most visible and important ways to reduce conflict and improve the organizational health of the enterprise.

Like a cardiac patient with a weak heart, organizations with poor organizational health are not equipped to respond to the stress of exponential change. To boost your organization's health and to decrease the stress put on your business, I recommend designating some people from within your organization to act as meeting facilitators.

Equip these people with new knowledge about meeting facilitation and group dynamics. Offer them opportunities to put these new skills into practice and learn from those experiences.

If your enterprise is looking to Scrum and other Agile software development processes to help you respond to exponential change, then the best people to fill the meeting facilitator role would be your ScrumMasters and Agile coaches.

I recommend that ScrumMasters and Agile coaches adopt a teaching stance to help the various groups within your enterprise to improve their processes and structures so that they can become self-facilitating.

When the ScrumMasters and Agile coaches focus on teaching groups to become self-facilitating, this will bring about lasting change in people's mental models about meetings, solve the important issues brought on by *exponential growth* and rally organizational health.

What You Have Learned

☑ The effects of exponential acceleration on markets.
☑ The difference between Moore's Law and the law of accelerating returns.
☑ The Six Ds of exponential growth.
☑ The importance of a healthy organization.
☑ Empirical learning as part of a modern organization.
☑ The exponential company.

1. Do you remember the difference between Moore's law and the theory of exponential results? How do they affect your business?

_____

_____

_____

2. Is there a product in your company that has followed the six Ds?

_____

_____

_____

3. In broad terms, what do you think a healthy organization requires?

_____

_____

_____

4. Which aspects of the empirical model do you think need to be strengthened in your company?

_____

_____

_____

CHAPTER 2

Finding a Suitable Solution in a Complex World

CHAPTER 2

"Simplicity does not precede complexity, but follows it."

Alan Perlis, Computer Scientist

I bet your library and mine have much in common. You probably have dozens of books on Scrum, Agile, Lean, software development, Business Agility, team management, and the like. But you probably have fewer focused on the human factors for leading change in a company facing exponential markets, and you probably have few on accelerating the adoption of new habits and practices.

Achieving new habits and practices requires a variety of skills and a basic understanding of organizational patterns, software, frameworks, neuroscience, psychology, system thinking, business, leadership, and coaching. You must also be able to alter course without causing counterproductive emotional states.

It's easy to find books and other media telling us *what* practices are needed or where we should reach. It's harder to find information on *how* to confront change in the era of exponential acceleration. Effective transformation initially demands the reorganization of a company's structures, processes, practices, and skills. You'll also have to revisit the company's power distribution, as well as the company's vision and mission. You need to understand how people interact, what motivates them, and, above all, the right time to embark on a change journey.

There are effective ways to deal with new challenges. However, they require time, may cause disruption, and might temporarily cause feelings of insecurity among the team. But there can be no real evolution, nor will you be able to face exponential growth, without undertaking your change journey.

From the more-traditional point of view, using linear growth techniques or processes, you can employ different approaches to lead a business transformation. Some will have greater impact, unleashing a series of big events, while others will be more specific and constrained.

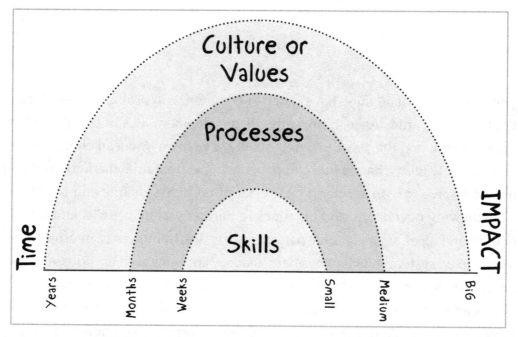

FIGURE 2.1: Impact of change from a more-traditional point of view (linear growth process)

Transformation is the new company's weapon of choice to help it confront challenges from competition, the digital era, and artificial intelligence. Transformation is also an antidote, helping companies build structures that are strong yet remain flexible enough to withstand the fluctuations and surprises of a globalized market.

Nowadays, companies and independent professionals specialize in business transformation. Events, conferences, websites, and consultancies are specifically designed to help you channel organizational transformation. I've seen numerous presentations on the challenges arising from change, and I always end up with the same question: *What is it that makes a company truly exceptional and able to confront the new exponential market rules?*

You've probably seen the trick where a magician makes a rabbit appear out of a hat. It appears natural, even easy. You could replay a video of the trick in slow motion and still not discover how it's done. In the same manner, the change occurs naturally in exponential companies. Those within feel as though they are part of the initiative. They contribute, push, enjoy, and, when they least expect it, find themselves on top of the mountain.

In more-traditional organizations, individuals invest much effort and time to urge such transformation, and they try to convince others to evolve the processes they themselves created. But there can be no real change unless there's first an honest alteration of behaviors. It's no longer valid to think individuals will try to improve something when up to that point they've been taught to follow orders from a superior.

In the exponential organization, employees enjoy themselves as they grow and evolve. They think collaboratively and achieve shared goals. They openly share what they wish to learn from each situation, create new habits that can be expanded to the rest of the company, and reflect within the team on how to take better action. All of them want to become more experienced and perfect their practices. They offer reciprocity and help each other, and they strive to improve how they connect with other employees.

Consider this from an economic point of view. At exponential companies, such behavior translates into higher revenues, greater profitability, rapid adaptation, and a faster return of capital invested.

As we learned in the previous chapter, healthy companies greatly outperform those that are not, and you should keep this in mind when considering future change initiatives.

I used to work for a *"healthy"* consultancy in the UK. Their company values were displayed in every office, and every week they'd send an email with the photograph of a prestigious golfer to remind us of the importance of their values. I can only suppose they did this because something wasn't working properly. I imagine you wouldn't want a superficial strategy, framework, or process that was only good for people to follow blindly. This is what many companies ask from me, but deep inside, they know they long for a healthier life within the organization.

Change is Complex

The following questions will help you think about the change as you take your first steps:

- ▶ Who could inspire change or make it contagious?
- ▶ How can the company culture help?
- ▶ What are the intellectual and emotional factors during an individual's personal-improvement journey?

The change should be initiated by someone who inspires, someone people truly admire. This isn't the same as the person who believes people trust them, and it doesn't have to be the person with the highest role or salary.

Don't worry if you are new to the company or if you feel uncomfortable leading a change initiative. Later in the book, I'll show you effective ways to create a great impact by implementing minuscule changes (micro-habits).

A lack of support isn't an excuse to halt change on the curbside, either. Many consultants wait to carry forward their idea until company leaders fully understand the problem, but this only leads to valuable time lost. I have experienced this on several occasions. I've scheduled appointments, or simply waited for the CEO, to talk about the company's dysfunctions or about adopting the Agile mindset. They often had other priorities, and what was important to me was merely an extra task to them, just something more to do. *How could they not see that the world had changed? Why wouldn't they take the lead?*

There are three common reasons why leaders delay the start of a change initiative:

1. They can't see a clear sense of urgency.
2. They want to wait until other large companies demonstrate that the implementation of concepts is successful or that the techniques are mature enough.
3. They want to wait until the approach has been studied by academics, there's sufficient research material in books or conferences, or until same-level peers in other companies begin to talk about the subject.

They lose months and years looking for the ideal moment. Opportunities are missed, and the organization is excluded from seeing change as something positive and natural. Companies have more than enough heads to decide whether something is good and to adapt appropriately. But on many occasions, what's required is only a small push and modification in the foundations people use to make decisions.

Look at the history of Toyota. For over 30 years, Toyota led innovative change in the global automotive industry using Lean techniques. It took American companies that same amount of time to get on par with leading companies and start using the new "*mindset.*"

Simply put, every occasion is a good opportunity to carry out a change. All you need is to ensure that your company is healthy and to procure the right tools, processes, or work styles. If these aren't met at your company yet, Chapter 5 lists modifications to main habits so that the company can become healthier and so that the change can become exponential.

I'm sure you're a good communicator, that your colleagues appreciate your help, that you work well with others, and that you're good at sharing ideas. But *what else is needed?*

The following **six principles** will set you on the right mental path and help change your world:

1. **It's always a good time to make a change**—another person's delay is not an excuse to wait!
2. **Believe in your idea**.
3. **Share your idea**.
4. **Accept feedback** and improve how you reflect on it and internalize it.
5. Have **passion** for **collectively** bringing the idea forward.
6. Assume that **decisions made by others**, who do not support your plan, **can always be changed**, even if they are firm decisions. Chapter 4 will show you how the brain works, and how to employ techniques that facilitate this point.

Your company's culture also has an influence. If you compare the different places you've worked, you would probably offer a different solution to the *same problem* for each of these companies. This is because of the company culture. Culture has a significant impact on the speed of implementation of your change plan. Everything will progress faster if the business supports innovation and encourages healthy habits. And if it promotes communication and encourages individuals to reflect, learn, feel safe to experiment, and even fail, then this is a plus.

> Change will not come if we wait for some other person or some other time. We are the ones we've been waiting for. We are the change that we seek.

Barack Obama, 44th President of the United States

For a change to become **contagious**—a **midpoint** state between **traditional linear** change and the required exponential growth change—employees must be empowered to take ownership of your initial idea, improve it, and make results their own. They must possess enough mental flexibility to set their egos aside and alter course at any time. They need to discover how to deal with their emotional sides and the emotional sides of others in a consistent manner. And they need to recognize that this personal learning journey is a long one.

You'll need to first invest in personal preparation and analyze the organizational patterns and attitudes in your favor. Once you understand how to implement the change—I promise I'll be more specific in upcoming chapters—you'll succeed at making it **contagious** first and **exponential** later.

Exponential means you'll have a community of motivated people, teams that feel like activists, business partners that are like colleagues supporting your initiative, and a culture that looks more like a social movement than a rigid set of values stuck on a wall.

Remember, change is a journey that requires you to realize that any modification in processes, policies, or work styles affects people in a very personal manner. Processes can't be changed, nor work rules or agreements put in place, without forever altering how people think. For this reason, it's essential that you have the proper tools to accompany you on your journey.

The Formula for an Exponential Organization

Amancio Ortega knew little about business when he started working at a clothing store in the city of La Coruña, Spain, at the age of thirteen. Nonetheless, he went on to found a small clothing manufacturing company in 1963, before he'd even reached the age of thirty. In 1977, the success of his designs prompted Ortega to install the first of his Zara factories in Arteixo, a small town of around 31,000 inhabitants. During the next few years, his company, Inditex, began to grow rapidly, reaching a rate of one worldwide store opening per day, including openings for several of their other brands (Pull and Bear, Oysho, Massimo Dutti, Bershka, and eighty more).

Customers love Ortega's products, and several of my own friends will attest that they cherish the innovative quality of their designs so much that they can't live without them. I'd always believed that product quality was crucial in any service, so I was surprised when Zara failed in several areas in a quality test carried out by the Beijing Consumer Association on twenty brands (fourteen Chinese and six international). According to the association, several of Zara's products had labels that did not correctly indicate fabric composition, and the product faded after its first wash. It seems that people pay less attention to product quality if the products are innovative or if they fulfill their purpose.

Is innovation the secret component for an exponential organization?

Around 1995, the company Artemis presented the WebTV service in the United States. WebTV was a cutting-edge product that allowed people to surf the web on their TVs. The product made it possible to bring the internet into homes that could not afford a computer, thus making web browsing possible for those with limited computer skills.

This innovation led to Microsoft buying the company in 2001 and renaming it MSN TV. Microsoft appeared to have a brilliant strategy, as it would allow the company to market a cutting-edge product in a familiar market with a million paying subscribers. Microsoft created an updated version of WebTV with a more powerful graphics processor to satisfy users who wanted to make video calls and record television programs simultaneously. This was a success from the standpoint of innovation! But a few years later, Microsoft shut down the service. Among other reasons, the software lacked the expected quality, and a number of issues compromised security for users.

Perhaps innovation is only part of the formula, and the key to success lies in more-traditional methods, such as having a proven strategy and short customer feedback cycles. *Could this be so?*

Coca-Cola has always been a world leader in soft drinks. In 1980, leaders at Pepsi decided to roll out an aggressive marketing campaign to position their drink within youth sectors. That same year, Coca-Cola lost customers until it only held about 24 percent of market share.

Coca-Cola leaders decided to act. They established a solid strategy that included changing the formula of their star refreshment and creating a product sweeter than Pepsi. Their roadmap was set up with a strategy that validated the new taste with a sampling by 200,000 people. Weeks later, the new product was out, and the original formula vanished from shelves. *What do you think happened?* Over 400,000 calls poured in from angry customers, and hundreds wrote complaint letters expressing dissatisfaction with the new drink. *How was it possible that Coca-Cola could make a mistake in their strategy when market research had yielded positive results?* Fifty-three percent of customers had approved and liked the new Coca-Cola!

The answer? Consumers were motivated by more than just the taste of the drink. When the research was conducted, the premise was that taste was most important. But this isn't the only component of the success equation. Customers make purchasing decisions based on habits and emotional factors such as nostalgia and loyalty, and this hadn't been taken into account.

Concrete numbers are useful because they give the conscious mind something to do, but it's our emotions that decide what is true and guide our decisions. It took the company less than three months to announce their return to the original Coca-Cola and abandon the tested and innovative product strategy.

You must consider factors broader than innovation and fast feedback loops with the customer. Many of the executives I speak with have a firm understanding of how and where to reduce costs (cost and efficiency), but we know that wealth is created differently in the new economy and exponential markets. You also need expertise in other areas:

- Being able to create a plan with exponential characteristics (able to expand without physical limitations)
- Having customers as cocreators of the product and understanding their motivation.
- Engaging individuals of different ranks and knowledge within the company with a shared sense of purpose and responsibility.
- Understanding that making a change is simply complicated, as it involves complex feelings and behavior patterns.
- Noting that the solution to a problem needs to be considered from different viewpoints, utilizing different forms of reasoning (*reframing*).
- Using short cycles to experiment and change rapidly.
- Ensuring that people feel safe.
- Always having a definition of minimum and acceptable product quality (Definition of Done) that is nonnegotiable in the face of market pressures, so that the quality of the product or service remains constant and high.

Reframing is a powerful set of cognitive techniques that allow us to analyze a problem from different points of view, guiding us to temporarily think as the person with the problem or from the perspectives of those who observe the problem. This makes it possible to reach different conclusions, with different assumptions. This practice encourages new neural connections and results in innovative ways of thinking that help the company evolve.

Today, innovative solutions and ideas are needed to replace simple transactions that focus merely on a small portion of what we can observe. When an honest focus is placed on clients, they feel exhilarated. A focus on the client helps build bridges, the client becomes a cocreator, and the organization can better understand how he or she thinks.

When you treat employees as potential clients, it provides a safe space where they can feel part of the organization. This results in employees who further contribute to the creation of an exponential company.

Techniques for reframing and brain functioning, applying neuroscience for change, are fundamental, as they help executives use different forms of reasoning. When this is achieved, individuals begin to listen more, and information gains new relevance. The result is constant improvement and products that are ahead of the competition.

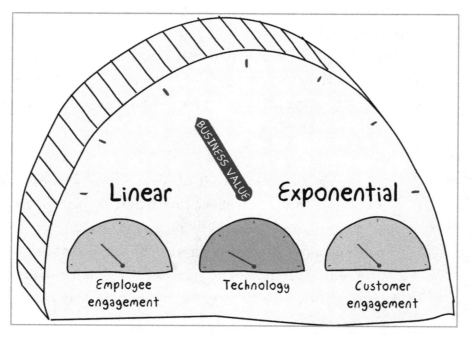

FIGURE 2.2: Speedometer of an exponential company

All plans require interrupting linear forms of work and technologies to replace them with exponential habits and tools. Otherwise, you won't be able to adapt your plan when the business goes from growing 10 percent to 10^2. In addition to leaders who can expand processes rapidly, you will also require technologies, work and learning styles, increased interactions with the client, and much more. The speedometer in Figure 2.2 helps us see the relationship between these areas

- Technologies that need to move from the linear to the exponential.
- Structures used to engage the client and the way that those structures scale up.
- Structures used to engage employees and the way that those structures scale up.

Later, you will see how knowing more about neuroscience (Chapter 4) and understanding the five habits before starting a change initiative (Chapter 5) will allow your company to become exponential.

The art of Predicting the Future

When I travel, I often bring along my racing bike. I generally use a special sports transportation bag to protect the frame and wheels, especially in the airplane cargo hold. I've taken it upon myself to include instructions, in several languages, stating that nothing should be stacked on top of the bag. But more than once it has ended up at the bottom of a pile of heavy suitcases. The story repeats itself over and over: When I return from the trip I have to take the bicycle in for maintenance and I pretty much already know what parts will have to be repaired or replaced.

But unless we're talking about machinery, with elements that fit and work together using predictable and repetitive tasks, it's difficult to forecast the future. In modern companies, much can vary. Companies are exposed to global markets with constant innovation, political surprises, cybersecurity issues, changes in world geography, diseases, and a whole array of events that affect us all.

In the past, plans were set to reduce and contain variability and to secure a constant workflow. But in the same way that a teenager needs to be in contact with the world to learn faster, a company needs to use such variability to its advantage. Without rapid changes, you cannot create differential business value or achieve greater innovation, and this would ignore the economic importance of the success formula. We mustn't focus only on stability. Instead, we must learn to observe what surrounds us with a different lens.

Around the end of 2017, a telemarketing company conducted a market study to capture opinions on a mobile-banking application belonging to one of the largest financial institutions in Catalonia, Spain. A high number of respondents expressed dissatisfaction and rated the software poorly. As a result, the bank probably invested time and effort trying to create an endless list of possible reasons, which led to new objectives and a change in the vision of their mobile product.

In reality, though, Catalonia was in a process of potential separation from Spain, and those opposed to Catalonian independence were impulsively responding negatively to the mobile product survey—their answers did not really reflect their feelings toward the software. Cases like this remind us that we must analyze many factors to understand the source of variability. This implies that we must be able to understand that we are facing complex—but not complicated—scenarios.

The Complication of Being Complex

A change within a company is a complex problem, and to solve it you need to think differently. It's useful to recognize a fundamental distinction made by those of us dedicated to helping and promoting change. The terms complex and complicated are often confused. They are used interchangeably in company conversations: *"The company's processes are very complex!"* or *"The organization's strategy is complicated!"* or *"The solution to this grave matter is complicated!"*

A complicated problem is one with a definitive and correct solution. We may not know what it is, but if someone, perhaps the subject matter expert, finds the solution, the result will be immutable over time. The following are complicated problems:

▶ How many four-digit numbers are there such that the thousands digit is equal to the sum of the other three digits?

▶ How many linear meters of bricks will I need to cover that wall?

▶ How many customers have we received feedback from?

Being complicated indicates that it may be hard and take several steps to find the solution, but eventually we will have a definitive, stable, and predictable response. Generally, something complicated can be solved by an industrial machine. The automation of a car assembly plant is a complicated problem. Something complex, on the other hand, requires a different thought process and involves different areas of the brain.

These are characteristics of genuinely complex problems:

▷ There is no 100 percent correct solution to the problem; there are simply different perceptions of what could be the most *appropriate* solution.
▷ The situation may have elements that are illogical or not fully understood despite our best efforts to analyze and rationalize these elements.
▷ There are multiple people involved with different expectations and points of view, which often seem irreconcilable.
▷ There is a high human factor influenced by social or cultural conditions.
▷ The environment on which the situation is centered is politically charged.
▷ Resistance is different because the problem involves varying aspects, many of which carry emotional repercussions.

Imagine I leave you in a room with a whiteboard for solving an equation. Sooner or later, you'll be able to solve it and find a logical and definitive solution. This will activate an intrinsic reward system in your brain that will generate satisfaction and keep you fully motivated.

Now imagine that I leave you in the same room with three of my nephews and two of their friends, all between six and eleven years of age (and forgetting to mention that the latter are the worst behaved at school). I ask that within the next three hours you implement a strategy that will control their behavior, and that this strategy should be predictable and replicable on future occasions. The challenge is much greater here!

The first challenge requires linear thinking (if A = B and B = C then A = C) and has a consistent relationship between cause and effect (complicated). For the second challenge, the relationship is neither clear nor linear, and neither are cause and effect (complex). With linear and rational thinking (complicated), we have a definitive solution. However, in a complex situation, there isn't a single solution, but rather several suggested recommendations.

Which of these cases most resembles the problems at your company?

Imagine you are part of the Stradivari family and want to build Stradivarius violins. The challenge would require that you have the proper knowledge and coordinate the necessary people. The creation of this product presents a lot of variability, because it involves specialized, constantly interacting people and manual, ever-changing work. Any alteration of the chain (value stream) would lead to unpredictable results that are complex to solve. If we add that each new violin must include innovative features, working times would increase exponentially because of an increase in the complexity of human interactions.

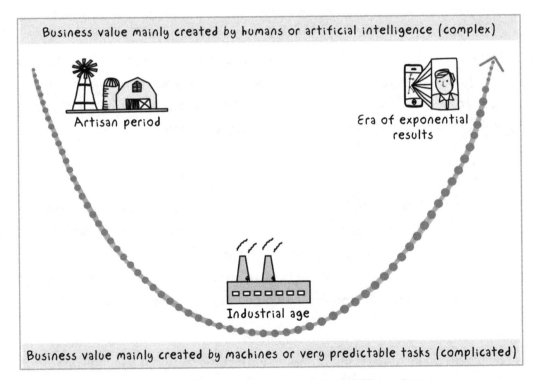

FIGURE 2.3: Business value creation differentiator

If we used a machine instead of crafting the violin manually, the differentiator in business value would be mainly industrial equipment. The better the machinery, the faster you can produce your product. If there's a problem, it would probably suffice to change gear or standardize the processes to resolve it. If machine failure were predictable, you could calculate the exact number of violins you would lose that month and alert your customers. Here, the cause and effect are clear and consistent, and a solution to the problem can be reasoned by linear thinking. But as of 1995, three factors began to alter this scenario:

1. The ability of any company to approach global markets.
2. Acceleration due to the Internet and artificial intelligence.
3. The need to be highly creative and to have a differentiated product.

Nowadays, much of a company's success consists of creating plans that can grow exponentially with innovative products, putting a high number of minds to work together, looking for creative solutions, and connecting an idea with a previously nonexistent market. This is clearly something complex.

Part of the solution is to actively involve the individuals with the problem, turning them into cocreators of the solution (customers, business partners, etc.). Help them think differently and encourage them to solve the matter as a complex problem instead of a complicated problem.

Trying to solve something complex with rules for what's *complicated* only aggravates the problem and makes the solution appallingly tangled when it's struck by reality.

The Trap of Tools in a Complex World

Imagine a group of people who lack good communication and trust but who could become an unstoppable team by changing their interactions. If you were to install a software application for them to communicate better, this would only exacerbate the problem and increase conflict. There would also be a rise in bureaucracy, because it would require the installation of the new software, account and password management, and an increase in time sitting in front of a computer to cooperate—which would unavoidably diminish face-to-face communication.

This type of action is very common and may be well-intentioned, but it's particularly dangerous if the company doesn't realize that social problems (complex) aren't solved with IT tools (complicated) or new methodologies.

Parties involved in complex problems often suffer from shortsightedness. As the saying goes, "*When all you have at hand is a hammer, everything around you will look like a nail.*"

Remember that there are important benefits when company executives understand the difference between the complicated and the complex. When this happens, they usually begin to see things through a different lens.

The Illusion of Change

A few years ago, I helped with the Agile transformation of one of the largest airlines. To offer new routes under a unified brand, they had bought out another company from a neighboring country. The change seemed simple. The planes would be painted with the new logo, employees would be sent on training programs, processes would be standardized, new publicity would be rolled out, and new uniforms would be made available. Within a few months, everything would be ready for the new start. But in reality it took years and faced much resistance, because the employees of the acquired company thought of their brand as part of their own culture and country.

This provoked a politically charged, hostile environment where people chose sides instead of becoming business partners working toward a common goal. It took years to establish a healthy environment and center employees' focus on the business value again.

When companies simplify or try to solve a complex problem as if it were complicated, employing linear thinking, they end up resorting to what I call the simple loop decision process. This response is derived from a reasoning style inherited from the industrial era. Our education is based on a time that no longer exists, and we're trying to adapt the reality of our organization to an obsolete toolbox.

When I started programming back in 1987, a unique version of programming applications hit the market every one to two years. In 1997, Microsoft offered an update for its operating system every six months. With such long time spans between updates, we could still employ linear or traditional thinking. Today, you and I update mobile phone applications several times a week, making it difficult to use traditional techniques. Leaders are constantly confronted with challenges of exponential acceleration, and these challenges are different from those that their predecessors faced.

Most of the people I help have never been trained to plan for changes in highly complex and uncertain environments. They feel comfortable breaking problems down and solving them sequentially, but this only results in a simple loop decision.

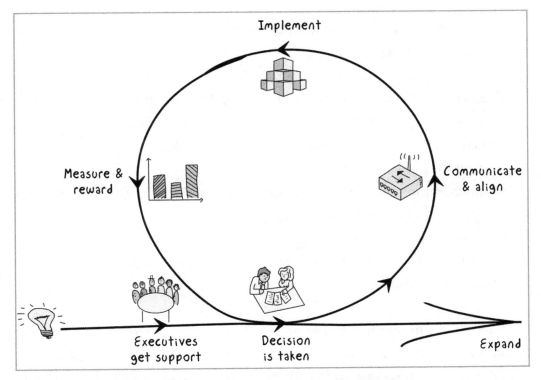

FIGURE 2.4: The simple loop decision process

Don't get me wrong, linear thinking works perfectly fine for certain scenarios, but we're entering a moment in history when focus must be placed on changing the way we reason, our habits, and how we validate our conclusions. The important thing is not to solve problems analytically and procedurally, or to follow strict steps, but to use different types of intelligence to achieve our goals. The simple loop is an almost automatic solution that goes unnoticed by many. It's healthy to make it visible to start examining the foundations of the organization.

These are the intrinsic steps that we take when using the *simple loop decision process* in a company:

1. **Executives get support for the change**. Support is strengthened by negotiating and convincing other executives that the proposed solution is best.
2. **Decision**. A plan is decided on; one which will usually affect people uninvolved in the decision.
3. **Communication and alignment**. The change is shared with the rest of the company and tacit alignment is sought.
4. **Implementation**. The original plan is implemented.
5. **Measurement and reward**. The plan is measured and adjusted, and explicit reward is offered to those who met set objectives.

This cycle can be repeated in different ways. When we have the results (measurement and reward), a new decision is made, communicated, and implemented. And so the cycle continues. Sometimes specific departments push the change plan. On other occasions, leaders do. But in any case, communication flows from top to bottom with a strong goal of alignment.

The people issuing direct orders or communications are often not the most appropriate for conveying a message. The purpose of the simple loop is to ensure the implementation of the change by means of measures that specify whether the results have been aligned with initial expectations.

Explicit rewards (a "*carrot*": money, higher position, etc.) are common for motivating individuals. If there's a discrepancy between the original plan and reality, new measures, rules, or processes to reinforce the path are added. The plan will be considered successful and the transformation complete when metrics reflect the expected values.

Simple loop decisions originate from an incorrect premise, one that ignores emotions, collective intelligence, social patterns, and how the brain reacts in the face of change. Processes and structures resulting from a simple loop decision do not create sustainable behavior over time. Even if there were a peak of positive reaction at the start of the implemented plan, it will usually be followed by a lack of interest or low adoption. There is no real change unless mindsets and habits are altered. This has much to do with how conflict is faced and how the mind resists change.

The Non-linear Cause-Effect Relationship of an Action

Many companies build trust with their employees through personal conversations, creating programs that support their work and goals, and through consistent, visible forms of communication. This mutual trust can last for months or decades, but one day a small error or misunderstanding can erode the work built over many years.

In traditional management, a problem is usually approached with a *"big plans = big changes = big impact"* mentality, but in a complex system, such a large-scale intervention might have the opposite effect. A minuscule modification could encourage positive behaviors and lead to exponential effects. The person who made the mistake could apologize, honestly and in person to those affected, and the company could hold a session that answers the question *"How are we better, and what has Mr. X's situation helped us learn?"*

I was a client of a British bank that had a high rate of credit and debit card fraud, much of it related to the theft of credit card numbers from people's mailboxes. The company could have developed an extensive strategy to improve the situation with complex processes such as checkpoints and constant measurements to determine whether the intended objective was met. But the bank decided to alter only one habit (or micro-habit). The bank would send envelopes containing bank cards using images or logos that weren't associated with the bank. The employees just needed to take envelopes from a different place.

This resulted in a noticeable reduction in fraud, with minimal effort and without having to change existing processes. Altering a small habit can alter the direction of the entire company and restore confidence.

In another example, employees of a software-development firm received an order that only a maximum number of high-severity software defects would be tolerated. From three hundred errors per month, the teams reduced this to fewer than fifteen. It certainly looked like a big achievement!

The change was established in a short time, which seemed like great progress for the company. But through an informal agreement, the team had started cataloguing high-severity defects as medium or low, thereby giving the impression that the change was a success. Obviously, the solution didn´t solve anything. It merely tricked the system and was probably the result of having used the simple loop decision process for years.

You know now that the cause–effect relationship isn't always linear. I will share more on this in Chapter 4.

From a Bird's Eye View to Low-Level Flight

Analyzing a complex problem as though it were complicated can be a useful technique to provide parties with a bird's eye view of the situation. This provides general insight and teaches you more about the beliefs and initial thought patterns of the parties involved. For example, imagine addressing a meeting with the following beliefs:

▶ The SAP department always completes its work on time, but other development teams delay the final solution. We should make a contingency plan and increase control over the teams. Let's recruit three new bosses.

OR

▶ Employees can't do their jobs, and they require more training. We should communicate this and develop new training strategies. Let's call in all the learning providers and begin in two weeks. In three months, all employees will be aligned.

Both ways of thinking exhibit traditional cause–effect linear patterns of an action. Here, a great change is addressed with a specific plan requiring coordination and control. *What would happen if the SAP and development teams sat in the same area, worked in pairs, or self-organized with respect to their goals? Which micro-habits would be easier to change and return the greatest positive result?*

Seeing a complex problem as *complicated* makes it possible for a group of people to channel initial conversations and create working agreements before analyzing the situation as complex. It also allows the observation of individual tendencies and understanding of the *"lens"* they should use to see the world.

In a typical episode of the TV series *Undercover Boss*, the owner of a company visits one of its branches as if he were an employee. Initially, he has a simplified understanding of the problems the branch is facing and an idea of the actions he'd take to solve the problems (complicated). But once in contact with the reality, the boss realizes that the problem is different (complex) and that it requires different information and skills to improve the situation.

Before proposing a solution, temporarily abandon your role and invest time to work in pairs with those who are actually facing the problem or require the change. Take time to absorb information, collaborate, and help. At this stage, do not judge the individuals or processes. Be part of the team, foster curiosity, talk, and question as much as you can.

In his election campaign, Donald Trump said he had a plan to improve the American health system, and that it was simple. Once he became president, after analyzing the problem with several officials, he announced that the health-system matter was an extremely complex problem.

The first step in creating a successful business is to determine whether you will require techniques to solve a complex or complicated problem. You have to gather firsthand information, talk without prejudice to several parties, change hats, spend time working with the individuals facing the problem, make the situation visible, and be aware of existing social patterns.

A good exercise is to write down the assumptions, values, and beliefs you had before initial contact with the team members. Identify patterns and explore your own reasoning process, because this often goes unnoticed and expresses itself in automatic responses. If you're comfortable, make the process visual and share it with those around you. If you'd rather not share it, analyze why, and you might find that you need to include something else in your personal-improvement plan. Remember that once you share something, you begin to use collaborative intelligence, which includes learning to manage feedback.

Pay close attention to changes in expectations when people discover that an apparently complicated problem is complex. Observe how they act in the new scenario. Who is still trying to use linear reasoning to solve the problem? Who is starting to look at the situation from a different point of view?

From the Good Idea to the Change Plan

In 1884 in London, Thomas Parker built the first electric car to be produced on a large scale. The vehicle was a popular method of transportation in the late 1800s because of its comfort and ease of operation, unmatched by gasoline cars of the time. Yet despite this early appearance of electric cars, we will only start using hybrids on a massive scale around 2022, and only in some countries, with the general public forced to continue to wait for electric cars to become more viable.

I used to think that anyone would readily adopt a good idea without delay or hesitation. I figured a good idea plus a plan equaled certain change. I now realize how impossible this is without a prior understanding of basic social, psychological, and organizational functioning. Simply put, having a good idea and a business plan is far from enough.

The first steps are to bring the problem to light, use collaborative thinking to analyze the problem, and explain the foundations of complex and complicated problems. Later, you can focus on getting support from within the organization to gain more traction.

Above all, remember that training courses, PowerPoint presentations, or a leader's desire for a better company will not lead to cascading change throughout the company. Old techniques such as the *"stick and carrot"* no longer obtain the best results. Real change results from using techniques that turn transformation contagious and exponential. And these new tools are the ones that you will learn about in the coming chapters.

Are You Tasked with Driving Organizational Change?

By: Dr. Sebastian Vetter, *Innovation and Strategy Consultant*

Traditional change management relies on linear thinking in a stable world. You conduct a status quo analysis to define the current state (**A**) of your organization.

You then define a clear future state (**B**) you want to achieve. You are looking for the shortest distance to get from **A** to **B**. Therefore, you make a plan and a roadmap with sequential steps you need to follow. With each step you take, you move closer to your desired future state.

$$A \quad\quad\quad\quad\quad\quad\quad B$$
$$\cdot \longrightarrow \cdot \longrightarrow \cdot \longrightarrow \cdot \longrightarrow \cdot$$

While this linear way of thinking about organizational change has proven successful in increasing operational efficiency and cutting costs in the late 90s it falls short in today's VUCA world (volatility, uncertainty, ambiguity, complexity) where effect-result relationships are exponential, chaotic or simply unknown.

- ▶ How do you approach change when there is no defined future state?
- ▶ How do you navigate change when there isn't a path you can follow?

▷ How do you stay on course if there are external forces that influence your speed and the direction of travel?

One of my clients, a leading professional services firm was experiencing these challenges. The task was to install a business unit that would envision how the future for the whole organization could look like and act as an accelerator and instrument of organizational change. The challenge was to figure out how this unit should operate and stabilize in order to best fulfill its' mission.

You can learn more about VUCA in the following article: *en.innova1st.com/20A*

The organizational context this unit was to operate in can be characterized as ambiguous with multiple stakeholders voicing conflicting demands, the occasional hostile response from the corporate immune system and powerful political forces.

The first thing to be aware of is that in an ambiguous environment not seeing the path you should follow is normal because there is none, no one has walked here before. You need to become comfortable with ambiguity as you will face some unknown unknowns.

As you don't know exactly what your future state will look like you need to have a strong vision of what could be, and you need to share this vision with your team. Start moving as soon as possible, hit the market with whatever you've got. Don't spend too much time with planning and overthinking, you need feedback from your customers to see what works and what doesn't.

Action creates speed and speed creates momentum. Run experiments on how to engage with clients, how to organize yourself, how to approach leadership, how to run meetings, how to track key performance indicators, etc.

See what works and what doesn't. A hard thing to realize is that failure is an option. What you are tasked with is hard. It has not been done before. You can actually fail. You can run out of money, lose the trust of your organization, lose valuable employees or fail at the market.

Why do I say such a depressing thing no one wants to hear? Well firstly because it's true, there are so many change initiatives that have failed. Secondly because I want you to understand that navigating change in a VUCA world is not an easy thing to do and that you can't do it on your own. You need to be humble, you need to have a team that shares your vision and supports you when the goings get ruff.

Think about the people from the south pacific venturing out in their canoes in a quest for new land. There was no path to follow, they did not even know if there was any land to discover. They must have had a strong belief that there could be land. Navigating by the stars they were able to change and to correct their direction of travel. Some canoes have reached New Zealand but... *how many canoes did they send out that must have vanished somewhere in the Pacific Ocean?*

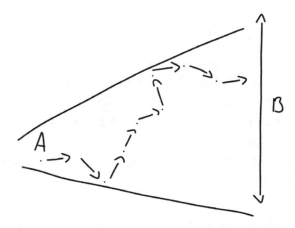

It's impossible to find the shortest path to an unknown destination. It's about exploring and learning and sailing with (and against) the wind and using currents to create momentum.

Knowing when to pause in times of decreasing winds and when to pull out the rudders and start rowing. The key is to keep going and to continuously course correct based on what you learn along the way. In order to successfully navigate change in a VUCA world you need to:

- ▶ Become comfortable with ambiguity.
- ▶ Create a strong vision of what could be.
- ▶ Start moving and gain momentum.
- ▶ Have a mindset of experimentation.
- ▶ Continuous measure results and course correct accordingly.
- ▶ Be humble and realize that you can actually fail.

Those elements might sound like soft skills; believe me they are not. They can make or break your change journey.

What You Have Learned

☑   Some ideas that will help you think when you start a change initiative.
☑   The six principles to change your world and people around you.
☑   The non-linear relationship between cause and effect in a company.
☑   The differences between complicated and complex problems.
☑   The simple loop decision process.
☑   When it's feasible to successfully use the complicated thought process for a complex problem.

1.   Have you ever missed any of the six principles of change?

_____

_____

_____

2.   What are the differences between complex and complicated?

_____

_____

_____

3.   Describe a time when you analyzed a problem as complicated when in fact it was complex. What would you do differently if faced with the same problem today?

_____

_____

_____

4.   Can you identify three instances where a simple loop decision was made?

_____

_____

_____

Learning to Change your Company

CHAPTER 3

> "Change is the law of life. And those who look only to the past or present are certain to miss the future."

John F. Kennedy, 35th President of the United States

The power of a single individual or group to peacefully alter the fate of hundreds of people, and even entire civilizations, is amazing. We've seen it in history and we observe it every day.

I truly believe that every person can think and act as an agent of change. For companies, every employee is a potential change agent.

Thinking it's impossible to modify the company's direction because you have a lower salary or lack authority is an outdated belief. I regularly see well-intended revolutionaries materializing changes where there was once only a desert. Being an effective revolutionary doesn't mean having to go against current practices, being the strongest, or having the highest salary. It's about knowing how to sit at a table with a firm point of view and help people connect with a better future. *So what's needed to make this happen?*

You might be considering transforming your company into a more sustainable model, trying to achieve greater competitiveness, or looking for possibilities to implement new products or services. To achieve all of this, you need to start with an idea and an explicit vision of change that enables those around you to walk in the same direction, talking and dreaming together of that better future.

The First Steps Towards Change

Every change starts with someone with a different point of view and a passion for achieving something. If that person also possesses the right skills and mindset, he or she will help others take over the idea and turn it into a roadmap. For this to happen in a company, people must be able to see the beginning of that near future, trust the person who facilitates the change, and have no associated fears with modifications to their status or role.

I've often heard conversations stating that *X is better than Z, that Waterfall is better than Agile*, that *using estimates is better than not using estimates*, or that *less hierarchy is better than rigid corporate structures*. You can argue along these lines to prove a point, but we know scientifically that this less-than-positive thought process leads to unfavorable mental behaviors that increase resistance and alienate people's support.

When a high-impact change materializes, we say there's been a **company reorientation**. This reorientation alters original strategy, making it possible to reinvent the organization. But for this to happen, you must first establish that powerful vision of change. Ask yourself, *What do I wish to achieve? Why must I do it now? What's the intended benefit? Do I have the capabilities to make the change or develop the product?*

Your vision of change can motivate people to modify a specific area of the company (software development, marketing, human resources, etc.) or the processes of the entire company. But don't confuse your *vision of change* with the *corporate or product vision*. Both are equally important, but they have different objectives.

The corporate vision speaks about the personality of the organization and how it will achieve success through its values, principles, and unique abilities. You won't be able to implement a change if your company doesn't have a clear company vision with a consistent message about what is said and what is done.

All visions instill emotions and indicate opportunities for reaching the new state. Visions bring to light the challenges that have to be faced.

An extraordinary vision of change should be easy to understand, occupy no more than half a sheet of paper, be able to be expressed within sixty seconds, be intellectually sound, and have great emotional appeal. It must constantly be reaffirmed by company leaders to remind people how important it is to go in that direction.

I have seen more-traditional companies build large transformation plans. But nowadays we know that profound impact within an exponential growth company does not have to rely on a plan of great magnitude. This is where your vision of change will work its magic.

Creating a Powerful Vision of Change

Having an explicit vision of change helps everyone imagine and aspire to a better world. It also creates alignment within the company. This vision is one of the tools that will allow you to have greater impact. A vision of change also makes it possible to diminish feelings of uncertainty, which in turn leads to positive psychological attitudes and brain activation that largely eliminates the fear of failure.

> If you do not know where you want to go, any road will take you there.

Cheshire Cat, fictional cat in Alice's Adventures in Wonderland

Start with a draft of your vision of change. Support your vision with numbers or other relevant information. Humans are usually motivated by positive messages that connect them to their own purpose and emotions—and that contain at least one of the following four items:

- **Numbers**: $123.874, £10.723, €253
- **Stories/Anecdotes**: I remember once when...
- **Analogies**: The new product will be as important as the discovery of penicillin!
- **Emotions**: Gestures, tone of voice, emotions sparked through your stories, etc.

When you create a vision of change, you become the **sponsor of the initiative**—unless you are embarking on a transformation of great magnitude within a very large organization, in which case there will be multiple leaders. As a sponsor of change, you'll have to count on the day-to-day discipline, time, and commitment for clarifying the change strategy and supporting those who need to understand what's happening.

To be a good sponsor, you will need to work on the following:

▶ Reinforcing the change's message and increasing its visibility.
▶ Removing any initial obstacles.
▶ Promoting a healthy environment with values that match the change vision.
▶ Inspiring people and leading by example.
▶ Connecting people and resources to support the change.
▶ Pulling the "*political strings*" to facilitate the strategy.
▶ Always helping when requested.
▶ Evaluating economic factors.

When taking a new path, people often have conscious and unconscious fears about how their role and position will change within the company. That's why you must repeatedly **clarify the rights, obligations, and expectations of each position during the transformation** of your organization. Remember that the sponsor is not there to control. The sponsor is there to lead using motivational techniques.

I know from experience that you'll face situations where managers and other employees will have a dire need to know if the proposed change is viable, and this will generate a lot of nervousness. You'll need patience when communicating your vision, because people have different perspectives, expectations, and personal challenges.

To create a vision of change, bring together a small group of people in a room. Your goal will be to collaborate on a message that includes real (informal) stories that are meaningful to those who should change.

Years ago, a close friend presented an improved mathematical formula for the calculation of motor vehicle accidents to the board of directors of the National Association of Garages in his country. He believed that the results of this formula would motivate the executives to change their existing accident-evaluation processes and habits. The workshop seemed to go well. He spoke for two hours on how accident scenarios would be calculated, the reasons why the formula should be used, and its benefits. But at the end of the presentation, one of the executives stated that no one had understood the formula and that they didn't see why they should change the way they did things.

To avoid a situation like this, the creation of your vision of change must be a collective effort. Those around you should also take ownership. Adopting your idea is an important part of their day-to-day life as well. Keep in mind that you can count on several visions of change, depending on how many change plans you have. But your vision of change should always be connected to a single company vision.

The Importance of a Sense of Urgency

A sense of urgency plays a crucial role in the success of your plan and in consolidating a change. People won't feel energized if the vision is static, if a document is written by someone who isn't part of their reality, or if it doesn't matter whether the change is implemented immediately or within three years.

There must be a clear sense of urgency before taking the first step. This sense of urgency is not a group's frantic activity following a PowerPoint presentation, nor is it created by a meaningless date. The sense of urgency you need results from the following:

- External pressure from markets or competition.
- Abrupt changes in the organization.
- The economic consequences of inaction when facing a new market challenge (cost of delay) or understanding what action to take for urgent change without destabilizing the health of the organization.

▶ Clients who understand and support the change plan and would like to see the advantages as soon as possible.

▶ A deadline with a significant penalty if not met.

▶ Positive and visible results when removed obstacles lead to a new reality and a company with greater adaptability.

▶ Employees who recognize the benefits of change and who urgently want to change.

Without a clear sense of urgency, such as a random deadline set by management, there can be no real and sustainable alteration of behavior, and the change will begin to lose traction after a few months.

Before taking your first step, you must collaboratively identify the sense of urgency and make it explicit in the vision of change.

Learning to Change

I usually ask executives, "*What do you want to learn from the transformation that you're about to start?*" On many occasions, I am met with silence or a response that only includes the desired outcomes (what they want to obtain from the transformation, or part of the objectives).

I've worked in large corporations that spend millions of dollars a year in the management and communication of the change strategy. But very few invest money to empower people to take the transformation as a learning experience that will change the way they think.

For many years, our education has rewarded those who simply follow a process correctly or offer a quick, single solution to a problem. But this differs from what is needed today to increase innovation and deal with volatile market situations. We must offer multiple solutions to the same problem from different perspectives, and we must question others to encourage the evolution of how they work and think.

What would happen if you could teach techniques so that people could solve problems using new perspectives, and thereby evolve how they reason and work? Your vision of change would need to include one or two lines that explicitly reference the expected forms of reasoning and learning to be attained from the change.

Asking Powerful Questions

Before creating your vision of change, you will have to do a little research to determine what will help you start that journey and provide initial traction. You can start by asking questions that will identify the foundations for that vision of change.

Below are sample questions you could ask in your company when you need to change to better serve your clients:

1. **Determine the sense of urgency.** *Why is change needed right now?*
   What is the status quo, problem, or opportunity that prompts you to think that now is the right time to make the change? What aspect of the current situation does not support the interactions for adapting to the era of exponential markets?

2. **Try to understand what inspires people.** *What inspires them to change and what company values do they need?*
   Studies in human psychology suggest that people usually want to change when an acquired benefit is double that which is left behind. Try to talk to them and learn what would inspire them to change their current path. This requires identifying what brings hope and the values that you'd like to see strengthened by the change. To get these answers, ask questions such as, What would inspire you to change? What values would you want the company's transformation to strengthen?

3. **Verify the expected goals.** *What are the objectives they want to achieve?* How will you know when the change is making progress or has been completed? What is the expected result? What are the expectations of the company versus those of the employees? What simple indicators could be applied to know that habits have been integrated sustainably as part of the new working style?

4. **Check what should be modified.** *What do they think should be changed?* What's expected to change? What change is optional, desirable or mandatory? Is it a change of interactions that also requires a change in processes or behaviors? Is it something more complex that would modify part of the culture? If the company grew exponentially, how would we make the vision or change sustainable?

5. **Determine what could be learned.** *What would they like to learn? What are their personal challenges?*
   Try to understand what employees would like to learn if they choose to take the journey of personal development. They can write a prioritized list of goals and objectives. Think about the common objectives so that all groups can align and work together. What would they like to learn each week? What is the personal challenge that impedes them from going in the new direction?

6. **Identify current opportunities.** *What benefits come from the change?* What will the people, team, or company gain with the change? How will this make the organization a better place?

7. **Determine what the concrete product/service/personal risks are, and the required milestones.** *What are the risks and celebrations?* Think about the risks at each stage and how you will celebrate when these risks are mitigated. What support will be needed from the rest of the

organization? What will inspire the team at each stage to feel proud of being part of the initiative?

8. **Establish a high-level roadmap for the change.** *Can you create a roadmap that supports your change plan?*
   Is the change something that can happen within a few weeks, months, or years? Remember Chapter 2, where we talked about some changes taking years while others take weeks or months (cultural versus procedural). How often should the roadmap be updated and in what way?

While the first six questions offer help in creating the change vision, the last two make it possible to think about specific steps (execution).

Collaboratively Creating a Vision of change

Collaborative visions of change are powerful, as they enable all those affected by a plan, as well as those in charge of supporting the change, to become cocreators of the strategy.

To create a collaborative vision of change, you must organize at least two 90-minute sessions. It's a good idea to invite the managers, the sponsor of the initiative, and the groups of people who need to change. Carefully consider who should attend, keeping in mind that this is not a meeting for the simply curious or for those who will not be contributing anything relevant at this initial stage.

In Chapter 6, I will explain how to create a Transformation Team to help implement a plan that is strongly supported by a vision of change, great strategy, and the necessary training or coaching.

At the start of the session, introduce the problem you need to solve in no more than two minutes. Place everyone in random pairs, which will allow different points of view to be expressed in each team. Give them sticky notes, pens, and space to move about. Avoid settings such as a meeting room with a large table, as this reduces interaction.

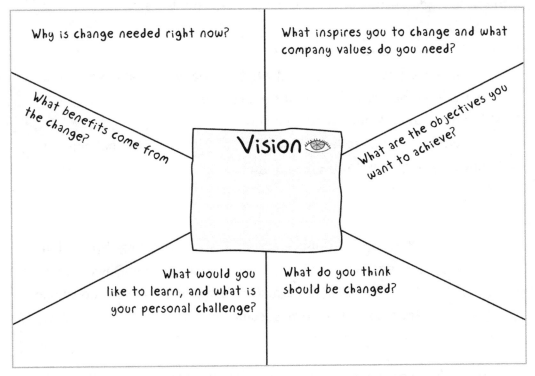

FIGURE 3.1: Change canvas, ©Erich Bühler

Write the following on the first area of your canvas: "*Why is change needed right now?*" Give the teams eight to ten minutes to discuss and write up to three answers on the sticky notes. As they discuss, share some of the other questions for the same point to help them deepen their thoughts on the subject.

Once the five to eight minutes are up, give the pairs two minutes each to come forward, place their sticky notes on the canvas, and share their ideas with the rest of the participants. This activity will not only help you align expectations but will also instill in your team a sense of being cocreators of change.

Feel free to add your own observations or ask questions, encouraging others to do the same. Open questions will allow you to discover new points of view, challenges, and areas you hadn't initially considered. Continue in the same manner with the second question, repeating the process until the end.

1. Why is change needed right now?
2. What inspires you to change, and what company values do you need?
3. What are the objectives you want to achieve?
4. What do you think should be changed?
5. What would you like to learn, and what is your personal challenge?
6. What benefits come from the change?

You can learn more about how to ask thought-provoking questions in Eric E. Vogt, Juanita Brown, and David Isaacs's book *The Art of Powerful Questions*, which you can download for free at *en.Innova1st.com/30A*

You will discover many ideas and points of view that will make it possible to start thinking about that powerful vision of change. At the end of the session, it's a good idea to thank the participants and provide them with information about what will happen next.

As you can see, this type of activity allows the team to brainstorm and explore different points of view, eradicate doubts, create alignment, listen to powerful phrases, and develop intelligent slogans that stir emotions.

In the second workshop, you should bring out the canvas from the previous session and spend at least ten minutes summarizing the ideas that were generated. Then ask participants what would happen if they opened their favorite newspaper the next day and found a headline and a short write-up (five to ten lines) talking about the company and the change they were about to implement. *What would the story say?*

Give them ten to fifteen minutes to write the story using the information provided in the previous session. Once time is up, ask them to come forward, read their note, and paste it in the center square. Remember to encourage participants to ask questions, add comments, and express their concerns. This crucial stage enables them to mentally prepare for what comes next.

As soon as you're ready, start writing the first draft of the vision of change. Draw inspiration from the different stories and ask for feedback from participants. Invite them to come forward and add their thoughts on the board. In the center square, you can start by writing phrases like these:

We change because...
Our personal challenge is...
We want to learn because...
We improve because...
We're inspired to change by...

Don't worry if this exercise is difficult at first. It takes a few minutes to warm up before words start pouring out. Often, it will be necessary to keep participants from side-tracking toward the solution (that is, they must refrain from creating a strategy or trying to establish the steps to implement the change). There is often anxiety about taking that big leap, so indicate that this will be tackled in later sessions. You can note any questions to answer in the future or at the end of the session, as appropriate.

Remember that your vision of change should take up no more than half a sheet of paper and should be able to be read in a maximum of sixty seconds. Once the session is over, share the initial vision draft and thank the participants. Inform them that the next steps will be related to the "*how*" (that is, the strategy).

As you can see, these meetings are essential to align people and help them feel involved. **Remember that the vision of change must be created collaboratively**, so any modification should be communicated and discussed before it is set.

Setting Up the Transformation Team

Unless yours is a small company, you'll need a team that supports you every day as you carry out the change-implementation strategy. In traditional companies, this group of employees is usually dedicated to controlling the progress of originally established goals. But the group acts differently in a company that faces the exponential growth of markets. Here the focus needs to be on constantly helping improve the company workflow and making decisions with the little information available.

In my experience, a Transformation Team usually comprises between three and five people for every hundred individuals affected, and the team requires an important commitment (in many cases, up to 100 percent availability). Members of this team must have strong mediation skills, be willing to learn, be well respected within the organization, and possess the power to remove obstacles within the company. You should expect the following activities from a Transformation Team:

1. Improving transparency and supporting the message and the change strategy.
2. Demonstrating behaviors consistent with the values of the vision of change.
3. Bringing to light the dependencies between areas of the company and facilitating their removal.
4. Helping unlearn old practices, skills, or processes and replacing them with new ones.
5. Creating necessary connections between people (or individuals with resources) so they can solve problems independently.
6. Helping understand the new ways of thinking.
7. Ensuring that the necessary alterations are made in the operations of the business to facilitate the change.
8. Ensuring that other areas of the company or senior management understand the reason for the change.

9. Creating formal and informal structures to support the flow of information within and outside the teams.
10. Helping to find, recruit, or invest in new capabilities that support the vision.
11. Taking care of team logistics.
12. Accounting for the economic cost of decisions and the impact of any decision that would cause a delay (Cost of Delay techniques).

One of the key aspects the Transformation Team should focus is on how individuals feel about the proposed change. Many employees might feel threaten or resist change for several reasons. A good way to reduce resistance is by making sure that everyone understands what makes them feel intimidated. Whether individuals welcome or resist change depends on whether one or more of the following needs are threatened:

NEED	Threat (example)	Reward (example)
Status (Social Status in relation to others)	Giving advice, direct instructions where low trust exists, losing influence or moving people to new positions with apparently less prestige.	Creating positions with more prestige than the previous ones, receiving positive feedback, building a safe environment, etc.
Certainty (Ability to predict Outcomes)	Not knowing what other people expect.	Having a clear vision, goals and transparent expectations, refocus people on what is certain right now, etc.

Autonomy (Sense of control over destiny)	Being micro-managed.	Allowing people to solve problems and self-organize around their work and to manage their workload.
Relatedness (How the person is part of the tribe)	Meeting new people all the time or not having time to establish quality relationships.	Having stable teams, a friendly environment, knowing what motivates people and amplifying it, etc.
Fairness (Perception of being treated fairly)	Non-transparent values, shy away from behavioral issues, etc.	Everybody has access to information, everyone has a say, etc.

Table 3.1: SCARF model by David Rock

Leaders and members of the Transformation Team should openly talk to the individuals affected by the change and try to bring visibility about their fears, frustrations, hopes, needs, and beliefs. If one or more needs are threatened, the behaviors might spread across the company and that will stop the new initiative from becoming contagious.

When planning a change, it is a good idea to use the SCARF model to frame questions that help uncover the real causes of resistance. Once identified these areas, the impact can be lessened by positively strengthening those needs. Finally, ensure those affected by the change feel that the Transformation Team is part of their day-to-day work and not viewed as an external group. In Chapter 6, I will show you how to prepare a Transformation Team for the change.

Understanding the Importance of Commitment in Employees

Remarkable companies treat their employees as if they were potential customers. When this isn't the case, individuals do not commit to change plans, and without commitment, it will fall solely on your shoulders to push the initiative. I can tell you from experience that this scenario is not professionally or personally sustainable and will eat away at those in charge of the initiative.

Months ago, I had a conversation with a manager in charge of the largest supermarket group in New Zealand. This person, although exhausted, told me she had to be in the office every day to make sure her team was aligned and would achieve their goals. The team exhibited low morale, motivation, and commitment. After being repeatedly scolded by management, they did not feel safe, and this led to dysfunctions in their interactions. They would passively smile in meetings as they accepted any workload imposed by their bosses—even though they knew they wouldn't be able to handle the workload.

Unfortunately, such situations are not an exception. I imagine that you have seen similar situations in other companies, where people only dedicate themselves to completing their tasks and are not actively involved in improving the organization.

In its report on the state of workplace in 2016, the Gallup consultancy revealed that only 13 percent of the world's workforce is committed to their work (32 percent in the United States). Recent studies indicate that there is a clear and direct correlation between the financial performance of an organization and the level of employee commitment to their work and change. To achieve strong employee commitment, the transformation must be carried out in an environment where everyone can feel safe, learn every day, and make highly visible collaborative decisions.

When individuals do not connect with their work, they leave it up to the majority to indicate the way they expect others to solve their problems, and they do not feel capable of developing their own skills. What do you think are the reasons why the people in your company do not feel strong commitment?

Below is a list of the reasons I usually encounter:

- Transformation plans where leaders or managers arbitrarily decide not to involve the affected groups in the decision-making process.
- Excessive multitasking, heavy workload, or a lack of positive recognition for successfully completed tasks.
- Insufficient emphasis/investment in learning.
- Lack of quality time to reflect on the processes and interactions.
- Outdated working conditions that hinder work (lack of security, trust, more than a single priority, destruction of shared knowledge, etc.).
- Lack of a realistic vision for the company, change, and product.
- Inability of people to self-organize to solve problems.
- Lack of direct contact between clients and the employees who create the product or service.

One of the most important assets of any company is **shared knowledge**. Many organizations have high turnover, and they might not know how to manage this turnover. Because of this, shared knowledge is often lost, resulting in high hidden costs. Inevitably, this delays learning, innovation, and adaptability. Everyone loses motivation while the company loses its traction for change.

Shared knowledge is the learning that results from the interactions of a team during the time they work collaboratively on one or more tasks. This includes information and skills, but also shared mental models (forms of reasoning, interpretation of expectations, and the understanding of problems). This knowledge can rarely be maintained in documents and is the *"secret recipe"* that gives the business its competitive advantage.

Employee turnover radically increases the loss of shared knowledge. Research carried out by Deloitte's Global Human Capital Trends in 2018 indicated that 78 percent of business leaders rated staff retention and commitment as urgent or important.

Three types of attitude directly affect the results of change in a company:

Committed Employees	Those who will help you to implement the change. As soon as they understand your vision, they will do everything in their power to take it forward and remove any obstacles that arise along the way. They will actively think about how to improve processes and interactions.
Uncommitted Employees	They will do the work but will not feel motivated by their tasks. Tasks will be a job to be completed before they can go home.
Employees disconnected by their own choice	This group is dissatisfied with the work and makes their frustration clear by actively undermining committed workers.

Table 3.2: The three types of employees

The first group (**committed employees**) makes an additional mental and physical effort to evolve interactions and processes. They work with passion and feel a deep connection with the vision of the company and its change strategy.

Uncommitted employees often leave the company if they do not find valid motivation. But they could become highly committed allies if you involve them in the process and give them the opportunity to decide and alter the plan. This can be done through activities that provide them with the necessary space to influence decisions and with sufficient visibility to understand the initiative.

The biggest risk to the change plan are unhappy employees who choose to **disconnect** and will show their lack of satisfaction by undermining the change strategy. They may be difficult to detect because they do not appear hostile or harmful. But if you pay attention, you will see that they have little or no concern for the client, produce high levels of conflict, and will complain about a situation without offering solutions.

It is easy to confuse people in this group with those who have an antiquated mindset. Nevertheless, they will be on your side if you provide them with support and corresponding recognition.

In a company I helped in the UK, a graphic designer who had worked for nearly two years with a multifunctional Scrum team decided that she didn't feel ready for the challenge. She was comfortable in the company but had decided to disconnect from its vision and goals. Obviously, her attitude generated high-risk situations, with high emotions that hindered others from reaching their goals. The organization decided to move ahead because it did not want to assume the cost of recruiting and training another individual. After a few months, the other employees were focusing more on the processes and less on their interactions. They lost motivation and began to disconnect from their daily tasks.

A good alternative here would have been to have a timely and crucial conversation—an open, honest, and transparent talk between the disconnected employee and someone they respected. If it isn't possible to connect the change plan with what matters to an employee—their goals and purpose or learning—the plan will have little chance of surviving.

Many consultants call it WIIFM (*What's in it for me?*), meaning that individuals need to know the benefits they will receive from a change and fully understand why they must change before they will attempt to do so.

Here are some things you can do to make people feel motivated during the transformation of your company:

1. Provide employees with the business context.
Explain the context that has made a change plan necessary. Share the vision, strategy, data, business goals, contractual issues, and any topic that can provide information on the situation.

2. Help understand the constraints.
Help people understand the constraints of the company, be they limited skills or unavailable resources. Help them also understand limitations such as dependencies that can't be removed in the medium term or aspects that are dragged from the past and that will have an impact on the change plan (technical debt, archaic processes, etc.).

3. Use the real capacity.
Ensure that employees can choose the workload they consider most appropriate, according to their knowledge and availability (Pull System, Kanban).

4. Connect people with the client and the purpose.
Ensure that individuals understand the client and why the change is needed. Nothing is more motivating than knowing that you are helping real people.

5. Give time to discover and reflect.

Many teams have no time to think, reflect, and discover how the new change strategy could affect them. Ensure that employees have the time to do so and ensure that managers reaffirm this practice.

6. Gamify the matter.

Use games for people to have fun while reinforcing positive behaviors, values, and principles. Create an environment that encourages healthy competition for achieving goals so employees can witness their progress. Don't forget to offer rewards to increase motivation.

7. Create suitable metrics.

Ensure teams can collectively understand and collect simple metrics that measure the progress of change. Also ensure that any local improvement has a positive impact on the rest of the organization.

If you decide to use gamification to impact behaviors, make sure you use games that make people feel good at the end of their day/sprint. They should see the progress they have made towards something that matters to them. Every gamification initiative should leverage the following techniques:

- **Dynamics**: motivate behavior through scenarios, rules and progression.
- **Mechanics**: help achieve goals through teams, healthy competitions, rewards and feedback.
- **Components**: track progress through quests, points, levels, badges and collections.

In Chapter 6, you'll see how to connect many of these points with a Transformation Team.

The Story of Peter

I've known Peter for many years now. We met in Uruguay when I had a company that created software tools for corporations. I still remember the day he told me that he had an innovative idea and that he wanted to set up a business.

During startup, he had only a few employees. Communication between them was mainly face-to-face. There was mutual trust, they knew what others thought of the company, and they understood its vision and strategy.

At that time, the company's size was easily manageable, and information traveled quickly, informally, and with low levels of distortion. Every day, internal and external feedback helped avoid wrong paths or decisions.

I must admit that there were gaps in the company. Some skills were scarce, but everyone was happy to collaborate and share their knowledge, even when overly busy. Teams would meet if there was an urgent problem, and they exchanged ideas until the problem was resolved. You could see what others were doing, because the actions were observed in the office and the progress was seen on physical boards. They were happy, and it seemed as though it would last forever.

During that time, no one thought it would be necessary to transform the company or that explicit values would be desperately needed to align the entire organization.

Peter didn't know that core values are the most important aspect of a modern organization. They establish basic limitations as to how, where, and why to compete. They dictate how people will behave socially and how everyone will provide visibility of their work. He didn't even suspect that a small change in those values could affect the five basic foundations of the organization.

There is no universal truth, but regardless of the size of a company, the following pillars will always exist:

1. Company vision and strategy
2. Clear distribution of power in the organization
3. Behaviors / social systems (how people behave, interact, and make their work visible)
4. Structures and their connections (hierarchical structures) that help employees
5. Control systems (how people and things are controlled)

When one or more values are modified in the organization, a cascading effect occurs upon the other areas. Although it may seem like common sense, employees do not always stop to reflect on the importance of employing a strategy that will produce a chain of changes. When all the pillars change, we say that the company has undergone a transformation.

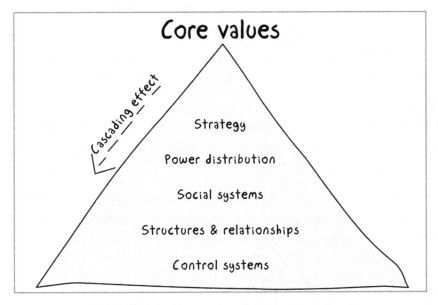

FIGURE 3.2: Core values cascading effect

Peter wanted me to help his company succeed, and he completely trusted my opinion because we had a relationship based on friendship and respect. One day, he told me he wanted to start a transformation and begin with the software teams. He'd heard about the miracle of SAFe (*Scaled Agile Framework*) and LeSS (*Large-Scale Scrum*), and he wanted to try them.

Unfortunately, he didn't believe me when I told him that starting with a change in the way we coordinate people or how employees are controlled (control systems) would be a slow way to transform.

Control systems are procedures/processes designed to verify, regulate and supervise people and their outputs.

Modifications in coordination and control are weakly associated with changes in people's mindsets. Many companies are convinced that by becoming digital they can transform quickly by simply altering the way people work. In fact, some might choose to modify processes to promote change. But to really alter something, you need a radical disruption that breaks the patterns of organizational inertia and helps individuals learn new ways of thinking.

Agile and the Scrum framework have an important role here. The *Agile Manifesto* contains principles that Scrum aligns to and that result in important disruption, such as putting the customer and employees first, the self-organization of teams, cross-functional groups, and real feedback from the client and the rest of the company. Pay attention to Scrum's values and think about how they could impact your company:

Courage - Team members have the courage to do the right thing and work on tough problems.

Focus - Everyone focuses on the tasks of the work cycle and the goals of the Scrum team.

Commitment - People personally commit to achieving the goals of the Scrum team.

Respect - Team members respect each other as capable, independent people.

Openness - The Scrum team and its stakeholders agree to be open about all the work and the challenges of performing the work.

Scrum offers a minimum set of rules, such as a fixed work cycle (*Sprint*), a single priority for work (*Backlog*), time to reflect (*retrospective meeting*), and recurring meetings to empower people (*Daily Scrum, planning*, etc.).

Back to Peter and his company . . . he didn't ask me about Scrum, but he was lucky. A few months after launching his product, the small business became a success. This attracted the attention of hundreds of customers and a lot of capital. The immediate result was the creation of new departments, roles, and rules to better serve their clients. This positively impacted the company's economic stability and helped predict actions to be taken in the medium term.

He decided to move to new offices and needed to create a logo that better identified the corporate culture. It was clear to all that the growth of the company had brought new benefits—but also additional processes.

One day I heard someone mention that better performance was needed and that this could only be achieved by focusing on cost reduction. I also heard that they wanted to add new departments to address this issue. Within the company, everyone began to get used to the idea that each time there was a new corporate requirement (cheaper and more reliable service, higher quality, faster speed of the market, etc.), a new role or department would be added to deal with the matter.

As the company and the number of departments and roles grew, the number of associated processes increased. Along with this, more bureaucracy and dependencies were created. Little by little, the flexibility of the organization diminished, and it became more difficult to determine if the value delivered to the client was right.

Because the company was growing, everyone figured it would be a good idea to abandon the physical whiteboards that had been used since the beginning. These were replaced with a software tool to increase collaboration. Soon after installing this software to manage tasks, they began getting rid of the physical boards and their sticky notes.

With the new tool, not everyone had the same visibility. It was now necessary to ask for usernames, passwords, and permissions. It was also necessary to learn how to use the application, and a new department was created to oversee this. As a result, visibility decreased, and complexity and transaction costs increased. No one had realized the impact that a small change of habit would have. People were happy to send tickets and emails back and forth and were confident that this would exponentially increase their productivity.

One month later, they opened two new branches in nearby countries, and the following Monday Peter said that he wanted to achieve a clear corporate identity in all his branches. A new business-alignment (Brand Management) department was established to reaffirm the existing core values and ensure the entire company had the same foundations. Greater stability was achieved, which allowed people to better understand the unique character of the company and establish an internal legitimacy for desired behaviors.

Working with Peter as a consultant before his company's exponential growth, I had noticed the continuous feedback between employees and clients. But as the company grew, informal communication channels had been standardized and replaced by coordination structures through processes in all corners of the company.

The Transformation Team announced the new vision of change and strategy with a small event, and they sent everyone an email with the company's new values and principles. To increase visibility, inspirational photos were hung in the meeting rooms. Rules were also adopted to comply with the new vision, and a recruitment system was established to find candidates for the new profile. At that time, Peter did not know that his company was going through a period of convergence.

FIGURE 3.3: A convergent period ends and another one starts

Companies often confuse a period of convergence with a transformation, but these are different situations.

An organization has many periods of convergence, one after another, during its life cycle, but these stages do not alter the company. They **reaffirm and evolve the organization's initial ideas**. During a convergence stage, there is no disruptive change. The values and most of their strategies remain intact. Forces move to **support the status quo**. Each time a new period of convergence begins, stronger interpretations of the current situation are created, and these are commonly reinforced by new processes and practices.

A period of convergence is a stage where organizations elaborate, reaffirm, and increase existing structures and control systems to offer greater alignment with their core values and strategies.

The longer the convergence period, the more difficult it will be for a consultant or any other change agent to make a radical change. There will be more obstacles to remove and greater institutional resistance, both psychological and procedural.

As the converging periods come and go, the status quo is reinforced by what we call **incremental change**. In traditional companies, these stages increase dependencies and complexity, because more interpretations and standards are usually added after each adjustment.

Something similar can be seen in many governments, where convergence periods result in hundreds of laws, rules, and guidelines—but there's no real transformation. It's better to reboot the system with a focus on simplifying processes.

In most companies, convergent periods add or formalize new rules or habits around their initial beliefs. I've seen many teams loaded with bureaucracy, reports, metrics, and guidelines resulting from many years of incremental change.

Moments of turbulence are one of the triggers for the reduction of complexity. I remember an episode in a company that was about to lose an important client. The organization went into chaos as they questioned many of their processes and beliefs. They finally simplified their forms of communication, methodologies, and standards, and this helped them win the client back.

I realized that the only way for Peter to run, grow, and transform his organization was by simplifying the company with a clear vision of change. Unfortunately, this would only happen if he and his company experienced real problems, such as a sustained period of low performance or high competition that resulted in the questioning of their beliefs and how they worked.

One morning, I read in the newspaper that a group of companies was coming to the market with products similar to Peter's. I imagined that the likelihood of their executives receiving the information from that news was extremely low because the organization had gone through long and successful convergence periods.

I waited for management to become aware of the news, but it never happened, as their focus was exclusively on the improvement of their processes.

In April 2015, I had to transfer to Chile to help another client. For several months, I heard little of Peter's company, so I figured it must be fine. When I returned to Spain, I was surprised to find a different Peter.

He'd gone through a couple of interesting stages, and I was glad to see he'd learned a lot from them. Initially, he'd decided to compete with the other companies by reducing costs: He hired cheaper labor and reduced the quality of the products so they would hit the market faster. He also tried to expand his software department to produce more applications, but he encountered a lot of pressure, a shortage of skills, an increase in bureaucracy, unhappiness, conflict, and a decrease in business value for the client. It was not a good time for him. But he learned—a lot.

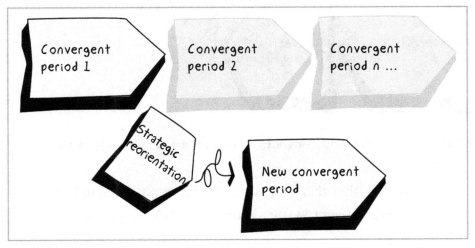

FIGURE 3.4: Strategic reorientation leads to new convergent periods

During the year I was in Chile, Peter remembered I'd mentioned the *Cost of Delay techniques* for decision-making and that he should look for exponentiality for the areas of his company that were scarce (knowledge, resources, etc.). This helped him set a strategic **reorientation**, which meant a short period of **discontinuous change** because of a new radical strategy. And this led to a new alignment, which caused some turbulence and alterations in the distribution of power, control, social systems, and organizational structures.

At that point, he understood the impact that changing values and principles had on the pillars of an organization.

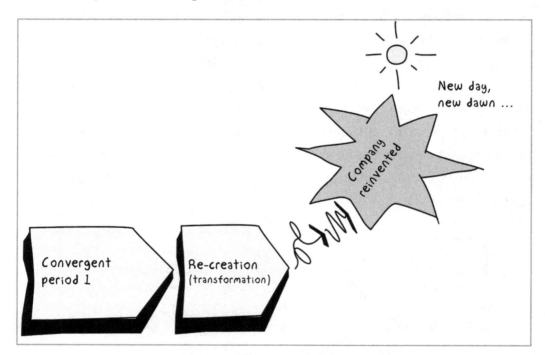

FIGURE 3.5: A company reinvents itself after a re-creation (transformation)

I had the feeling that this **re-creation** (transformation) had been the most extreme and exciting event in the history of Peter's company.

During a re-creation, all or some of the company's values change, triggering a cascade effect upon the other pillars of the company. Re-creation is how organizations reinvent themselves. Consultants and change agents usually refer to this as business transformation.

I thought Peter was going in the right direction and that his organization was evolving because of honest feedback from clients and employees. He was actively working on reaffirming those informal channels and reducing the complexity of their processes, metrics, and forms of interaction. The company had a powerful vision of change that motivated them to move forward together.

My work with Peter was done. I was happy to have participated and witnessed the growth and change of his company.

Reaching Sustainable Change in the Company

You can use several approaches to achieve sustainable change, but for all of them you'll need people who are able to connect informally and analyze opportunities and problems from different points of view.

Regardless of what you want to modify, it is always a good idea to experiment first with a small part of your organization and then expand. This allows you to demonstrate that the concepts work and to know in advance how to scale these new ways of working to the rest of the company.

Many initiatives entail testing of new company values. People need to feel safe, but they must also be able to leave their comfort zone. You won't be able to guarantee success until you have acquired knowledge through experimentation in real scenarios.

If you promote the right conditions in the organization, you'll see that people will gradually take ownership of your vision and strategy. If all goes well, they will start thinking about expanding these ideas through the company without you constantly pushing the initiative.

You're probably wondering what techniques you can use to implement a change in the company.

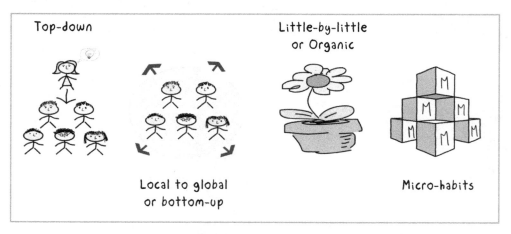

FIGURE 3.6: Four approaches to transform your company

I'll show you four approaches, though you'll have to use a mixture of them based on the situation and the level of motivation in your teams.

Making a Change by Implementing a Top-down Approach

In a top-down approach, leaders or senior management create the vision of change and define the strategy. This approach is common where decision-making is centralized in the higher ranks of the company. Here, managers usually make preliminary studies and evaluate the benefits, costs, and affected areas. They verify the progress of the strategy and its subsequent implementation. It isn't surprising that more-traditional companies make *simple loop decisions* (as illustrated in the previous chapter) during the execution stages of a change plan.

Imagine that the CEO decides that the minimum unit of work is two people and that all tasks must be done in pairs. My experience indicates that this type of behavior is difficult to implement in a sustainable manner. However, because the director has the authority, employees will assimilate it as something that is expected and part of their role in the company.

The biggest drawback in top-down approaches is that the change can be seen as an action imposed by management. Such a situation can lead to interpersonal conflicts and greater resistance in the long term. *Do employees do it because it is mandated or because they feel inspired and want to learn and improve?*

> People do not resist change. They resist being changed.
>
> Peter Senge, Scientist

The initiative's success in these cases will depend on whether a positive and trusting relationship develops between those who implement and execute the strategy and those who will be affected by the change. It's a good idea to use rules that decentralize the control of economic decisions (in other words, to allow others to learn and make decisions without consulting you).

In the aeronautics company Boeing, assembly-plant workers can make design changes or substitutions of aircraft materials of up to $300 as long as the change results in savings of at least one pound off the aircraft's total weight. In these cases, the decentralization of decisions encourages creativity and learning while decreasing pressure on the upper layers of the organization to supervise all tasks.

The top-down approach can also prove useful when you need to adapt the whole organization to new principles, or when structural changes affecting the pillars of the company need to be implemented.

Just remember that it isn't realistic to manage a top-to-bottom change when market alterations are constant and knowledge requirements are difficult to predict.

Such is the case for the software-development industry, where you need various roles and constant collaboration from different areas to create a single product. If you think about it, the interventions here require specialized and scarce skills, or experts far below those who order the change. Generally, this kind of specialized knowledge isn't found higher up the corporate ladder, so making top-down decisions logically increases the risk. In this case, you can use a variation of the top-down approach where strong leadership fosters the auto-organization of individuals around their objectives.

Steve Jobs led the consumer-technology market and created exceptional devices with cutting-edge designs. When Jobs launched the iPhone in 2007, he stated that his vision was to have a computer, the software, and a touch screen within a single device.

Apple rarely listened to focus groups or included market trends in their phones. Jobs usually expressed what he wanted through a vision, enabling his teams to self-organize and implement his plans, change strategies, and metrics.

As you can see, a single approach can lead to different tactics and deliver different results. If you lead with a clear vision, you can allow room for those involved to create their own change plan and determine how they will proceed through the self-organization of their tasks and responsibilities. This creates space for innovation and for teams to make decisions and learn without having to constantly involve middle management.

Initiating the Change: From the Local to the Global

In the local-to-global or bottom-up approach, gravity works backward—and with different rules. This type of change is common in software-development or digital companies.

The exponential acceleration of markets initially requires that software teams are closest to the client. IT departments commonly use the Scrum framework, which encourages several positive habits:

- Self-organization of the team around goals and daily tasks without the need for management control.
- Working side-by-side with clients and focusing on business value.
- Technical excellence in everything that is produced.
- Fixed length work cycles (*Sprint*) of one to four weeks.
- End-of-cycle reflection sessions on what could have been done differently and action points to improve processes and interactions.
- Daily team meetings to promote visibility and coordination among team members.

This way of working generates knowledge quickly, so it's considered by companies as a platform toward the transformation of the entire organization (re-creation).

Constant face-to-face communication between team members and clients provides a high level of information exchange. In turn, making collaborative decisions accelerates the development of ideas. Individuals feel more motivated because they are the main actors in their change strategy. They will, therefore, do everything in their power to achieve success. This includes taking over the improvement and evolution of their practices, processes, and interactions.

Management, however, encounters many inconveniences during the first months of using Scrum, because managers have to stop themselves from controlling people and start focusing on removing obstacles.

Some may feel that they lose power, and this could generate setbacks. In the next chapter, I'll explain how to deal with this issue.

When implementing Scrum, or any other modern framework, you'll see that companies usually employ pilot projects, allowing them to test an idea and reduce risks. A trial period is usually established for a limited number of teams to use the new rules, values, principles, and practices. Once the change proves its value, new habits and knowledge often spread quickly to the rest of the company.

The expansion of the pilot project to the rest of the company may vary depending on the risk or uncertainty about the change. In some cases, the first pilot team finishes, and a second pilot group begins. Other companies prefer an overlapping approach in which the second group starts a few weeks before the first pilot group has finished.

When you use pilot projects, remember these three important points before expanding them to the rest of the company:

1. This type of project requires highly motivated people, which could cause the rest of the company to be depleted of appropriate talent as key employees are transferred to the pilot teams.

2. It's a good idea in the early stages to use automated processes and artificial intelligence so you know in advance the scarce areas or resources and start thinking about how they will become exponential in the near future.

3. When expanding the learning of the pilot teams to the rest of the organization, you could inadvertently introduce the problems of those areas (the unhealthy habits) into the rest of the organization. Pay special attention to this.

A successful change requires more than quickly disseminating knowledge to the rest of the company. The efforts to transform the company from the bottom-up creates the approach and the initial conditions for sustainable change, but they're not enough to achieve it. A high level of employee motivation is needed for bottom-up transformations to be successful.

Embarking on a Change by Introducing It Little-by-little

Another alternative is to introduce new ideas little by little (organic). In this approach, you implement each process or practice until you complete a larger goal.

Imagine that the goal is to implement a framework that has six practices: You will implement one and wait until you see that the adoption has been successful. Then you will continue with the second, and so on, until you have completed the proposed plan. Management usually approves this approach because it entails a small experiment with constrained and controlled results. Because the cause and effect of a change tends not to be linear, the addition of a minor new practice could be really positive or very negative. These in turn will either move the company in the right direction or cause the initiative to quickly lose traction. Losing traction can be an inconvenience, because it often leads to a return to old habits. If this happens, you should analyze the cause of the loss of motivation and reformulate your plan or use the micro-habit technique that we'll explore later on. You can create an organic change when there is no clear sense of urgency, if the risk of implementing everything at the same time is high, or if you need to experiment with something small because you do not know if it will solve the problem. In any case, you'll need clear metrics that allow you to detect a setback as soon as it happens.

Making a Change Using Micro-Habits

Micro-habits are actions that require little effort, or minimal motivation, to complete. Over time, micro-habits build slowly upon themselves until they result in something significantly larger.

The beauty of a micro-habit is that you can make a huge impact without large amounts of energy, major plans, or coordination. This is because of a psychological phenomenon known as the behavioral impulse, which I explain further on. Basically, once you start a micro-habit, you have a better chance to build a longer-lasting habit.

Some years ago, I taught seven simple techniques so that Product Owners could say "no" indirectly to their clients or stakeholders, and I also taught a small micro-habit to reaffirm these techniques. That small change made it possible to reduce queues of unnecessary requirements, increase team morale, and increase innovation. A small habit with a great impact!

Micro-habits also help in making personal decisions in cultures where group decisions are prevalent. I share more about micro-habit techniques in the next chapter.

As we've seen, employee commitment is needed for an incremental and sustainable change. Remember that incremental implies that it has a clear story line between the progression of the different plans (which support each other) and a connection with the vision of change. Sustainable means that you will not have to push it every day. Instead, motivated individuals will take over the change plan and help it grow and evolve.

Regardless of the approach you use, you must be able to demonstrate that any change initiative can be easily capitalized. For this, I suggest you follow these seven recommendations, which will enable you to create your own approach:

1. If you start with pilot projects, **invest several days on the liftoff stage of the initiative**.
2. **Make learning and economic benefits visible.** The change will come easier if it translates to economic advantage for the company in addition to being a way to test new ideas, values, or ways of working.
3. Ensure that the pilot project **demonstrates** areas that could be **automated** or supported with artificial intelligence to convert limited or scarce (linear) resources into exponential ones.
4. During the first stage, focus on **removing obstacles** to facilitate experimentation. You can also expand your idea to other teams to ensure you're on the right track.
5. **Use your clients as much as possible.** They are a huge network of brains that can offer valuable feedback, come up with solutions, and help you detect shortcomings in your strategy.
6. When you **expand the new processes**, framework, or other solution to the rest of the company, focus on **high-priority problems**. Begin by removing blockages that restrict the organization from competing or better adapting to the markets.
7. Finally, focus on **accelerating** those areas of the company that make it possible to **develop capabilities**, so that your initiative is sustainable in the long term. This may include changes in infrastructures or the use of a technology to accelerate knowledge.

A good change approach also requires that you understand the way people act upon change. In the next chapter, you'll learn key change techniques related to neuroscience, psychology, and organizational patterns.

What You Have Learned

- ☑ How to create a powerful vision of change.
- ☑ The characteristics of a sense of urgency and learning.
- ☑ Techniques to create a vision of change in a collaborative way.
- ☑ The role of the sponsor and the transformation team.
- ☑ The different levels of commitment in employees.
- ☑ Different approaches to implement a change.

1. What four types of messages should you include in your vision of change to make it powerful?

2. What are some of the sponsor's responsibilities when implementing a change initiative?

3. How can a sense of urgency be created?

4. What are some of the tasks that a Transformation Team should perform?

CHAPTER 4

Preparing Your Mind for the Change

CHAPTER 4

❝We are what we repeatedly do. Excellence, then, is not an act, but a habit.❞

Will Durant, Philosopher (based on Aristoteles)

Congratulations! You've established a new framework in your company and now everything revolves around leading with innovative concepts, practices, and processes. Your organization is making decisions based on business value, everyone is aligned with the principles and new habits, and most initiatives seem to be on track. But then progress begins to lose traction. You decide to speak with the team members, because you believe the problem might lie in a lack of general knowledge or understanding of the ingredients of an exponential company.

To your surprise, they do know about the exponential acceleration of results, they have mastered techniques to analyze complex problems, they are practically experts in Agile, Scrum, Lean, eXtreme Programming, mindsets, and frameworks, and they have the support of their managers.

They also know that company transformation has ceased to be optional and is now an imperative business requirement. They acknowledge they must change as often as needed. But the initiatives continue to lag, and you wonder what could be wrong.

A senior manager from a company I helped some time back once said, "*Logic always prevails and people will modify their opinions if they are shown evidence and a good reason for doing so.*" This belief resulted in meetings with empty chairs, because employees were too busy to attend, trying to "put out last-minute fires."

You can't alter how people work or think without remembering that our brains are not built to accept change or contradictory information easily.

One Monday morning, I was heading out to hold a workshop at an Agile conference in Austria. To be honest, I've never liked getting up early, and I hardly notice my surroundings until I've been awake for a few hours. I remember, though, that the plane was full and noisy. I was focusing on the material for my presentation when I overheard someone speaking about something that caught my attention.

Four people next to me were fervently discussing human rights, Trump, and the situations in Europe and Catalonia. Each had their own ardent and well-developed point of view, based on information that seemed factual and solid. The conversation drifted to other parts of the world, such as North Korea and the United States, and then to the 9/11 conspiracy theory and the explosives allegedly placed by the US government in the parking garages of the towers. Finally, someone concluded that humankind had never reached the moon.

At first, the thread of conversation seemed rational, but it progressively became less so. They took turns pointing out that Armstrong's moon-landing photos showed no stars, that there couldn't have been waves on the flag because there's no wind on the moon, that the astronauts' shadows couldn't be real . . . The more any of them presented their "*scientific*" evidence, the more the others would disagree.

Although I'm not particularly sociable in the mornings, I decided to interject—before someone concluded that Walt Disney had produced the moon landing, which would only lead to someone saying that the filmmaker was being held in deep freeze at some top-secret base in the US near Roswell . . .

> We must be careful not to believe things simply because we want them to be true. No one can fool you as easily as you can fool yourself!

Richard Feynman, Physicist

I offered what I felt to be an irrefutable piece of information: On the moon, there's a laser reflector (Laser Ranging Retroreflector or LRR) installed by Apollo 11 during its mission. Its main objective is to reflect back a laser fired from Earth to measure the distance between the two. I added that the reflector has been in operation for over four decades.

After hearing me out, though, they were still far from convinced, and they attempted to invalidate my claim with dozens of new arguments. They continued with their rhetoric, adding that no one could have filmed Armstrong because the radiation would have melted the cameras, and that the delay in communications was less than it should have been considering the technology at the time. How was it possible that logic did not prevail and that these individuals did not change their minds after hearing me? I'd forgotten how several surveys sustained that between 6 percent and 20 percent of Americans, 25 percent of Britons, and 28 percent of Russians believe that humans have never landed on the moon.

Then I remembered something I've seen play out in companies for years: Rational arguments are not very effective at altering people's beliefs or behaviors. Our rational brain is equipped with evolutionary neurological mechanisms that aren't particularly advanced, and information that differs from our personal beliefs is perceived as a threat.

For the most part, forms of reasoning learned during early childhood guide our opinions for the rest of our lives. When we hear contradictory information that threatens our dogmas, the mind, instead of accepting it, focuses on finding fault or inconsistency. The mind creates arguments against the information instead of establishing brain connections that allow new forms of reasoning to develop.

This is what we call confirmation bias, which refers to the way in which our brain draws conclusions. Confirmation bias was initially demonstrated in the 1960s by Peter C. Wason, a cognitive psychologist at University College London.

Confirmation bias is the process of putting together a selective collection of evidence to affirm a position. Many employees or groups tend to favor information that confirms their preconceived ideas or hypotheses, regardless of their accuracy.

We see it all the time in companies: a team that doesn't talk to the client but makes decisions about what the client might like or dislike about the product, or a Product Owner who creates several user profiles and makes decisions without face-to-face feedback from clients (or only collects it every several months).

We also observe confirmation bias in discussions: someone who tries to lead others by pushing the idea that their process, framework, or anything else is better (for example, Agile vs. Waterfall, SAFe vs. LeSS, etc.). Going back to the airplane story, you might be intrigued to know why conspiracy theories arise—an explanation, by the way, that could help you better understand how to lead a company.

As individuals, we have a psychological need to create clear structures in our minds when observing the world around us. At the same time, we try to reconfirm our existing beliefs in everything we see. By doing this, we attempt to predict patterns and behaviors in others, helping us decide how to act in the short and medium term. But this mental process can be a trap if we are not aware of it.

This confirmation bias helps people feel more secure and minimizes the activation of the amygdala, the region of your brain responsible for detecting threats. This can cause problems, as it doesn't allow you to clearly and objectively judge the information before you.

Remember that confirmation bias is the human tendency to seek, favor, and use information that confirms a preexisting opinion.

Overcoming the Confirmation Bias

Confirmation bias is less than advantageous for companies that must make frequent decisions because of constant changes in their markets. A good way of overcoming this bias is to use a different kind of question.

Case in point: The management team of a company was considering the launch of a new top product to maintain its privileged position. They convinced the rest of the group to conduct market research to explore its viability. Within days, surveys, focus groups, and competitive analyses were all set in motion.

The decision was clearly emotional, and those responsible didn't realize that their views and actions were being strongly influenced by their feelings and would only result in reconfirming their initial, and very possibly misguided, beliefs. The market research team began asking questions that the managers themselves had recommended, questions that were, of course, biased. As a consequence, the results were exactly as expected and reconfirmed the managers' initial hypothesis.

So how can you, and should you, minimize confirmation bias in your company?

How you ask questions and measure results are part of the answer. To discover preferences, instead of asking, "*Do you think* _____ *is a good idea for the product? Would you be interested in it?*" you can ask consumers to classify the characteristics of their ideal service or product.

Another option would be for someone on the team to play devil's advocate while another takes on points of view that the group doesn't commonly take. For this, you need to know what the more uncommon and common perspectives are in the situation.

Confirmation bias can be present in any part of the organization. For example, during a personnel-selection process, someone from HR might sit down with a candidate and ask them to sell their skills to the company. If the candidate fits the role, they may be asked questions that lead to expected answers, such as, *"How do you perform under stress, and can you give me an example?"*

Logically, the person is expected to provide an appropriate answer, because the work surely has high levels of stress.

To reduce confirmation bias in cases such as this, it's necessary to change how questions are framed. One of my favorite techniques is to use the opposite scenario: Why do you think you are not the person for this job? What should this product fail to do when it hits the market? What do you dislike about our service?

Asking more-open questions allows the brain to reason differently. Questions that begin with How are another alternative: *How do you think you can help our company?*

Confirmation bias is extremely difficult to overcome, both in your personal and professional lives. People don't like to be wrong. Our minds will always look for evidence to show that the chosen path is the right one and that anyone who disagrees is moderately wrong. Applying neuroscience of change helps us understand processes and influence mental patterns to allow leaders, change agents, and consultants to make better decisions during a transformation.

Change and Learning in Traditional Companies

Many companies believe that providing more information will help people do their jobs better and make better decisions, but this is only partially true. We are not designed to acquire knowledge that could alter our reasoning or related behaviors, and it's a challenge to make a group of individuals acquire new habits.

We're prepared for a world of linear and progressive evolution, where one fact leads to another and the discovery of something is nothing more than the accumulation of previous events. We've lived this way for many generations, and that's what we've been taught since we were very young. We all carry childhood *"baggage"* (what we learned as children), and this permeates our reasoning, our beliefs, and our behaviors as adults.

Except during extreme situations, such as natural disasters or other life-altering events that abruptly change our habits, you'll abide by rules learned during childhood when making sense of your day-to-day decisions. Your brain considers situations that do not fit with your way of thinking as a threat. You don't perceive the resistance directly because it takes place in your subconscious, but it reflects in your conscious self in the form of arguments that will seem coherent and well founded.

You'll probably agree that it's difficult to identify the origin of most resistance and friction when you try to lead a change. Instead, we tend to simplify the problem and solve it as if it were a complicated situation, although, in reality, it's complex.

Traditional change management tactics from the eighties more closely resemble obedience training than psychology and neuroscience; that is, leaders promise bonuses and promotions to those who agree to the change (the carrot) and punish those who fail to do their job or obtain poor results (the stick).

The results of several investigations carried out by McKinsey & Company showed that around 70 percent of change initiatives fail. *Why? How can you make yours more successful?* The connection between a change (or decision) in the company and how brain processes produce healthy habits is rarely evaluated, but this is key to understanding the source of institutional resistance and dysfunctions you are likely to encounter when working with teams. The neuroscience of change offers a window of opportunity. You can help people become more aware of their shortcomings, make better decisions, and be more open to learning, evolving, and acquiring healthier habits that match Agile and modern company needs.

The Key to Success

Regardless of the country, company size, or culture, there's always a factor that will condition the success of your next change initiative. *Can you imagine what it is?*

Change initiatives require certain ingredients so that the desired behaviors become exponential (that is, for people to offer low resistance to change and be open to new ideas, with positive and proactive attitudes toward learning). They should also be willing to modify how they think when they come across information that contradicts their beliefs or reasoning.

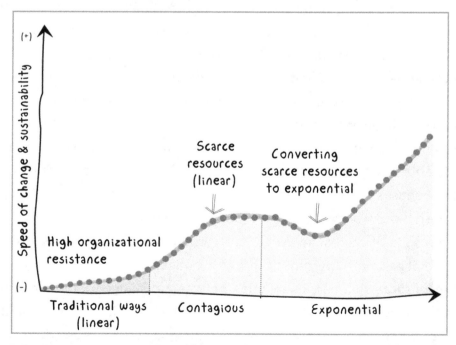

FIGURE 4.1: Ways to make a change and corresponding sustainability

Allow me to clarify the difference between exponential and contagious. In a company where change is **contagious**, nearby departments (uninvolved in the change) observe the change and adopt or copy some of their ideas or processes. If they find something interesting or useful, they will add it to their own toolbox as a new skill. But keep in mind that contagious mechanisms become very complex if you try using them to expand a practice, technique, or framework throughout the rest of the company.

In a business transformation where change is **exponential**, the result is different. Here, members of departments that surround those who are changing will feel that their own ways are outdated. They will fervently want to copy, understand, take over, and evolve the new processes. They feel it's no longer possible to maintain the status quo, that their world has changed, and that a door has opened leading to a better individual and group life within the organization.

To achieve this, focus must be placed on evolving all the minds of the organization—and not just some departments in the company. People must be able to achieve a state of continuous well-being despite constant change.

Many organizations begin by improving and making their software processes more adaptable (**technical agility**). This makes it possible to build a company more flexible and responsive to market disruptions. But while it is a good initial strategy, it's not enough to increase the adaptability of the entire company (**business agility**). To accelerate change, continuous improvement in five dimensions is essential:

Technical agility — Changing software as quickly, cheaply, and securely as possible.

Structural agility — Changing the organization's structures and procedures by running experiments while minimizing the impact on organizational health.

Outcomes agility — Delivering results even during turbulent times to respond to changing market conditions.

Social agility — Connecting well with other employees or with customers in rapidly changing environments, thereby achieving highly collective performance.

Mental agility — Reframing challenges to find new solutions even during stressful times.

If the brain cannot accept emerging situations and realities (**mental agility**), then employees will rarely adapt to new market conditions. When the context changes, people must be able to find simpler and more innovative habits (or micro-habits) that allow them to better connect with each other, with customers, and with strategic partners (**social agility**). The company must be able to experiment and deliver results, even in times of high turbulence (**outcomes agility**).

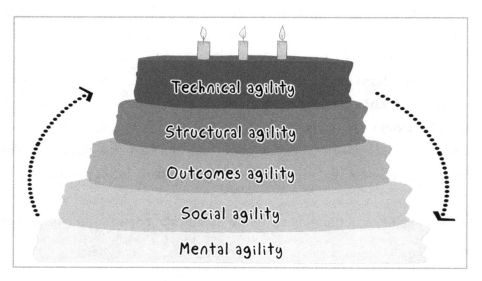

FIGURE 4.2: Different types of agility, Erich R. Bühler

Inspecting and evolving roles and processes actively and collectively (**structural agility**) is also essential to continuously deliver results. The processes must be supported by new technologies that allow minimizing or empowering limited resources of the organization to turn them exponential.

The synergies produced from these five dimensions improve the flows of knowledge and innovation, increase business agility, and facilitate the change of people and products.

When transformation becomes exponential, people are motivated, and it is they who push the new small habits (micro-habits) and want to share their experiences. They are thirsty to learn more and make the change. They also find that the practices or processes they use locally can be expanded to the rest of the company without restrictions, and this is true even if the company, or team, grows suddenly.

A micro-habit is a small action that requires minimal effort or motivation to complete. The accumulation of micro-habits can have an important positive impact. In general, a micro-habit takes no more than a second to commence and sixty seconds to complete. It's repeated over and over during the course of a day or week. It's a fundamental "technique" to make a change plan become exponential.

Exponential change also makes it easier to find solutions that enable teams to convert limited resources or linear forms of difficult-to-expand work into new ways that are easily scalable. This will lead people to feel comfortable with the constant changes. I have seen change initiatives where leaders have tried to expand a framework to the rest of the company using linear thinking. The consequence was that the processes or frameworks could not be adapted as the number of teams that used them increased. So it's necessary that you understand how the brain functions, accepts change, and regulates or adds new habits and behaviors to confront situations in constant change.

The Science Behind the Change

In recent years, brain-analysis technologies such as electroencephalography (*EEG*), magnetoencephalography (*MEG*), and functional magnetic resonance imaging (*fMRI*) have allowed us to track how the energy of a thought flows through the brain, in the same way that we trace blood flowing through our circulatory system. We can also see different areas illuminate according to the type of thought.

This scientific base helps us understand how we react to change and supports the new style of leadership needed to get ahead in the era of exponential results. It also brings us closer to understanding how people react best to business transformations.

Neuroplasticity is the *"muscle"* of the brain. It facilitates the improvement of what is done and thought by generating new neural connections. It takes place as the result of learning, new experiences, or reframing. According to Hebbian theory, neural connections can become stronger or weaker depending on how often the thought process is repeated.

Understanding the neuroscience of change and how we process ideas and make decisions is vital in developing new ways of managing the company, making it simpler and much more flexible. You need to be able to identify techniques and teach people how to acquire habits that help establish new brain connections, reconnect existing behaviors differently, and develop knowledge in an environment that is perceived as safe and positive.

This is what's called **neuroplasticity**, defined as the art of increasing neural connections, thereby resulting in new habits and behaviors. Neuroplasticity helps people evolve and reason differently.

Evidence indicates that employees who work in companies where tasks provide an appropriate level of challenge, and are performed collaboratively, benefit from improved brain neuroplasticity. Change agents, consultants, coaches, and leaders should focus on creating opportunities for people to increase neuroplasticity. As a result, employees will become more motivated to learn and actively seek to evolve the way they interact and reason.

Your change plan (which includes its strategy, training, and implementation) must provide challenges, encourage taking risks, and even make people uncomfortable in a way that leads to success. Analyzing situations from several points of view helps create new neural connections. This is why collaborative decision-making also encourages neuroplasticity.

Pilot projects are a good example, because they make it possible for employees to experience new emotions, ideas, processes, values, or principles in a controlled and safe space.

The Power of Emotions in Decisions

During a company transformation, employees often believe that a new plan presented by management puts their role in the company at risk. This thought process means that all the information evaluated by the person in the following weeks will be judged negatively—without them even realizing it!

Your brain has emotions that are connected to the same channel through which decision-making information flows (the *limbic system*). In other words, **your thoughts and actions are colored or biased by your emotions**. This peculiar phenomenon makes some things you observe look better than they really are— or alternatively, utterly miserable. The ability to take a nearly instantaneous posture toward a situation has been an important element for evolutionary survival. We react first, and then we analyze. That first reaction automatically colors the situation and, without you realizing it, influences how you'll process subsequent information. Sure, such a process can be useful if you're at the entrance of a cave and a bear appears in front of you, but it's not an advantage if you need to react calmly to an instance of stress in the company.

Take this example: You're in a meeting room and a manager comes in and explains a delicate situation. Before solutions become conscious in your mind, your brain will have already taken an initial position based on your emotions. This is also true in the design of products. A customer will prefer a functional feature of a product that generates a greater emotional charge over another that produces less emotion.

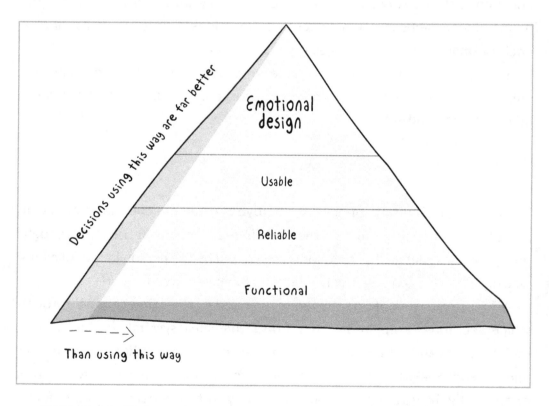

FIGURE 4.3: Minimum Product Increment and emotions (Source: Aarron Walter)

Logic only comes into play if emotion allows it, and you must take this into account when leading a change strategy. When an initiative has a clear purpose and people have fun from the beginning, that positive state will tilt the bascule favorably, and this will happen before they are even able to reflect on ideas.

Involving employees in decisions is important, and they should be able to self-organize around their tasks and speak openly about their concerns, expectations, and challenges. As before, how you phrase your questions will influence everything else: What's the personal challenge you see in this plan or initiative?

This question allows you to talk about the difficulties within the company and helps connect emotions with the initiative and put minds in a receptive state.

Research performed by Gallup and others has confirmed that there's a clear relationship between emotions and employee commitment in a project, but also between their levels of cooperation and resistance. Therefore, **you need to include the structures to support the role of emotions in your change strategy**, and for these to be clearly associated with goals and objectives.

Applying Neuroscience to Change

There wasn't much talk of digital companies twenty years ago. There were no specialized roles in Agile transformations, nor dozens of lectures on the subject. During 1999, I spent many long hours in front of a computer writing the first book on Microsoft Visual Basic .NET in Spanish. Because of this, I thought it would be a good idea to learn something new that would also get me moving. And thus, for several mornings that summer, I took windsurfing lessons. This new activity allowed me to take on a new challenge and occupy my mind with something unrelated to software development. Every day, before heading out, we'd meet with the coach on the beach and review the ecessary protocol and how to respond in case of emergency. Luckily, *Río de la Plata* doesn't present particularly strong marine currents, making it perfect for novices like me.

On my second day, I could already mount the sail and tie different knots to adjust the board. On the third day, we got into the water and completed our first practice session. The instructor taught me how to raise myself onto the board and to stay there for a few seconds. For a beginner like me, it was tough. The waves rocked the board and made it difficult to balance. But within a few days, everything became simpler. Windsurfing felt like a reward for my efforts.

I was struck by how mentally fatigued I felt at the end of each session. When undertaking a new activity, the part of the brain just behind your forehead, the **prefrontal cortex**, has to make a considerable effort to understand and learn what you are doing. This same prefrontal cortex is also the most advanced region of your brain, processing ideas and allowing you to draw your most elaborate conclusions.

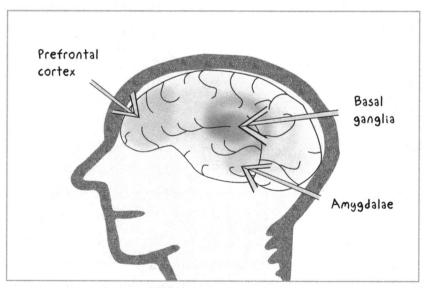

FIGURE 4.4: The human brain

Regardless of whether it is something as intangible as a new process in your company, a computer language, a programming technique, or a physical activity, the prefrontal cortex consumes a huge amount of oxygen when faced with the challenge.

This is why you felt so tired those first days at your new job or when modifying your routine. So it's important to understand that people will feel more tired and their motivation may decrease because of fatigue during a period of change.

Soon, my windsurfing progress was smooth sailing. I found it easy to stand on the board and even talk with my instructor while doing maneuvers. I practiced the same movement over and over again, which strengthened my neural connections. These new connections began to easily recall how to pair up with others and achieve the expected result. At this point, your **brain's hardware**, the **basal ganglia**, is activated to store the experience, just like a hard drive.

Located in the central part of your brain, the basal ganglia consume little energy. Thus, when new tasks turn automatic, you can carry them out almost without thinking.

My biggest challenge started when I had to learn to stand on the board, keep my balance, and move the sail in the right direction. I had recurring and irrational thoughts that told me I wouldn't ever be able to achieve it. It does seem there's always a critic around when you're trying to do something new and different.

Something similar happens with people's feelings at the beginning of a company's change initiative. Our brains seem to oppose the change and generate resistance to new habits—and then there's the fear of failure.

Understanding the Initial Resistance

When you face a challenge, a big change, or a new task, your prefrontal cortex uses high amounts of oxygen. When this happens, the amygdalae are activated almost automatically.

The cerebral amygdalae are two separate structures (the left and right amygdala, each the size of an almond). They are crucial in the detection of threats and are commonly referred to as the "*smoke detectors*" of the body.

The amygdalae secrete chemicals into your brain when you are in protective or intimidated mode, and this causes you to react and protect yourself from perceived threats. As a response to severe threats, the amygdalae can also cause visible physical reactions in preparation for an abrupt muscular response (*fight or flight*). Your heart starts to beat and pump faster, your face changes color, and your breathing speeds up.

These brain structures are crucial for our survival in environments where information comes at us from several directions at the same time and where situations change rapidly. But the amygdalae can also take control of the brain and insert negative thoughts and emotions, trying to sabotage your plan and bring you back to your comfort zone. This happens to almost everyone affected by a change plan that widely modifies how we work or our role in the company.

> As a leader, you can't let emotions such as stress, fear, or anger control your behavior. Though it takes time to perfect, there are ways to control negative emotions and guide your responses.
>
> Will Yakowicz, Journalist

According to a study conducted by an international team of scientists led by Dr. Antonio Gil-Nagel (Madrid, 2016), the amygdalae require less than 100 milliseconds to activate, but it takes longer (some investigations claim 250 milliseconds) for thoughts to become conscious.

Because of this, the information you have when you reflect on an idea has already been filtered by the amygdalae—and the bascule has already tipped.

In workplaces that require the amygdalae to remain on constant alert, people tend to focus more on strict processes and routines and less on improvements or innovation. This creates a temporary disconnect of *your thinking brain* (the prefrontal cortex)—the region that helps you reason, learn, and solve problems with creativity.

Imagine you're in an important meeting and something increases your level of stress. All of a sudden—*WHAM!* Your amygdalae are aggressively activated! Your perception of reality changes, learning is interrupted, and your reasoning skills go back to archaic times.

Either individually or as a team, write down three things that have worked well for you during the day and for which you are grateful. Research shows that this practice is one of the best ways to increase optimism and happiness, because making what's positive in our lives visible helps decrease the activation of the amygdalae.

Back at the office, the amygdalae are also activated when people or teams are overloaded with goals, tasks, and impossible deadlines. In these cases, people become paralyzed and the likelihood of reaching goals is reduced. The ideal solution is simple—empower employees to choose their tasks according to their understanding of what they can handle. You can use *Kanban techniques* to balance the workload and create a *Backlog* to ensure that everyone self-organizes around their work.

Activity within the amygdalae decreases when *short work cycles* are used (days or weeks), because uncertainty is decreased. The Scrum framework works remarkably well for this, provided that no unfinished activities are dragged from one work cycle to the next.

During a company change or transformation, look for situations where the amygdalae might be taking control or influencing decisions. If you see this happening, teach and remind people to use their thinking brain instead of falling victim to their emotions. You can initially help people focus on their breathing and take breaks to pay attention to their thoughts. In similar situations, I generally ask the following questions to help people regain control:

▸ Do you have any evidence to support the validity of these negative thoughts?

▸ What evidence makes these thoughts or concerns relevant?

▸ Is there anything that could disprove these negative thoughts or concerns?

If stress occurs during a meeting, take a break. Upon returning, ask attendees the above questions. Answering these questions will help them focus on the facts (instead of emotionally charged thoughts) and will gradually activate everyone's prefrontal cortex, our thinking brain. The more positive evidence you can bring to light when answering the questions, the easier it will be to combat the negative thoughts triggered by the amygdalae.

The *reframing techniques* explained in Chapter 5 are also excellent alternatives for increasing tolerance for new or different situations.

The Effect of Emotions on Memory

Memories are not static information stored and retrieved by the brain. They are thoughts that are re-created and highly influenced by how you think. Memories are recalled according to how a person reasons, and our interpretations of the past vary as our reasoning changes or evolves.

Companies where teams have acquired new ways of thinking often change their interpretation of past events. But memories are also affected by a person's emotional state. Individuals in a positive state of mind tend to regard past experiences more positively, and these kinds of emotions are stored in the basal ganglia.

If past events have a strong negative emotional charge (heated discussions, conflict, etc.), these memories will be stored by the amygdalae and kept in very *low-definition*. This means that any present stress scenario, with minimum resemblance to a stored negatively charged situation, will automatically result in a similar reaction, be it physical or mental.

Here's a good story for you. I was walking through the English countryside with a couple of friends, when one of them went into a panic as we were making our way down a narrow path by the side of a lake. I noticed how his heart rate shot up and that he was on high alert. It only lasted a couple seconds, and he quickly returned to normal.

His amygdalae had activated, confusing a branch with a snake, and it had caused him to react the same way he did when he had come *"face-to-fangs"* with a cobra in Africa!

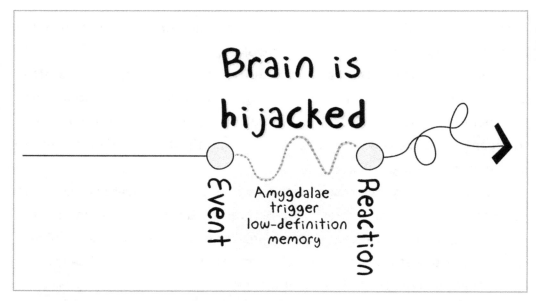

FIGURE 4.5: The amygdalae and the emotional hijacking of decisions

Have you ever tried to give feedback to someone in front of their team, only to have them respond aggressively? This may have happened because the person's low-definition memory caused them to impulsively feel as though they were being criticized and humiliated in public—like a dreadful flashback to when managers did this instead of offering positive, constructive feedback.

Imagine you're leading the implementation of a new framework, but weeks into the implementation you discover that traction has been lost. The amygdalae of your team members might be activating because of memories from when a new method only served to exert more pressure or control over employees. Your team could be confusing the framework you're trying to implement with the feeling that was instinctively generated by their amygdalae.

To overcome situations like this, positive experiences must be created, and any negative thoughts must be spoken about explicitly, with total honesty and openness. Speaking up will help employees consciously understand the new reality and, as a group, establish strategies to detect moments when that often-misleading smoke detector is activated.

Many companies use the Scrum framework with its retrospective meeting. These meetings are crucial, as they make it possible for individuals to develop conscious ways to establish group tactics to deal with negative experiences from the past. But I've seen organizations where a process improvement meeting is called retrospective, and they are not the same. Process improvement focuses on the future versus examining the past, and it has less impact on the way people reason or on how they deal with high stress situations that activate the amygdalae.

For a **retrospective meeting** to be effective, participants must not only focus on the improvement of processes but also actively challenge existing premises and how people interact. This includes thinking about the following:

- The emotional content of what has taken place during recent weeks.
- All human interactions: within the team, with other individuals, with other groups, or with the client.
- How processes or tools can be improved and how to help people feel more secure.
- Premises for current problems and how to question them.
- Areas that, due to market exponentiality or company growth, may make the team feel insecure.

At the end of a retrospective meeting, the team should have one or two action points, as well as feedback for the entire company. These fundamental areas for improvement can be measured and monitored to track progress.

Retrospective meetings are a necessary habit for adapting to exponentially changing market conditions. Without them, any improvement will occur in isolation and make it difficult for the entire company to adapt and grow.

Symbolic Threats

Anxiety can be produced by symbolic threats such as meetings between departments or with leadership, public speaking, incorporating new habits or frameworks, changes in the organization, or even working with people you don't know well. The amygdalae aren't activated only by low-definition memories or physical danger, but also by these types of perceived threats.

Humans are particularly sensitive to alterations in role or reputation. **The possibility of change in rank is one of the most aggressive threats an individual can be confronted with,** and this is where the activation of the amygdalae can be especially disproportionate.

Unfavorable status situations occur when people feel, implicitly or explicitly, that their position within the organization will be lost or diminished, when they think that others will have greater opportunities or privileges than them, or when they believe that others may have more access to information or key individuals.

Situations like this will cause a rapid increase in the levels of cortisol, the hormone that plays an important role in helping the body respond to stress. The result is an abrupt obstruction of the thinking brain (prefrontal cortex), encumbering our ability to make rational decisions.

When the Agile mindset or Scrum framework are in place, hierarchies in the organization are often flattened. This is when teams begin to self-organize around their goals and tasks, causing middle management to play a different role.

Generally, managers transition from a more-controlling role to being leaders at the service of their groups (servant-leaders). The shift causes an unconscious slip in their perception of rank within the organization. As explained before, this can lead to the aggressive activation of the amygdalae. The result is often an increase in resistance and less flexibility toward change.

To avoid this, your plan should include formal and informal arrangements that help people understand that their rank in the company will not be reduced. This should be supported by action and communication plans accordingly.

As this is a sensitive issue, it's necessary to reiterate the message more than once and in different ways to keep the brain's defense mechanisms at bay.

For any planned change, you should carefully consider any modifications in the position or status of employees. It's especially difficult to address these issues when embarking on a major transformation in a large organization, as numerous people are involved. But the initial public information must be, at the very least, sensitive as to how the change could affect employees.

It's a good idea to involve those at risk of feeling a loss of status with their new role. Participating in the impact assessment and helping to design the strategies will help them maintain their sense of role security.

The Effects of Unsolicited Advice in the Company

We all know that person who loves giving advice—especially unsolicited, chiming in with *"Why don't you . . . ?"* This is a common and well-intentioned practice in many companies, and it usually seems like an innocent enough question or statement.

In more-traditional organizations, suggestions are usually handled through formal channels, while in more-modern companies, they are handled informally and publicly.

We all know that opinions come at us from all directions and in all shapes and sizes. We sit with clients to create products of excellence and allow them to advise us on how to do it better. We encourage teams to tell us how to perfect their interactions, and we meet to analyze how we could have acted more effectively in the previous work cycle.

Giving an unsolicited opinion or piece of advice is likely to be interpreted by the recipient's unconscious brain as though it's being dictated to them by someone of a higher rank, or by someone with more knowledge in the matter.

Giving advice can feel great, but neuroscience tells us that unsolicited advice is considered the second greatest threat to the amygdalae. I'm not telling you to refrain from giving advice, but you should consider the objective of the advice and the best way of sharing it. On many occasions it's preferable to use guiding questions that lead the recipient toward the conclusion.

Feedback should have clear rules. One way to achieve this is through *Jim McCarthy*'s perfection game, a retrospective exercise that helps activate the correct areas of the brain and enhance the positive acceptance of feedback. The perfection game has three prompts that must be answered:

Rate the product / service / interaction with me / change plan / etc. on a scale of 1-10

What I liked about _____ is . . .

If it wasn't perfect for me, what would make it a perfect 10 is . . . (list what needs to change)

Divide participants into pairs and have them stand or sit face-to-face. For the first prompt, each pair will rate different situations, interactions, or services received from their partner on a scale of 1 to 10 (*1 = not so good and 10 = excellent*). If there's nothing they think could be improved, they would indicate a 10. If they feel the result could be doubled, then a 5 would be indicated.

Answering the next prompt ("*What I liked about . . .*") makes people focus on the qualities and strengths of what was delivered. This situates the brain in a more-open attitude and identifies personal skills, interactions, or anything else that the person performs positively and that can be used by others for continuous improvement.

The last prompt ("*If it wasn't perfect . . .*") makes employees focus on the actions or behaviors that could be added or improved to increase the value of what was delivered. **Thinking about how you will provide the feedback is more important than how the other person receives it**.

Use the *perfection game* to discover strengths and stimulate positive and creative thinking using the feedback obtained. Individuals might feel uncomfortable on the first few occasions, but the activity will foster new experiences.

Although this technique is simple, it stimulates creative thinking and makes it possible for the initial subconscious positioning to be positive. It also improves the quality of conversations—all because individuals must not only provide a rating but also proactively give suggestions when their assessment is low.

I have played this game with executives and senior managers of organizations. After overcoming initial apprehension, it has always provided benefits and led to continuous improvement.

Remember, you can only play this game when people feel safe in their working environment.

Small Changes, Great Impact: Micro-Habits

Imagine you're responsible for improving processes within a department that requires innovation. You've spent a few days with the team and witnessed how their challenges differ, almost daily, because of constant changes in the market. That variability causes motivation to fluctuate in disproportionate ways. For weeks at a time, people love their tasks, but during other weeks, frustration sets in.

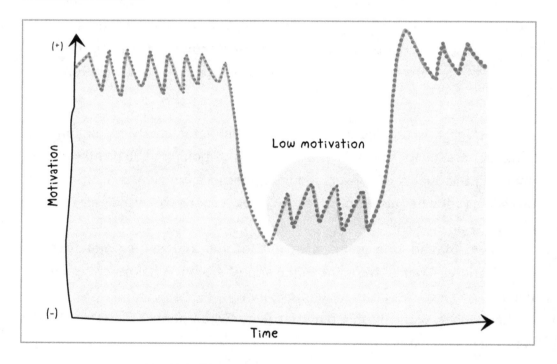

FIGURE 4.6: Fluctuation of motivation levels

During motivation highs, it's easier to implement changes or tasks involving important structural modifications. During low periods, it will be a challenge to make even small alterations in any process.

If employee motivation is too often on the lower side, then it won't be a good idea to make structural changes such as implementing a new methodology or framework (Scrum or other). It would probably cause a rapid loss of traction in your plan, increased conflict, or greater resistance. The following ideas can help motivate your team:

- ▶ Involve participants in making decisions that have an impact on their processes and interactions or on the product/service.
- ▶ Use short work cycles. This will allow employees to see the impact of their work on clients or other areas of the company.
- ▶ Propose small goals that can be achieved in days or weeks.
- ▶ Empower them to choose their workload according to their capacity. This will make them feel responsible for their own work.
- ▶ Reflect on what could have been done better and the potential impact on personal interactions.
- ▶ Create a Transformation Team or similar group that provides support and removes obstacles.
- ▶ Ensure there's a clear vision of change or vision for the product.
- ▶ Use software to automate processes that are difficult or where skills are scarce

Decreasing multitasking and having a set of small tasks prioritized by business value (a Backlog) will help keep motivation high. In the case of software-development teams, unit tests that constantly and automatically verify product quality (*Automated Tests*) might bring greater emotional stability to the group and a substantial gain in positive traction during a change plan.

There is also a direct relationship between the business value delivered to the customer and the way in which habits are established within the organization. We know of this relationship after many years of observation of the habits and micro-habits of employees, the correlation with their work environment, and the success in achieving goals.

The initial definition of business value that I shared with you in Chapter 2 may help you establish healthy habits in your company.

The Foundations of a Micro-Habit

Half of the actions carried out in a company—reasoned decisions to the untrained eye—are actually small, subconscious habits. That's why they require little motivation and are an ideal technique for teams with low or fluctuating motivation.

When a person learns a new task or activity in the company, the prefrontal cortex of their brain is activated. As the new task is controlled and done with greater fluidity, the experience begins to move toward the basal ganglia (the *brain's hard drive*), responsible for automating the work. The brain stops feeling this activity as a reasoned thought and considers it a reaction (or habit) ignited in response to a stimulus. This process allows the task to be carried out repeatedly with minimal effort.

You might think that it'd be difficult for people in your organization to alter the way they work or follow processes, because they've worked the same way for so many years. But many habits are just a huge set of micro-habits— meaning that they are automatic behaviors instead of reasoned decisions, as one might think.

The implementation of micro-habits can be successfully used when motivation is really low and other transformation techniques could fail.

Imagine you intend to take on a sport to improve your health, but you're not a big fan of physical activity. You'll need a lot of motivation to join a one-hour gym class. However, going downstairs every time you can would require less willpower, because this option requires less effort. It's also something you already know how to do (ability), and you have a clear stimulus that will fuel your effort—leaving to go shopping, for example.

A micro-habit works because of something called **behavioral impulse**, or *virtuous cycle*. When we make a small, positive change, this motivates us to make other small changes that are also positive. The sum of these creates an important change.

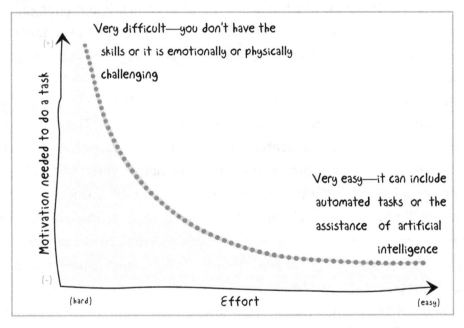

FIGURE 4.7: Motivation and effort needed to do a task

To the left of the graph are the actions that need more motivation, and to the right are those that can be performed almost automatically. As motivation increases, people are willing to take on greater challenges. On the contrary, when motivation decreases, the difficulty of the challenges must also be lower.

The skills each person possesses also affects the tasks they can perform. If I ask you to travel forty feet (12 meters) on a bicycle when you don't know how to ride one, it'd be impossible for you to complete the task and you'd feel frustrated, even if your motivation was high. If, on the other hand, the task is partially automated (by a machine or computer application), it would require less effort, and the person would gain the same positive reward as if the task had been completed manually.

You should be aware of the motivation level of those affected by the change plan. Otherwise, you could use the wrong tools. High motivation provides an opportunity to carry out more complex modifications. In these cases, you could alter processes or key behaviors to achieve maximum change, add a new framework, or transform the values or principles of the organization. This would allow you to obtain a significant impact in the near future (within weeks or months).

The members of a team I helped during a period of high motivation decided they wanted to work in pairs to increase shared knowledge. They also wanted to use disruptive and sophisticated tools to improve product quality. These decisions established the foundations for the coming months and had a great impact on processes, interactions, and other work habits. But if motivation is low, you'll have to think about micro-habits that will allow you to reduce barriers (remove blockades, increase skills, etc.) so that crucial behaviors can be reached at a later stage. In other words, making small changes that pave the path for that major change in the future.

At another company, I ran an experiment in which no meeting could last more than fifteen minutes. As a result, people connected informally (micro-habit), and information flowed more quickly within the organization.

Identifying and Establishing New Behaviors in Teams

At an investment bank, I helped a group that was constantly interrupted with requests from other departments. The situation stemmed from a lack of clear business value. For years, individuals on that team had to go to extra lengths before they could concentrate on their own tasks. Because of this, multitasking was high, motivation was low, and the quality of their results was poor—among other issues.

When faced with a complex task that required maximum concentration, they worked in pairs. Frustration grew when they were interrupted. They decided that whenever there were two people sitting in front of a computer, they would put a visible *red sign* on the desk. They informed their colleagues that when the signal was up, they were not to be interrupted.

This action increased their motivation and the quality of the product and decreased the amount of multitasking they were forced to perform—it certainly also reduced the fatigue they felt at the end of the day. Their self-esteem and confidence for future tasks increased. It taught people the importance of having rules to maintain a constant workflow. It also demonstrated the effectiveness of focusing on a single task. Without realizing it, they had linked an existing behavior with a new micro-habit: Each time they sat in pairs (specific stimulus), the red sign (micro-habit) went up, which resulted in not being interrupted and being able to focus on the task at hand (*reward*).

A crucial moment is that exact point in time when you have a stimulus that could initiate a different habit.

You need to know the four steps of the formula to identify a crucial moment:

1. **Identify the crucial moment or stimulus** that initiated the habit you want to change and link it with a new one.
2. **Be aware of the old routine or behavior** and of the desired new habit.
3. Keep in mind the **benefits of applying old and new behaviors**.
4. *CELEBRATE! You've integrated a new, healthier habit!*

As you can see, a crucial moment is linked to unleashing a new habit. The brain is able to create neuronal connections when something new is concluded successfully. We call this behavioral impulse (or *virtuous cycle*). It's of vital importance that there's an internal reward that helps the new micro-habit turn into a sustainable routine.

When I add a new healthy habit into my life, I might (discreetly) applaud myself, offer myself a word of encouragement (*Good job, Erich!*), or give myself a pat on the shoulder as a way of celebrating my small success, thereby encouraging new micro-habits to turn into new routines.

The more often new habits are repeated, the more comfortable people, and their amygdalae, will feel. Repetition makes new neural networks connect more strongly, and you can learn more about this by searching *"Hebbian theory."* Links are established between these new connections and areas of the brain related to creativity and thought-out decision-making.

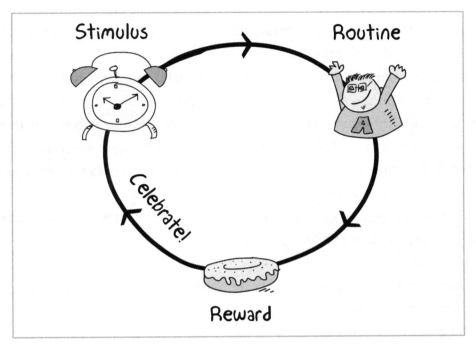

FIGURE 4.8: Micro-habit loop

You must also pay attention to the existence of vicious cycles where negative habits reinforce themselves. Such is the case of companies where people do not feel safe or where there is excessive control.

If you focus on making small positive changes, the behavioral impulse will help you progress toward clear objectives and limit the effect of false steps.

> If you want people to trust you, to feel a real connection with your culture, you have to trust them first. By demonstrating that trust, others will trust you.
>
> Ross Shott, Human Performance and Systemic Innovation Consultant

You will have to teach everyone to commit to new healthy habits, which entails first believing in them yourself. If no one outside the team at the investment bank had trusted the *"red sign"* technique, they wouldn't have included the positive routine into their daily tasks.

If you want employees to trust you and feel a real connection with the company's culture, vision of change, or product, you must first trust them and make sure they can test, fail, adjust, and try their new habits. For this to happen, you must help them recognize the crucial moment when they could go in one direction or another. If they don't see it, they'll miss the opportunity to change their world for the better.

Charles Duhigg, author of *The Power of Habit*, tells us that to isolate a crucial moment, it's necessary to recognize six areas:

Place – The exact place where the stimulus that produces the unwanted action/behavior occurs.

Moment – The moment when it happens.

Emotional state – How the person or group feels a moment before starting the old habit.

People involved – The individuals who are usually involved (changing individuals could start another crucial moment).

Type of behavior that is ritualized – The existing behavior or habit exactly before and after performing the routine to change.

Reward – The implicit or explicit reward that people get immediately after completing the action.

The more specific you are at identifying a micro-habit, the better the result will be. My recommendation is that you write down the place, moment (time), emotional state, the people around, type of behavior that is ritualized and the reward. You may need several attempts to identify this clearly. You will also have to create the new habit and ensure it is strongly associated with the initial stimulus.

If the change does not work as expected, you must be willing to try something different, something small and with a clear reward.

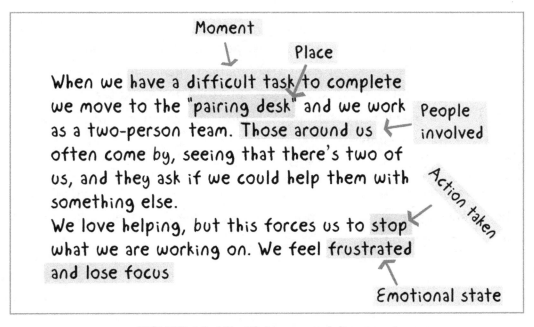

FIGURE 4.9: Identifying a crucial moment

Remember that no change plan is good if you do not know how to deal with the impediments that arise while attempting to implement it. In some cases, you'll need time and external support to set the new micro-habits in action.

Social pressure is important. If everyone performs an action, then the probability of others doing the same will be higher. Therefore, it's a good idea to ensure that those who have incorporated the healthy micro-habit are physically close to those still needing to adopt it. Sometimes you'll even have to change the physical layout of the office. It's not a bad idea to erect physical barriers to hinder unwanted habits, instead facilitating the desired ones.

Most of us will think twice about visiting the soda machine if doing so requires climbing four flights of stairs.

In some Asian cultures, people prefer to make group decisions, and they may feel uncomfortable when making them individually. It's possible, then, to build a set of micro-habits so that independent decision-making is not threatening.

Remember that the micro-habit technique can generally be used with any other change approach in your organization and that it's essential to create a remarkable organization.

When to Use Each Approach

You've learned, between this chapter and the previous, five approaches you can use to start transforming your company. You could end up using a mixture of them all, but there are situations where using a single approach will prove more useful:

- ▹ Top-down approach
- ▹ Changing from the local to the global (bottom-up)
- ▹ Habits (or change in processes)
- ▹ Introducing it little by little (Organic)
- ▹ Micro-habits

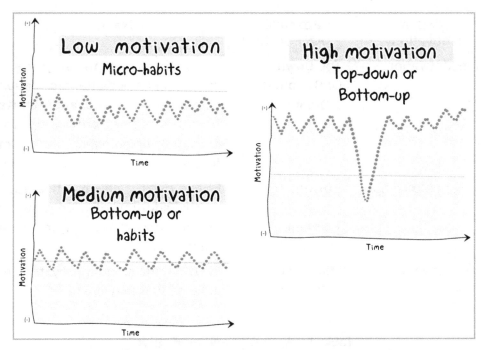

FIGURE 4.10: Motivation and possible change technique to be used

The organic technique can be used with individuals or teams at any level of motivation. Since you already know how motivation works and its impact on the speed of change adoption, it's a good idea to begin to relate this to different approaches.

Level of Motivation	Possible Approach	Example
High Motivation	Top Down Or Bottom Up + Organic	Executives or management initiate a business transformation (top-down) or the change starts from the teams (bottom-up; for example, implementing the Scrum framework).
Medium Motivation	Bottom Up or Habits + Organic	Habits mean a new practice, such as the addition of a continuous integration process in software teams.
Low Motivation	Micro-habits + Organic	Traffic-light signaling system to indicate that they are busy.

Table 4.1 Approach and motivation

Table 4.1 doesn't mean that you don't use other approaches if the motivational levels are different, but rather that you pay more attention when that happens.

An Individual Transformation to Achieve a Collective Transformation

By: Claudia Patricia Salas, *Human Resources Consultant*

As a human resources professional, I have been part of many organizational transformations in different countries and cultures. Reading Chapter 4 has helped me reflect on changes and micro-habits that I use every day. I believe the following:

▶ There is no absolute reality; we live in worlds that can be interpreted differently.

▶ We do not see things as they are; we see things as we are. We interpret reality according to how we think. Our judgment, beliefs, emotions, and biology influence what we see, hear, and feel.

▶ Humans have three major dimensions: language (mind), body, and emotions, all of which interact fully.

▶ Language plays a fundamental role in defining our behaviors: it creates realities.

Company leaders and change consultants must internalize and integrate these four points. New mental structures (reframing) are also essential for supporting a business transformation. Awareness of these paradigms has made me develop micro-habits that I apply daily as I listen to and observe people. For starters, I am wary of confirmation biases. I believe we see what we want to see, and we hear what we want to hear. These erroneous perceptions become attitudes and behaviors that can affect those around us.

A few years ago, I hired a professional for a technical position. He was a brilliant developer—but he always had something to complain about, and he expressed his criticisms aggressively. With time, I categorized him as confrontational and unconsciously started to treat him in kind: I was slow to reply to his calls and emails, my conversational manner became blunter, and, when he spoke to me, I came to expect a complaint. Gradually, my attitude bought out and worsened his most problematic side: my biases had caused real consequences.

You see, when we work with people, we risk falling prey to confirmation biases and prejudices.

When I started working in recruitment, I unconsciously showed prejudice while reading CVs and conducting my first interviews. After reviewing a CV, I would categorize it with descriptions such as *"unstable"* or *"friendly."* If the candidate was considering other offers, I'd think, *"She must be very good, which is why others are also contacting her."*

This kind of prejudice emerged instantaneously, lacking any rational argument or evidence.

To *"fight"* this, I developed a micro-habit that I have applied ever since. When I first pick up a resume, I look it over for no more than a couple seconds (stimulus). Instead of categorizing it and automatically rejecting or accepting it, I place it on hold (crucial moment). A few minutes later, I read it again, this time in detail. I perform this second reading with a more open mind. I go as far as saying to myself, *"Be careful!"* I repeat this process several times before finally contacting the candidate to hear his or her story.

Prejudice operates in our minds more than we'd like to admit. Uncontrollable thoughts are almost always activated when we receive a stimulus. The crucial moment to become aware of prejudice comes mere seconds after the stimulus, and this is when we can redirect our decisions.

When we work with others, discussions are something else to consider. The micro-habit I have developed for discussions is that when I hear an opinion with which I disagree, I immediately take a breath. After a pause, I state, "*I think that . . .*" I also add, "*From your point of view . . .*" This helps to avoid unnecessary arguments and conflicts, because it reminds us that there are different points of view—with the added benefit of increasing our neuroplasticity!

Over the years, I have become more empathetic and flexible with others. I have also changed the way I speak to myself. I have my own mental dialogue and have changed the words that I repeat to myself to transform my way of thinking. In addition to assuming new paradigms and concepts, I have also developed the micro-habit of speaking to myself more positively, even when facing the simplest challenges.

Changing your internal dialogue expands your possibilities and generates opportunities. To transform an organization, you must start by transforming yourself.

What You Have Learned

☑ The relationship between logic and beliefs.
☑ Confirmation bias.
☑ The effect of emotions.
☑ The initial resistance to change and how the brain responds.
☑ What micro-habits are and how to use them.
☑ Change approaches to use according to motivation levels.

1. Where in your company can you see confirmation bias, and what actions could you take to change those situations?

_____

_____

_____

2. What technique can you use to get positive feedback?

_____

_____

_____

3. What's needed to identify a micro-habit?

_____

_____

_____

4. Can you identify at least two micro-habits that could initiate new positive behaviors in your company?

_____

_____

_____

The Five Patterns to Make Change Contagious

CHAPTER 5

> "Good leaders make people feel that they're at the very heart of things, not at the periphery."

Warren Bennis, Organizational Consultant

For several years, we have been using Lean and Agile mindsets, the Scrum framework, and visual management tools (task boards, Kanban, etc.) to empower the organization to become more flexible and offer better solutions for clients. Many also know the essential attitudes that are needed to motivate people when implementing a change initiative.

Daniel H. Pink, New York Times bestselling author of *Drive and A Whole New Mind*, rightly said that for individuals to be motivated, they require three intrinsic attributes within their culture and daily tasks:

Autonomy - A desire to be self-directed.

Mastery - The urge to acquire better skills.

Purpose - The desire to do something that has meaning and is important.

This is a solid foundation for feeling happy and impassioned about work, but this alone will not make a change contagious.

I have seen extremely motivated teams lack the skills to create situations that make change contagious. For this to happen, one can't only look inward—inside the team. One must also look outward—at interactions with other teams. This initially requires that teams belonging to the same value stream have shared goals and a shared understanding of the problem.

Shared objectives help increase collaboration between teams, but they don't necessarily encourage surrounding groups to understand and adopt new, healthier habits.

Value stream represents activities (processes, people, resources, etc.) a team uses to build solutions that provide a continuous flow of value to customers.

You need to plant a different seed, one that makes it possible to evolve how teams reason, resolve conflict, take responsibility for tasks, view different expectations, and embrace other attitudes for turning the organization into a remarkable place. This is what I call *CREEP*, a set of five areas that I usually focus on weeks before starting a change initiative—and after the company has understood the needs of its employees; see page 92.

Focus on CREEP
some time before
starting with the
initiative

FIGURE 5.1: Focus on CREEP before starting your journey

Focusing on these five areas ensures that the subsequent plan becomes contagious from the liftoff stage and prepares the organization for the increase of the 5 types of agility (page 130).

C Conflict Resolution
R Reframing Mindset
E Exponential Strategy
E Expectations and Alignment
P Psychological Ownership

These areas can be analyzed and acted on in any order, depending on the situation. They can also be incorporated into existing habits within the company. Even if an initiative has already taken off, you can review these areas to provide the company with greater adaptability and speed.

Conflict Resolution

No matter how you define your workplace culture, the dynamics of interpersonal relationships play a key role in how objectives will be met and in the success of the business transformation.

It's practically inevitable that conflict in the company increases during periods of change, particularly when change is exponential. New roles are created, technologies are added, and personal interactions and work changes, as do the metrics. All of this can lead to an increase in uncertainty and conflict.

It isn't unusual to find company leaders stating that one of their biggest challenges is finding solutions to conflicts that occur every day as a result of unexpected situations. Many times, they unintentionally avoid crucial conversations because they feel they lack the skills to handle them, they don't want to hurt people's feelings, or they're unsure whether they can use traditional ways to solve a problem in the "*new*" company.

I've seen organizations investing more time trying to find solutions to this type of situation than supporting innovation, creating greater business value for their clients, or looking for ways to modify areas that work in a linear fashion to make them exponential.

Organizations unable to manage conflict positively will find it hard to accelerate change. It's therefore necessary to count on specific knowledge on how to build a solid foundation so that conflict can be used as a positive tool, helping you pave the way for continuous improvement.

In Chapter 1, I presented the *Runde and Flanagan* conflict resolution model so you could evaluate where your company stands in terms of conflict. Below I describe a behavior that can slam the brakes on your plan if you don't know how to manage it correctly.

In 1968, Dr. Stephen B. Karpman developed the **drama triangle** (persecutor, victim, rescuer). Although this was over forty years ago, it's as relevant and new to change agents and leaders today as it was back then.

The drama triangle consists of three roles that appear when a problem arises and creates utterly dysfunctional behavior.

FIGURE 5.2: Dr. Karpman's drama triangle

Victim - The person or team that feels victimized, oppressed, helpless, hopeless, and ashamed, and seems unable to make decisions for itself: *"They'll definitely fire us!"* or *"We did our best but could achieve no more!"* They aren't real victims. They only feel and act as one.

Persecutor - The controlling person, who is critical, oppressive, angry, authoritarian, rigid, and superior. The person who blames others for what's happened: *"It's all this person's / team's fault"* or *"No one does their job properly in this company!"*

Rescuer - The person who rises to help the victim, putting out *"fires."* This person acts with good intentions, often believing that their proposed solution or way of thinking is better. *"I'll help you solve this"* or *"I know the best solution. Let's sit down and do it together so you can finish the job on time."*

Even with only two individuals, this kind of relationship can exist. A single individual can also take on different roles, depending on the situation.

In my first years as an Agile consultant in England, I was hired by a digital recruitment company that wanted to adopt the Scrum framework. One of the teams (the victim) systematically accepted more work than they could handle. They regularly succumbed to pressure and wanted to prove that they could do better than before.

During the two-week work cycle, the Product Owner (the persecutor) kept adding small requirements, but at the end of the cycle he would publicly criticize the developers (the victims) for not finishing what they'd committed to. This resulted in a certain person from outside the group always offering to help (the rescuer).

This person would sit with the developers for long hours and, because he'd been their boss some years back, he'd make constant comments about the low quality of the code or what should have been done differently—thereby also becoming a persecutor. This situation repeated itself over and over, generating a lose-lose relationship for all. Over time, I could see that the participants began to **polarize** and become increasingly tense, and this resulted in resentment and a loss of motivation.

I have seen organizations inadvertently expand the drama triangle to the rest of the company. This dysfunctionality then becomes further entrenched in the culture, making it harder to eliminate. The drama triangle is a toxic pattern whereby everyone tries to manipulate each other in different ways. As you can see, this situation impedes change from becoming contagious and doesn't allow the company to adapt as intended.

Do you think the work environment is extremely conflictive? It may be due to a toxic **psychopathic** person. In a toxic environment, change cannot become contagious or exponential. A crucial skill for any change agent is to identify psychopathic people and use techniques in addition to those described here. Learn more about it here: *en.Innova1st.com/50N*

Leading Conflict Situations

It's crucial that you or the other leaders know how to effectively break this type of dynamic. This implies taking responsibility for the situation.

The first step is to understand how the damaging relationship operates and to realize that, in day-to-day situations, you could end up becoming part of the triangle. Asking yourself the following three questions can guide you:

1. What orientation do I adopt within the dynamic?
2. What action can I take to help us exit the triangle?
3. What skills, resources or, training do we need to better cope with these situations?

Let me give you an example. After a coaching session, the employees of a company agreed to always have three cards in their pocket (*victim, persecutor, rescuer*). They would pull out the most appropriate card whenever their conversation fell into the drama triangle. This helped them become more aware of the dynamics and enabled them to adopt healthier habits.

At a different company, I organized an activity in which participants acted out a recent situation. I then repeated the same situation, with participants exchanging roles. This allowed them to observe what was happening from a different angle.

We then used The Empowerment Dynamic (TED) to establish a new form of communication among the participants. TED employs a different perspective to "break" the dynamics of a drama triangle.

Created by David Emerald, TED focuses on balancing the way people relate to each other, learn, and take on responsibility. Three roles are fostered: Creator, Challenger, and Coach. The Creator takes advantage of his state of motivation to develop a product or service that people love. The Challenger focuses on providing learning and vision, and the Challenger also challenges the Creator with ideas that can become reality. The Coach understands how to ask powerful questions to ensure that the Creator understands the vision and that the Challenger does not enter into the trap of the drama triangle.

You can also employ a different approach by changing micro-habits.

At a company I helped, the software architects "*rescued*" Scrum team members on a weekly basis—whenever the team members faced difficult tasks. The architects would sit at the desks of the product developers and complete arduous tasks. This obviously offered a short-term solution, but it seriously deterred learning and the Scrum team's sense of commitment.

To remedy this, I suggested a rule that forever changed the habits they used to relate to one another: The rule stated that only members of the development teams could touch their keyboards. Architects could sit with the developers and explain, but it was the programmers who had to do the work.

Other techniques for conflict resolution include creating explicit working agreements that result in healthier habits, adding principles, or establishing new and healthier micro-habits to the groups. I recommend that you evaluate the situation and ask your teams what they think would be the most effective solution to their problem.

Reframing

In recent years, we have used techniques such as brainstorming and design thinking to create new opportunities and innovative products. Both are undeniably useful, as they help generate ideas for solutions based on innovation and creativity. But these techniques, which started in the fifties, have different objectives.

While brainstorming generates new ideas, design thinking focuses on innovation and empathy with the client to create products and services that better satisfy the markets. Design thinking also places consumers at the center of the scene, turning them into cocreators of the product.

Do you remember the "carriages and cars" example in Chapter 1, where people came up with new ideas and concepts but still used old ways of reasoning to analyze and solve problems?

The same could happen with these two techniques. Although both are very useful, they are not intended to radically alter the forms of reasoning that people have used for years. They do not focus on adding new mental structures, many of which may be contrary to the values and principles that people already hold.

If your goal is for those around you to reason differently, brainstorming and design thinking may be techniques to use initially, but it's reframing that will help you take that much bigger step.

With design thinking, people use familiar mental frames to solve a problem. The reframing technique forces individuals to use different forms of reasoning, many of which might not exist in the company. Both techniques complement each other and can be used together to accelerate the change.

Allow me to focus for a second on how your mind works when it tries to solve a problem. When you act on a situation, or need to make a decision, your brain's response is usually based on what was learned during childhood and information integrated at later stages. Your mind creates a story that gives meaning to a set of assumptions, guiding you in one direction or another.

People often solve problems using these same forms of reasoning (or mental models). Reframing techniques are thus of vital importance, because **when individuals can consider different points of view, they are also able to reach different conclusions**.

Reframing doesn't focus on getting more information but rather on "*rebooting*" the mind with a different "*operating system*," enabling it to reason through different perspectives. The result "*overwrites*" the tendency to which individuals are inclined, and in its place offers several alternatives.

From the point of view of neuroscience, reframing increases neuroplasticity, which makes neurons connect differently. Brain-imagery studies show how regions associated with learning and adaptation are activated while reframing.

Reframing doesn't only change our perception of reality, but it also affects the way we recall memories. New ways of reasoning will interpret memories differently, which will shape our present behaviors and decisions. In short, we replace old stories with new ones, completely altering the frame, using a different lens, or observing life (or problems in this case) from a different angle.

Reframing makes it possible for anyone to reason as a customer who dislikes the brand, a manager of a competing brand, a team that doesn't understand what's happening, or someone indecisive as to whether to acquire your service. And reframing does this through lenses or from perspectives that do not inherently exist in those looking for a solution, nor in those surrounding them.

By reframing, everyone can use alternative lenses. Imagine thinking: "*I will see the situation/problem this way. Now I will consider it from a point of view that challenges my assumptions. Next, I will look through a new lens and describe what I see and feel.*"

A person can adapt to any number of lenses or points of view. Changing our perception of reality has important positive effects on a personal scale (our emotions), a social scale (how we connect with others), and on the culture of the company.

The following are the benefits of reframing:

▶ **Internally**, reframing makes it possible to regulate emotions as it moderates the activation of the amygdalae.

▶ **Socially**, reframing redefines how we interact and collaborate with others.

▶ At a **company level**, reframing decreases the resistance to change.

In some cases, only two or three perspectives are used. For example, *"Let's put ourselves in the client's shoes and try to think like them."* Even if the mind temporarily flips sides, it might still use the original values or principles to evaluate the situation. This not only limits learning, but it also restricts a person's neuroplasticity and adaptability. This is what's referred to as the *"coin effect."*

Reframing techniques purposely employ varied perspectives during a single session to avoid this cognitive bias. A reframing session allows you to adopt several points of view, including some that might challenge your core values. This makes it possible to interpret the meaning of events and situations differently, with the bonus that a person can effectively regulate automatic reactions to emotionally charged experiences.

Further on I will share examples of how you can use reframing techniques in your day-to-day activities.

> Properly trained, a man can be dog's best friend.

Corey Ford (this is a great example of reframing)

I know from experience that many companies have a marked tendency to employ certain forms of reasoning. Because of this, reframing is crucial. Reframing makes it possible to increase adaptation, create new experiences, and help everyone understand different points of view, even when they are contrary to their own.

The clients I work with usually love reframing techniques. Once accustomed to applying them, they realize that thinking via diverse reasoning matters—very much.

Many change agents, coaches, and consultants struggle for months or even years to get managers to understand the importance of the Agile or Lean mindset. On many occasions, even after the managers have grasped it, they still succumb to pressure and go back to old habits.

This is because sustainable neural connections were not established, nor was the necessary learning internalized so that the behaviors changed in a sustainable way. I will present two reframing techniques so this doesn't happen to you and your team.

The first, and simplest, is called *Robinson Crusoe*. This is useful in situations where people are exposed to emotionally charged events such as abrupt organizational change. The second, called *Perceptual Position*, requires more preparation but will enable people to add new points of view, even when the perspectives of a problem are notably biased. For this, I will share an activity specifically designed for use within a company.

The Robinson Crusoe Technique

Imagine that you are the cashier at a gas station. One morning, you are ready to help the first customers when an armed person approaches you. The armed individual demands that you hand over all the money. The person then makes the same demand of each customer and finally leaves without causing any injuries.

You are traumatized and spend months mentally trapped within a situation that conditions all your future decisions.

Many people have experienced similar circumstances and have suffered for years because of them. Many have felt the need to change work because of the event. In situations such as these, the frame of thought is usually as follows:

THEFT = THREAT = EMOTIONS OF ANXIETY AND ANGER

Believe it or not, organizational change can be as aggressive to the brain as in the story above. Both might lead to not-very-positive emotional outcomes that condition attitudes, thoughts, memories, and future decisions. The day-to-day operation of a company might not completely resemble the previous story, but many situations do have a similar emotional charge.

In both cases, people react with fear and frustration, which is when the Robinson Crusoe technique offers a good starting point.

Being able to revisit an event with a different perspective will not change any facts, but it does make healthier emotions and conclusions possible.

Use the Robinson Crusoe technique in situations where people find it difficult to cope with a situation or when adding points of view is necessary because the existing options are negatively biased.

How to use the Robinson Crusoe technique:

Participants write fifteen to twenty lines describing a conflict situation or a scenario they are experiencing in the company. For the previous scenario, you would write something like this:

- A theft is an unpleasant event.
- The robbery made me feel helpless.
- The event has been the most unpleasant I've had in the last 12 years.
- Remembering the situation makes me angry and anxious.
- The situation made me feel useless.

Once done, direct them to add "*BUT*" at the end of each sentence and continue with something positive from a personal point of view. During the first few minutes, participants might find it difficult to change focus, but they will gradually complete each sentence with greater ease.

*A theft is an unpleasant event **BUT** it's an opportunity for a person with my ambition to have a better life.*

*The theft made me feel helpless **BUT** helped me see that the support of my coworkers is really sincere.*

*The event has been the most unpleasant I've had in the last twelve years **BUT** the probability of it happening again is really low. It could have happened anywhere!*

*Remembering the situation makes me angry and anxious **BUT** it also helps me rethink my priorities in life and focus on those things that really matter.*

The situation made me feel useless **BUT** *taught me to stay calm in emotional and highly stressed contexts.*

The first statement is particularly disruptive because it connects the participant's values with the thief's, but even the most difficult experiences provide a seed for something more valuable. Each statement redirects our attention toward a new point of view, allowing the brain to generate new emotions and neural connections.

Robinson Crusoe is a simple technique that can be used with groups, in coaching sessions, or even individually.

Using the Perceptual Position Technique

The second reframing technique requires more preparation, but it's useful to establish the foundation for a contagious change. This technique will enable people to use different perspectives when a problem has no apparent solution.

Allow me to share a classic story that illustrates the potential cost of solving a situation using other forms of reasoning.

In New York, occupants of a multistory office building complained constantly about the elevator service. Wait time at peak hours was excessively long, and tenants were threatening to terminate their leases and move to a nearby building.

Management authorized urgent work to determine the best solution to the problem. The outcomes revealed that no engineering solution would be economically feasible because of the age of the property and the available technology. The engineers told the bosses that they'd have to live with the problem.

The desperate manager called a staff meeting. Among the attendees was a recent graduated in psychology, and this young man brought a different lens to the meeting.

When giving ideas, the new member did not focus on the speed of the elevators, as other staff and tenants were doing. Instead, he focused on the fact that people were getting bored because of the wait. He suggested installing mirrors in the elevator access areas so that everyone would have something to entertain themselves with. He suggested the mirrors be placed inside the elevators as well. The company adopted the suggestion and started changing the elevators. The low cost of the change was an added bonus.

To everyone's surprise, the complaints stopped and the problem was solved—and now you know why so many elevators have mirrors.

This case of reframing occurred naturally because someone in the room took a completely different perspective.

Use the Perceptual Position technique to encourage people to face various problems and to solve them through different perspectives. This will help them increase their Mental Agility.

For a reframing session, you'll need a group of two to eight people, at least two hours, and room to move around. First, create ten to twenty phrases that represent different perspectives. Have them ready before the session. The following are some examples:

- Someone who wants to benefit from this situation
- A team member of a supplier company
- An incredibly successful entrepreneur who always speaks very directly
- The captain of a ship
- The competitor's general manager
- Someone who wishes stability for the company
- An employee, one month away from retirement

▶ A child

▶ Someone who likes giving advice

▶ Someone who wants to learn more about how to solve the problem

▶ A person who only cares about what is earned in the short term

▶ Someone seeking to reinforce his own interest

▶ A high-stakes risk-taker

▶ Someone who wishes to reaffirm the company's values

▶ A comedian who wants to rewrite the problem in a more comical way

▶ Someone who lives in a parallel reality where the situation doesn't exist and wants to know what's at stake

▶ A writer of suspense or poetry

▶ A time traveler who works in the company in 2030 and wants to teach us what he has learned

▶ An extremely traditional person

▶ A fictional character like Superman, Donald Duck or Cinderella (include your favorite)

▶ Someone who speaks only in metaphors

▶ The Little Prince (Lesson of the story: *all that's essential is invisible to the eye*)

Gather the team in a room and write as much information as possible about the problem in no more than five or six lines. For example:

"Seven of the twenty software teams in our company belong to a strategic partner. Each of our thirteen teams has specific roles and some of them are scarce. Several of the strategic partner roles are occasionally required on the company's teams. The partner doesn't allow people from their teams to be part of the company's teams. Within the next six months, the organization wants their teams to have access to all the necessary knowledge while maintaining the current speed of delivery."

Provide a card to each participant with the key questions (see below). Give them a few minutes to reflect and talk using their personal points of view.

KEY QUESTIONS TO THINK ABOUT

1. What is my view of (the situation)?
2. What are my values?
3. The situation makes me feel the following three positive emotions: . . .
4. What progress/improvement helps me achieve this situation?
    Think of progress in the following terms:
    ▶ Functional (what I do)
    ▶ Emotional (what I feel)
    ▶ Social (how I interact)
5. If I keep thinking and feeling this way, what personal reality will be created with this situation? If the scenario has not become a reality yet, would I like it to become a reality?
6. What would you ask if you were using the selected point of view?

Next, hand out a new perspective for each participant and provide five to eight minutes for them to discover the values and points of view so they can feel as much as possible like that person.

They can jot down ideas, draw sketches, or do anything they feel is appropriate to express their thoughts under the new perspective. When time is up, ask them to introduce themselves as their character. It's important that they adopt their character's values, especially if they are different from their own. They should move and even imitate the actions and voice of their character, but in no case should they make fun of them or be sarcastic.

They'll have fifteen to twenty minutes to discuss the problem from that perspective, point out the benefits, and offer different solutions. Optionally, you can give them five to ten minutes at the end to reflect on the positive points learned from that new point of view. Just remember to manage the time, because the goal is to try out as many points of view as possible.

As participants go through the different perspectives, capture the "social math" of the activity, with the central idea reflecting the new way of thinking/ framing (its essence).

For example:

(PERSPECTIVE) The general manager of the competition: The employees from your company are lazy, and they'll never have multifunctional teams like us.

(PERSPECTIVE) An incredibly successful businessman who always speaks very directly: There is no leadership in the company and that will make it impossible to change our contracts with suppliers.

(PERSPECTIVE) Someone who wants to obtain benefit from this situation: My way of thinking helps the company, and promotion in the company is what should be prioritized.

Along the way, you can ask questions, ask for opinions, pose situations, or do anything you consider useful for participants to practice with the new perspective. Try to have participants practice with at least eight or nine different perspectives—the more the better. You may need more time or more than one session.

The last part should take at least fifteen minutes. At this stage, ask each participant to consider the "social math" notes you took. They should choose, write, and share two perspectives they feel they hadn't considered at the beginning of the meeting and that could be useful in their daily work.

Steps from this point on will largely depend on your company's situation. One option is for the participants to commit to using the points of view selected in the session during the coming weeks. You could also have them take a perspective at future meetings and use it when making decisions. For either case, it'll be useful to hold another session to understand their progress and how the practice has helped participants use different points of view.

The goal of the reframing process is to pause our regular neural wiring and progressively redirect our attention toward a point of view that sets in motion new ways of thinking and reasoning, as well as different ways to interact.

Participants should adopt as many points of view as possible. If you encounter a lot of resistance within your team, start with a smaller group and with participants willing to try something new to improve the group.

Finally, you can change and adapt the technique as you see fit. The more points of view your team can practice, the better the result will be.

Exponential Strategy

Digital companies require a different DNA to help them adapt correctly if their business goes from growing 10 percent per year to 10^2. This implies not only scaling processes, but also the technology and the culture of the organization. To achieve this, it's of great help to use computer tools and technologies, but also to have new ways of working, learning, engaging employees, and interacting with clients.

> It's not enough to receive support, no matter how needed it may be. It's fundamental to know how to receive this support and to ensure that its result is exponential.

Kay Rala Xanana Gusmão, East Timorese politician.

The reframing techniques you learned earlier allow people to change perspectives more easily, consequently improving their ability to adapt. But specific skills are required to scale up a resource, skill, technique, or work style to turn exponential.

Think about how you empower people. If they see you as a manager pushing a change, you're not on the right track. If your products become exponential, you'll be unable to handle the consequent increase in requirements. Hiring additional managers or leaders might not be feasible if the growth is excessive. For this reason, teams should self-organize around their work and perceive their leader as the promoter of the change vision proposed by the sponsor.

The leader should also be seen as a mentor who teaches the practices that will replace linear methods of delivery and help these become exponential habits.

In the early stages of the initiative, you must clarify the new roles for the leader and the team members. This can be done by meeting with those affected by the change and talking about their expectations, challenges, opportunities, rights, and obligations in an exponential environment.

Gather the teams in a room and form pairs. Ask them to write down what they think their rights, obligations, challenges, opportunities, and expectations are during the coming change initiative. Then have each pair share and discuss the similarities and differences of what was written between teams. This dynamic can help people improve their alignment with the rest of the company, as well as their expectations, as they take on the responsibilities of an ever-changing environment.

Exhaustive detail for each role isn't necessary, but the participants should be clear about the differential value they will bring during the change, as well as how an exponential strategy will be supported. This may include tasks that begin to involve process automation, artificial intelligence, Big Data, and adapting how you engage employees and customers.

You must also reinforce the vision on "*why we are doing this*" on a recurring basis. It may seem like common sense, but in a company undergoing constant change, many lose sight of their impact on the value stream.

Having a clear understanding of why things are done, connecting with the purpose, and reaffirming this purpose help individuals and groups make better decisions and act more assertively in unforeseen situations.

Some time ago, I visited the development teams of a leading tourism company. They understood their roles perfectly and had been using the Scrum framework for a few months. Everyone understood the vision of change, its objectives, and the direction of its products. Despite their good functioning, a severe restriction blocked the growth of the organization.

The barrier was rooted in the great dependence between front-end applications and their respective back-end services. Managers were constantly trying to manage and remove those dependencies, but the tasks became increasingly daunting. The company's exponentiality made changes more frequent, and the problem was exacerbated because different parts of the same product could be developed by different groups of individuals. If a front-end team needed an unavailable back-end service to feed their application, they had to wait until the service was made public by their "*owners*." This was true even when the front-end team had the ability and skills to implement the back-end service.

A few weeks later, I facilitated several coaching sessions so that people could create a set of explicit values and principles for their interactions. The sessions focused on using different perspectives to establish new agreements that would govern how the teams interacted when a situation blocked exponential growth.

Following the new values and principles, the two sides began to share information in real time about the dependencies, and anyone was allowed to implement a back-end service. They acquired new social responsibilities, such as capturing collective intelligence and alerting the original author of the component about the change.

In turn, healthier actions or habits were also taken whenever there was a blockade. The new approaches or habits included automated testing, DevOps, and peer review of a new code.

Thanks to these new ways of working, the teams had more time to focus on limited-resource areas such as software architecture or specific knowledge. They could also focus on new goals that were gradually discovered because of the characteristics of exponential growth. This resulted in automating processes, abandoning linear methods of product delivery, and evolving existing processes daily.

The change quickly freed managers and employees, reduced process complexity, and made it much easier to multiply the delivered business value, thereby increasing everyone's motivation.

Within weeks, teams began to use communities of practice to learn from experience and spread knowledge to the rest of the organization.

You can learn more about Communities of Practice and their benefits in Etienne Wenger's paper: *Communities of Practice and Social Learning Systems. en.Innova1st.com/50A*

One of the decisions with the greatest impact was adding real-time metrics, which clearly changed the relationship with the client because they could observe daily trends such as user satisfaction or NPS (Net Promoter Score), percentage of retention, and monetization.

But being exponential also requires that we "*take advantage*" of the network of minds within reach of the company. Clients not only provide feedback. They can also help the organization think, and this is a requirement for any exponential company: using every network of "*minds*" to solve existing problems.

This can be achieved by transferring processes to clients or other networks through gamification, contests, or any other dynamic that solves problems the company is facing.

Every exponential enterprise must work in the following areas:

- Act as activists of a social movement led by a vision of change and of a product, where they self-organize to define clear patterns of interaction. This leads to a focus on creating a network of people and knowledge that results in an acceleration of shared knowledge and the rapid evolution of the best processes, methodologies, and architecture.
- Reaffirm why work is being done and the impact you want to achieve. Connect it with the purpose and goals of the business.
- Use short work iterations and experimentation cycles to promote fast learning.
- Use cloud technology to simplify the existing IT architecture (Amazon AWS cloud, Google Cloud Platform, Windows Azure, etc.)
- Automate processes employing linear growth to become exponential.
- Transfer problems to any existing "network of minds" so they can act as an external brain for the organization.
- Adapt plans based on real-time metrics or information provided by artificial intelligence and Big Data.

Work cycles and experimentation in an exponential company may become shorter as you progress. According to Ericsson Research, within four years data networks for mobile phones will reach speeds up to five gigabytes per second. This will make it possible for information to be collected daily and analyzed by artificial intelligence to determine in real time how to improve the product by removing characteristics or correcting defects.

The result will be translated into new tasks of analysis, development, and implementation, which will be resolved by teams with unprecedented speed. We will no longer talk about work cycles of weeks or days, but of hours or minutes.

A prime example of exponentiality is Amazon, where robots have been used in their warehouses for years. Amazon knew it would be impossible to grow linearly in certain areas and that automating their most important strategic activities—data and cloud storage—would provide crucial information more quickly for their clients, enabling them to make better decisions at increased speed.

In short, all exponential strategy should aim to increase the flexibility and business agility of the whole enterprise and not just of some areas.

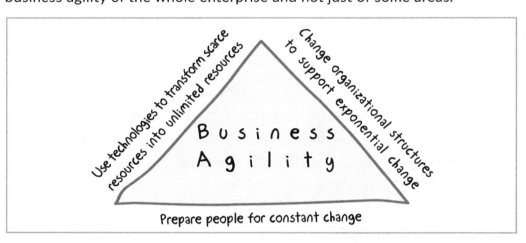

FIGURE 5.3: Three ways to increase business agility

To increase business agility, you need to alter organizational structures to have a better ecosystem, use technologies that support innovation and emerging technologies, help employees acquire new skills for dealing with constant change, and modify the management of limited resources.

As a change consultant, this requires you to help alter processes, evolve culture, change governance, and discover new ways of leadership in the organization.

Expectations and Alignment

Aligning the expectations of the value stream or company is the basis of strategic success when it comes to change. This is one of the secrets that enables sustainable transformation and contagious change. It requires an initial investment of time and effort to help with the alignment of shared goals and priorities. Everyone should be on the same page and move in the same direction and at the same speed.

Everyone must also ensure that the existing ways of work can function along with the new values and principles—and that no conflict is generated.

The engine of the organization has, as a single priority, to maximize the creation of business value for the client—as well as maintain its ability to quickly adapt. Many companies have diverging expectations because employees do not understand the company's vision or change strategy, the priorities of the business value to be delivered, or the required skills or capabilities.

You should recognize that every team member must strongly align with product and change visions, values, principles, goals, and the definition of business value if they want to acquire healthy habits.

When situations are constantly changing, it's easy to lose sight of the purpose for doing something. This is when a poor alignment is created, resulting in people who are unable to make good decisions about the cost or scope of their product.

If the workload increases and everything is given the same priority, employees will be so busy that they won't have the time or motivation to focus on the highest-ranked tasks or even on continuous improvement.

This can lead to enormous frustration. Many companies need to learn that they can't have everything and that, at a minimum, they must decide where to start or what to abandon.

You should collaboratively identify the departments to change first, areas with greater knowledge and a predisposition for change, and areas of linear production (with scarce resources, procedures, or techniques) that can be turned exponential.

It might be a good idea to implement the change incrementally, using any of the techniques presented in Chapter 3. You could also use a **change backlog**, as with the Scrum framework. This could help implement the change step by step.

You can also use great techniques to manage backlogs (for example, a clear definition of business value and good **backlog refinement** techniques).

The Agile mindset directs its alignment on keeping employees focused, improving processes, and delighting the client. The last can be supported by the following four areas (Figure 5.4 on the next page).

> In the absence of information about Value, of course the system optimizes for other things. Why should this surprise anyone?

Joshua J. Arnold, Agile Consultant

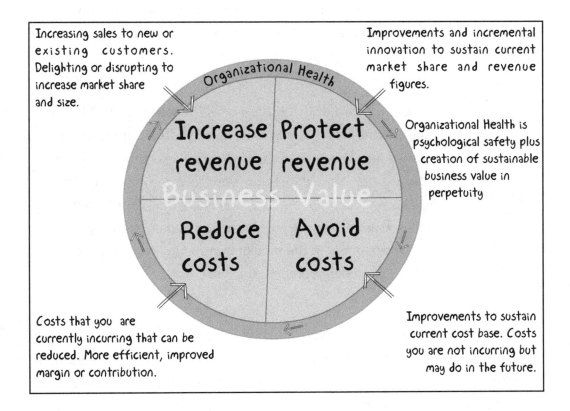

FIGURE 5.4: Features/actions here should maintain or increase org. health

Clarifying business value allows for the validation of ideas and alignment of expectations. Have in mind that a business value definition is generally associated to a specific business portfolio. Portfolio management is a particularly difficult problem to solve as multiple products initially compete for the capacity of the organization. Solving this problem requires a clear focus on what business value is and an agreed upon the way to work together. Subsequently, new elements can be considered in the business value equation, including the level of customer satisfaction, the impact of exponential areas or of those with scarce resources, and the weight of innovation. Once you have adopted an initial definition of business value, ensure that it is understood by everyone involved. This will be the solid foundation over which you'll create a good alignment.

Have you heard of the illusion of asymmetric insight? It is a bias in the way your brain processes information and knowledge. The illusion makes you believe that you know others better than they know you. As a result, you believe you know their expectations and make decisions based on that presumption, which can lead to misunderstandings and loss of alignment in the medium term. Making expectations explicit can help overcome this bias.

It's helpful to visualize and analyze the value stream and its evolution, not only to align expectations but also to understand that any activity in the organization must be improved. To achieve this goal, the **Value Stream Mapping** technique from the Lean mindset is of great help. Value Stream Mapping is a graphic technique that allows you to visualize processes and understand the workflow, information, and resources for creating a product or service.

Do you want to know more about *Value Stream Mapping* and *Wardley Maps*? A Wardley Map is an advanced tool to graph a value stream against evolution. Check *en.Innova1st.com/51B*

The goals must be clear and connected to a change or product vision. Depending on the change you intend to implement, it will also be necessary to consider how groups connect and align when they share the same goal.

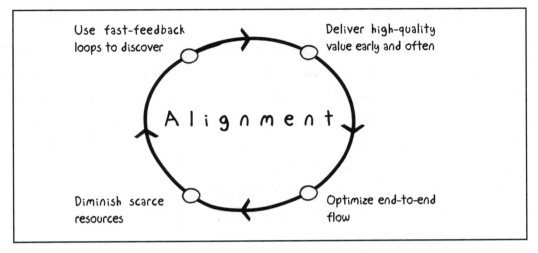

FIGURE 5.5: Principles for process alignment

It's necessary to align much more than teams and products so that the entire organization can more easily react to new situations, adapt, and create greater innovation. Enterprise-wide processes should align with the previous four principles (Figure 5.5). Following are recommendations to achieve a more effective alignment in high-variability environments:

1. Ensure you have a powerful vision and goals shared by teams belonging to the same value stream.
2. Constantly reaffirm the purpose of the change: *Why are we doing this?*
3. Have a clear and shared definition of business value.
4. Encourage people to feel comfortable verbalizing and sharing their expectations.
5. Use SMART goals: Specific, Measurable, Action-oriented, Realistic, and Timely.
6. Involve people who can positively influence the success of the initiative.
7. Employ very short work cycles (similar to the time-boxed Sprint used by the Scrum framework), learn, reflect, and continuously improve.

Psychological Ownership

If you're a Formula 1 driver, during your first races you will see yourself simply as someone who drives a high-performance car. As weeks go by, your effort and time invested will instill in you a sense of ownership of the vehicle. Without realizing it, your mind takes over the car, the goals, the strategy, and anything that could influence your future—even though the vehicle doesn't belong to you and you are only an employee of the brand.

This is what psychologists call psychological ownership. It occurs because individuals invest time and effort, contribute creatively, make decisions, and learn from what they do.

If you are curious about experiments related to the phenomenon of psychological ownership in companies, you can read the following investigation in the Journal of Organizational Behavior: *en.Innova1st.com/52C*

If you are a manager, you probably psychologically own the stages of the project, its successes, and its impact. You will feel strongly responsible and will expect others to possess the same level of commitment.

Until 2001, nobody had thought that there was a relationship between psychological ownership and the success of a company. From then on, many researchers began to carry out studies in traditional companies. But I want to go a step further and connect the concept of psychological ownership with Agile, digital, and exponential companies.

Software developers, for example, could take ownership of lines of code, modules they feel particularly proud of, a software infrastructure they developed, or a process or tool they created. This psychological pattern can occur even when the company clearly states that work produced during working hours is company property.

This ownership is a substantial advantage for the company. Because it does the following, it makes it possible for people to feel proud and to advance their careers by creating products of excellence:

- Increases people's commitment to their work.
- Helps increase motivation.
- Increases self-esteem and employee satisfaction.
- Helps create higher quality products and services.
- Makes those involved in a project want to continue being a part of it.
- Increases the desire to participate in the decision-making process.
- Helps groups set better goals and find better solutions.
- Increases shared knowledge.
- Decreases staff turnover.

We already know that psychological ownership is a key factor for any organization because it produces positive effects in the medium and long term. It also helps the outcomes of a change become contagious.

In many old-fashioned organizations, practices are often employed that considerably diminish psychological ownership because of the management style and excessive control (command and control), causing employees to have to ask for permission or seek approval to carry out their tasks.

In these cases, many will avoid involvement and will not aim for the continuous improvement of processes. They'll simply do their job as laid out and stick to the 9-to-5 working day.

The Scrum framework, for example, encourages each person to self-organize. They can decide for themselves what tasks they take based on their existing workload and they can also decide how they will implement these tasks. This has a positive impact because it increases psychological ownership as a consequence of individuals choosing their own future. *How can you encourage positive psychological ownership?*

The results of the Ownership Culture Survey (OCS) conducted on ownership culture in companies showed that employees considered fairness as the most important factor within the company for increasing psychological ownership. Fairness means that everyone is treated fairly, with reasonable rules, without preferential treatment toward specific individuals.

You can find a study on ownership in the company culture here: *en.Innova1st.com/53D*

In the same study, the second-most-important factor was a sense of community—the connection between peers. The third was the possibility for active participation—to be able to offer opinions and be included in decisions. *Have you ever considered these factors in your change initiative?*

If you do not have these values in the company (fairness, community, and participation), it would be a good idea to include them in the vision of change.

A good example is what happened to me a few years ago. In a financial company quoted on the stock market, they complained that the process for releasing a product to the market was extremely long and complex. The principal hurdles were legalities, because every application had to undergo long audits and complete hundreds of steps and forms before a new version could be released. The solution required that leaders trusted the employees, and for auditors and software teams to be empowered to find their own answers.

Several seemingly unshakable rules were broken, and points of view used for years were abandoned. That break not only increased motivation, but it also helped to create innovative solutions and make everyone more engaged with their work.

Instead of waiting for the end of the cycle to perform the audit, auditors and teams began to work side by side to develop the product. This simplification reduced the time to release a new version from two weeks to two days.

Psychological Ownership in the Era of Digital and Agile Companies

Some summers back I visited a client having trouble with his digital transformation. He had spent millions of dollars on assembling training plans, adapting their offices, and redesigning their corporate image. It was July and they hadn't even been able to meet the goals set for January. For some unexplained reason, the organizational resistance to change was enormous.

The managers were stunned. They came to think it was due to the profile of the individuals they were hiring, and they simply concluded that the hires were all useless. Managers reviewed the entire recruitment process and made several adjustments. The teams took over the candidate interviews, and this led to the implementation of a new protocol to determine if candidates matched the desired profile.

Despite this, the change initiative continued to crawl along. Still trying to improve the situation, they decided to bring in six people who worked remotely from their headquarters. This didn't help, but it did create a better working environment because local employees brought in remote team members they already knew and worked well with.

One day, talking to employees in charge of designing a crucial part of an internal software component, I discovered something rather impressive: The teams in that department were proud of the module they'd implemented years ago, but the change plan had proposed discarding it!

Because of this, albeit subconsciously, they'd been sabotaging the company's transformation plan. In different parts of the organization, they had created dozens of barriers that interfered with the plan.

As you can see, psychological ownership can become a headache if people are meant to create solutions they can be proud of, but are forced to discard them in a matter of months or weeks. How would you feel if you were told to give up everything you'd worked so hard for?

At Agile companies, we push to create more business value for customers and have greater commitment, but we do not teach people to get rid of their creations. Any company that requires high commitment and excellence, and provides products for exponential change markets, could put the change at risk if they don't know how to manage such situations.

The OCS states that managers and middle managers tend to give little importance to psychological ownership. As a result, situations and strategies for people to get rid of their creations aren't developed. Achieving this requires a systematic and safe way for employees to emotionally connect with the loss—and for this to be accomplished with transparency.

People place twice the value on anything that already belongs to them. Anything new should represent more than twice the value of what's being left behind. It's hard to let go of a cell phone, a house, a project you've worked hard on, or your role in the company.

One technique is to perform specific sessions to make the problem visible. You can use games and role-playing to allow people to discover and develop a plan of detachment with a positive attitude. I like the idea of holding celebrations when a new change plan is implemented or during the product liftoff stage. Here we explicitly praise what is being left behind and congratulate those who were part of it.

Can you see any kind of psychological ownership in your organization?

CREEP. The Five Areas to Consider

Much of what you have learned in this chapter is visible to a greater or lesser extent in your company. In some cases, you'll simply have to amplify positive habits, while in other situations you'll have to offer alternatives and ensure that people take ownership of them.

Organizational patterns and key psychological attitudes often have a common characteristic: They go unnoticed if we aren't aware of them. Think about when a child is first born. Suddenly, every TV ad, radio commercial, and billboard has something to do with babies and baby products. But it's not that this publicity wasn't there before. It's just that we have something in mind that brings it into focus.

Allow me to share the *Baader-Meinhof phenomenon*, or the frequency illusion. This illusion of frequency takes place because your brain is excited to have learned something new, and it results in selective attention.

Imagine your unconscious brain saying, *"Wow, this is amazing! I'm going to look out for it without really thinking about it."* And you start to find it everywhere. Your mind creates its own confirmation bias and convinces itself—even when you've only seen one or two baby commercials.

The same happens when you learn a new organizational or psychological pattern. Your brain goes *aha!* and you begin to see the world around you differently. You might even come to new conclusions regarding actions in the past.

Here's a trick you can perform in your company so that those around you can see the same things you do. Teach the patterns you think would have a positive impact on people and their relationships, so people around you can begin to see the patterns as well.

My personal recommendation is that, months before starting your change plan, you focus on analyzing and balancing each of the areas you have learned. Then observe the impact they have on individuals and teams. This will provide everyone with solid foundations so that the change/transformation becomes contagious.

What You Have Learned

☑ How conflict can occur and how to find solutions.

☑ How to enable people to incorporate different points of view (reframing)

☑ The Robinson Crusoe technique and Perceptual Position.

☑ The effects of exponentiality and how to prepare for it.

☑ How team expectations can support change.

☑ How psychological ownership affects the delivery of business value to the customer.

1. Any drama triangles in your company? What strategy could you use to overcome them?

_____

_____

_____

2. What could you do in a meeting to get participants to consider a situation from different perspectives?

_____

_____

_____

3. What are the effects of psychological ownership and how can you lessen them?

_____

_____

_____

4. What is the connection of this chapter with the five types of Agility (chapter 4)?

_____

_____

_____

Preparing the Transformation Team

CHAPTER 6

> "You're definitely a different person at different stages in your life."

Ben Harper, Musician

At some point, your company will decide to shift strategy. This will affect how people work and interact with others, and how organizational processes scale. The change usually originates from a combination of the following:

▶ Challenging market situations.

▶ A need to provide more value to the client.

▶ A desire to enter a new market.

▶ A need to increase revenue.

▶ A desire to protect the existing customer base.

▶ The possibility of avoiding additional costs.

▶ Mergers and acquisitions.

In Chapter 5, you learned several patterns (*CREEP*) that everyone in the company should be aware of before embarking on a change or launching a new product. This knowledge helps establish healthy habits and continuous organizational improvement.

The result of understanding the five patterns is to develop skills to do the following:

1. **Measure levels of conflict** and develop techniques to resolve problems in times of high stress or uncertainty.
2. **Consider various points of view**, including those of individuals with diverging motivations and values, when analyzing a situation (reframing).
3. **Recognize the impact of what is exponential** in the business and the techniques for learning quickly in these environments.
4. Accelerate results by enabling leaders and others to **maximize support from the company's network of external minds**, process automation, Cloud tools, artificial intelligence, and Big Data.
5. Understand **psychological ownership** and use strategies to help people feel passionate about what they do while still detaching from items they feel proud of.
6. Collectively **align expectations**, ensuring that goals connect with a powerful vision and a clear purpose.
7. **Improve** areas related to **how people work**. This can include gradually reducing batches, allowing people to self-organize around their goals, and making tasks and priorities (*Backlog*) visible.

In this chapter, I'll be slightly more prescriptive, showing you specific practices and steps for transforming the company.

Many will be excited about the possibility of starting a new change strategy and change plan. Some will probably need further confirmation as to the feasibility of embarking on the new change or product initiative. To assess viability, more-traditional companies use feasibility studies prior to a change plan. For these, people spend weeks—or even months—determining the risks, initial economic investment, and other aspects to finally decide whether to go ahead or abort the plan. But in an exponential company, it's essential to have techniques to reduce the effort and time invested and to face constant market changes.

Your organization probably has complex products that reach customers through different channels. As a result, there are different user experiences and life cycles. One of your biggest challenges will be to get departments that haven't interacted to come together to work more effectively and produce innovative and sustainable results. This entails drastically changing interactions and habits by teaching and facilitating techniques for working side by side.

The Scrum framework and the Lean and Agile mindsets have helped make this possible. If you look around, you'll find many practices that originated with these mindsets. However, none of these show the path for implementing a change initiative or the minimum requirements for them to be successful. It is therefore a good idea to learn effective techniques for starting a remarkable transformation.

Establishing an Initial Alignment

For a change to be sustainable, you have to involve teams and people with different backgrounds and skills, interests, and points of view. To achieve the greatest possible impact, teams must be aligned and self-organized around their objectives and tasks. It's usually necessary to arrange collaborative sessions during the initiative's liftoff stage, allowing individuals to learn and incorporate effective practices to adapt more quickly and techniques to connect and collaborate better.

During the development of a software product, the Scrum framework and Agile mindset focus on collaborating as much as possible. Short work cycles are used to reduce risk and uncertainty. At the beginning of an Agile initiative, change consultants generally recommend the following three stages:

Feasibility, purpose, and context of the initiative

An initial feasibility evaluation is carried out to know whether it makes sense at a strategic, economic, impact, or learning level. To determine if the change or product is viable, the *reason* for the opportunity, the purpose, and the expectations are analyzed and the focus is placed on creating an initial high-level alignment among executives, clients, and stakeholders. Unlike traditional companies that carry out this action at the beginning of the plan or once a year, exponential companies execute it over and over at different levels of the organization and in different ways.

Liftoff of the initiative

This stage prepares teams for the change plan or product. Some companies call this *inception*, consisting of group sessions lasting one to three weeks. This stage involves customers, stakeholders, change agents, developers, and all who need to know how to achieve a greater positive impact with minimum effort. This stage focuses on establishing the context and interactions between people and teams to discover *what* needs to be done. In some cases, the liftoff stage of an initiative is also used to *"reset"* existing teams so they can acquire new habits.

Planning, estimation, prioritization, and implementation

Finally, they prioritize and plan *how* the work will be done and *what* should be completed in the next days or weeks. Generally, work begins as soon as possible, establishing an initial scope and group commitment with respect to quality and expected outcomes through a *Minimum Product Increment*.

In Scrum, SAFe, Scrum at Scale, or LeSS, Product Planning sessions are run every couple months, while Sprint Planning sessions are held every week or two at the start of each work iteration.

In the exponential company, the feasibility of an initiative can be challenged by the information provided by Big Data, artificial intelligence, or any person in the organization, regardless of that person's rank. Here it's common to carry out the previous stages in a nonsequential manner and at different levels of the company. It's also possible to change course quickly or cancel a plan when it's no longer relevant. This allows for constant feedback loops, enabling the creation of shared understanding and purpose so that people stay aligned and can confidently change direction in moments of high uncertainty.

As mentioned in Chapter 1, the conditions of anything exponential make it impossible to see around the corner. Waiting for all the information before taking the first step is counterproductive. Everyone in the organization must act even when the information is incomplete. This presents one of the biggest differences from the way that traditional companies act.

FIGURE 6.1: First phases of an initiative

In exponential companies, the result of a feasibility assessment is no longer binary (yes/no) but consists of three possible responses:

1. **Yes**, we will continue with the initiative = **let's take action**.

2. We will **not move forward** with the initiative = we learned something and will dedicate ourselves to something else.

3. We do not have the necessary information, or we do not feel safe = let's take action—**a short experiment needs to be run**.

While the first two options are common in traditional organizations, the third opens the way to empirical forms of work that accelerate learning, allow for investment in stages, and enable better decision-making.

In a traditional company, during the first action, money is allocated to an initiative before any further step is taken. In this *top-down* approach, executives and management generally create and negotiate the budget for the coming months.

During this process, negotiations go hand in hand with traditional budgeting techniques, where the investment is more or less set in stone.

The problem is that these techniques contradict the fact that the world is changing quickly and that most of the knowledge for solving new challenges is not found in the upper hierarchies of the organization.

Rather than trying to calculate a fixed budget for the coming months or year, exponential companies need to base their budgets on the results of short work iterations/experiments frequently released to customers. This requires setting smaller goals along shorter time frames and taking the time to reflect on how processes can be improved.

An initiative's success can thereby be foreseen by the success of these short work cycles, and this removes the need for upfront planning and budgeting.

Using short iterations and constantly improving processes to react quicker to customers' needs will help your team budget initiatives in a way that aligns strategic goals with reality. This works well when teams are stable, people are motivated, and you no longer think of your customers as an abstract notion of a "company" you are serving.

Following this process provides full transparency and integrates your clients into every step.

Summing up, an important distinction of **exponential companies** is that they **allocate their budgets to initiatives that mirror the new ways in which they work**—and this is why the third action—**Experimentation**—is so important.

Establishing new habits for experimentation helps you carry out short work iterations that regulate your actions, guiding you to take small steps, particularly when there is little information. This allows the company to gradually allocate its investment while it discovers the problem to be solved. It also allows people to better manage the effects of uncertainty.

The following are pieces of advice that could help you create a simple framework to fund initiatives in your company:

1. Don't invest in a project. Invest in a value stream.
2. Ensure that clients and teams work together to establish initial expectations and that there is transparency regarding current obstacles or limitations.
3. Ensure that a clear process to refine the budget is established and that this process is known by everyone in the value stream.
4. Prioritize the work or experiments collaboratively.
5. Use your budget to create better products.

By following these recommendations, you will ensure that people in the organization develop healthier habits.

Feeding on Constant Experimentation

I've explained the importance of running short experiments—short, time-boxed activities that help you receive feedback from the client—but on many occasions those around you will have different ideas about what their objectives should be. Different expectations about the purpose of an experiment can cause a loss of alignment and conflicts of interest.

If you make the experiment's main purpose explicit, you will help everyone stay aligned and make it much easier to create the appropriate metrics, validate results, negotiate better, and find alternative routes.

A short experiment can have several possible objectives:

1. Generate a clear **economic benefit** for the client.
2. Acquire **learning** but not generate a clear economic benefit for the client.
3. Acquire **learning** and generate a clear **economic** benefit for the client.
4. **Remove a barrier** in the organization without a clear economic benefit for the client.
5. **Remove a barrier** in the organization with a clear **economic** benefit for the client and **learning**.

It's best that you help parties clarify goals; otherwise, invisible barriers could be established, hindering shared objectives and making mutual collaboration more difficult.

A financial client hired me to explain to her teams how to take small steps instead of undertaking extensive work. Management told me that under no circumstances should I use the word *experiment*, because participants might see it as a risky expression (this was a very traditional organization).

To ease everyone's concerns, we agreed to use the term *trial*. During a workshop, I focused on explaining practices and the positive reasons for performing small trials. At one point, a participant interrupted me and said, "*I have an idea! How about we use the word 'experiment' instead of 'trial'? It seems more appropriate."*

The teams had been using this type of practice for some time, but management didn't know. In addition, both sides had different thoughts as to the objective of the experiments. The moment turned into a good opportunity to explain the possible results I mentioned earlier and for all to start improving their alignment.

Lean Startup and Constant Validation

Lean Startup techniques help individuals take baby steps, validating assumptions or hypotheses via small experiments. Instead of implementing complex plans based on hundreds of assumptions, *Lean Startup* helps us employ a rapid cycle focused on *create-measure-learn steps*. It provides constant feedback on whether the time to make a drastic turn has come or whether we should continue on the current trajectory.

You can learn more about *Lean Startup* at: theleanstartup.com

An experiment can be strongly influenced by the emotions of the person running it, which could result in information confirming a particular point of view. But an important objective of the experiment should also be to determine the possibility of moving in other directions. In Chapter 4, we learned about *confirmation bias*. At any time, go back to that section to review the strategies for overcoming this mental pattern.

Using a Transformation Team

All employees should be responsible for facilitating a change, but initially it's common to have a group of people assigned to support the transformation of the company—the Transformation Team.

Modifications of processes, mindsets, interactions, values, and principles are significant activities and require specific skills to help remove obstacles and take the first steps toward change. A Transformation Team not only removes barriers but also teaches new concepts and practices, helps discover values and principles, and creates situations where people can give their best.

The Transformation Team should set in motion different techniques—bottom-up change, frameworks, and micro-habits—and teach ways to measure impact and make progress visible. One of the Transformation Team's most important assets is its ability to clearly identify levels of motivation and to suggest the most appropriate strategies and approaches for business readiness.

You want employees to take over ideas, improving them regularly, and you don't want the Transformation Team to be the only one helping with the initiative.

A Transformation Team isn't static. It should gradually disappear when its target group has the knowledge to make the change on its own.

At the beginning, you may be the only one who helps the sponsor, leaders, and other members of the company to create a draft of the vision for the change or product. But everyone should start considering who should be part of the Transformation Team, and eventually the Transformation Team should split into smaller and smaller teams until it disappears.

In my experience, a Transformation Team requires the following:

▶ Informal, hierarchy-free interactions between its members and explicit working agreements that establish healthy habits to be used every day.
▶ People with different areas of expertise and with the power within the company to quickly remove large-scale barriers.
▶ Internal use of the practices the team coaches to others and the curiosity to learn from the change teams.
▶ A passion for what they do and a desire to use different points of view (reframing).
▶ The ability to work as a team, even in situations where their personal values are challenged.
▶ Clear goals and a level of comfort working in pairs.

In Chapter 8, we will look at two change frameworks: ELSA and DeLTA. The first helps you promote a change when a sponsor actively supports an initiative. The second is useful for accelerating the transformation when you lack explicit support from the leaders of the organization.

The Transformation Team should be set up weeks before the start of a change plan. An executive leader or sponsor should also be part of the group or at least publicly express support for the initiative. This enables an initial removal of blockades and encourages curiosity from other executives and senior positions of the company. There's no single solution to all situations, but in my experience, the core group should include between three and five individuals for every hundred who need to change, and they should have 100% availability (at least at first). Members who are external to the company, such as an *Agile coach* hired for the mission, should focus on sharing knowledge with the rest of the team rather than taking charge of the change initiative.

Integrating Observers, Ambassadors, and Casual Members

Companies have different concepts of what a Transformation Team is. In more-traditional companies, these teams are made up of people selected by middle management with the aim of coordinating the work of other teams and completing the steps in an original roadmap.

In my opinion, though, the structure of a Transformation Team is somewhat different. Transformation Team members must be able to self-organize around their change objectives, their learning and skill-development, and the techniques necessary to cause greater impact on the teams who want to change. When the Transformation Team has these abilities, leadership can delegate decisions, management is freed from having to coordinate such tasks, and the organization is able to adapt quicker.

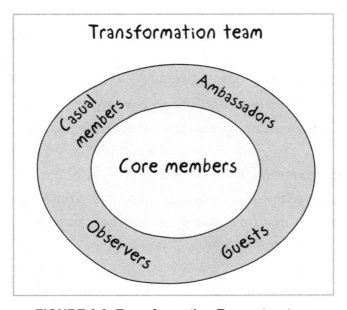

FIGURE 6.2: Transformation Team structure

A Transformation Team has core members but also requires a high number of collaborators (extended team).

Core members are individuals with experience in business transformations and who can devote most of their energy to supporting or promoting the initiative. They actively help those in the process of change. The core group often meets several times a day to review and adapt their strategy.

The **extended team** comprises the following:

▶ Casual members
▶ Ambassadors
▶ Observers
▶ Guests

Casual members (or casual participants) have good intentions and want to help, but they have little time or do not want to commit to the initiative because they need to concentrate on unrelated duties. They are willing to help you informally and want to learn more about how to make a change.

In some cases, casual members will support the initiative by delivering workshops or providing the names of people willing to share specific skills. They will lend a hand in the initial stages, helping to instill order, and will be grateful when their support is publicly acknowledged. Their participation often encourages others to mimic their attitude and collaboration with the initiative.

The **ambassadors** are the second member type. They are trusted and respected people within the company, and they already belong to teams in need of change. Their objective is to distribute information or replicate the learning sessions in their groups. They help maintain a constant flow of information in periods of high uncertainty and clarify possible misunderstandings. They also make it easier to scale the change initiative should it grow in a matter of weeks.

Ambassadors are usually happy to learn and gladly serve as members of the Transformation Team. They appreciate invitations to seminars and courses on new techniques or ways of working, and they enjoy working in pairs with core Transformation Team members. It's not rare, either, for them to join the core team at some point.

You could also have **observers**, individuals who want to learn or support the initiative but who can't commit to the team because of hierarchy, politics, or workload. Observers often contribute their opinions behind the scenes or provide people who can lend a hand. Sometimes, observers are senior executives who want to learn more about the plan but prefer to remain passive in the eyes of the organization.

Finally, from within the company, you will often receive **guests** wanting to know more about what is going on. They will come looking for new ideas they can replicate in their corner of the company or simply to gain new ways to work that they can apply in future initiatives.

If one of the objectives of the Transformation Team is for the company to implement the Scrum framework, then offer the article "*Measuring and Evaluating Scrum in Complex Environments*" at *en.innova1st.com/60A*

For knowledge to flow quickly and for the transformation to leap forward, the Transformation Team must be free of hierarchies and maintain informal interactions. This informal structure also makes it easier to scale the practices or techniques to the rest of the company.

Using the Advantages of the Principle of Reciprocity

In certain French schools, it's common practice that one teacher *secretly* cares for another during the weeks leading up to Christmas. When the unsuspecting teacher enters class, the room is *magically* ready—a cushion is placed on their chair or there's a bottle of water for them should they feel thirsty. This is called the **guardian angel**. This practice stimulates one of the psychological patterns with the greatest positive effect on people: **reciprocity**.

In a Transformation Team, the guardian angel is a powerful tool that establishes healthy habits from the beginning. Here, a core member will explicitly take care of an ambassador, observer, or casual participant, ensuring they have a better experience. Imagine that an ambassador needs to deliver a small workshop. Weeks before the seminar, the guardian angel could leave a book with information about the seminar topic on the ambassador's desk or even reserve a chair in a session with information of interest to the ambassador.

Reciprocity is a psychological pattern that creates an experience of giving back, and thus it brings about a positive mental feeling between two or more people. It helps establish good human relationships when there is little time to establish quality links, and it brings favorable exponential changes in the company.

I have seen how this habit spreads across companies. It's amazing to witness the increase in collaboration, trust, and empowerment that occurs in a matter of weeks, without the need for a great plan. This example confirms the nonlinear relationship between the size of a plan and its impact. Reciprocity is therefore an essential component in the expansion of any practice or framework.

Creating a Mutual Understanding

You have already handed over the draft vision of change and you have obtained commitment from core Transformation Team members. They've helped you identify possible members of the extended team, and now it's time to organize the initial ideas and set the first steps of the initiative in motion.

The first work sessions focus on creating a shared understanding of the situation and problem to be solved. When these sessions conclude, everyone should be aligned and know how to collaborate.

To achieve this, invite the core members, the extended team, the initiative's sponsor (if there is one), and people from the teams that need to change. As you will see in the Farm Market activity in Chapter 7, the same teams should select their representatives in these work sessions. Your goal during these meetings is to clarify underlying assumptions, validate beliefs, and clarify the scope of the change or product. In addition, you'll have to teach everyone to collaborate efficiently. *Have you ever used an impact map for this purpose?*

Impact Mapping, created by Gojko Adzic, is a quick and visual way for participants to understand what is happening, allowing them to structure their ideas and align with what is to come. Presenting visually has the additional advantage of revealing the shortest path toward achieving a common goal.

An impact map asks four powerful questions: *Why? Who? How? What?* These questions help to organize the information and enable everyone to open their minds to collaboration and building a shared understanding. Asking *Why?* as the first question is important, as its answer yields the purpose of the initiative.

Employ Impact Mapping when a group of people needs to know the purpose of an initiative, create a shared understanding, and align around objectives and tasks.

You can start by creating groups of two, ensuring that even the most timid members feel comfortable. Set up an open space where everyone can interact freely. One option is to remove excess furniture and place chairs in a circle. Keep the meeting environment as informal and relaxed as possible.

Use the first few minutes to present the agenda for the day and the purpose of the meeting. Then you, an executive, or the sponsor of the initiative should take a few minutes to explain the situation and the initial context. This can include a presentation of the initial draft for the vision of the change or product.

If there are questions from participants, remind them that these should focus on the purpose of the initiative and not offer solutions—at least not yet. It's common for people to want to offer a solution before arriving at a shared understanding of the problem.

Place a sticky note in the middle of a blackboard or wall with one of the following *Why* questions: **Why are we doing this?** or **Why is it important that we head in this direction?** Knowing the reason for the initiative makes it possible to understand its main objectives and react correctly if the information changes or unexpected events happen. It also lays the foundation for making better decisions about cost, scope, and timelines.

Without understanding the purpose, people will do the work without taking over the problem or self-organizing to find new solutions. Instruct participants to write down the answer and place answers in the center of the impact map. Don't forget to allow time for reflection on the conversations.

Help participants grasp the benefits of fixed-time work cycles during an activity by timing the parts of the session and getting feedback on the time used.

The second step focuses on answering **Who will be affected to achieve the goal?** to understand who—people or teams—will have to change or will be affected by the change. Keep in mind that areas or departments may arise that were not initially included or considered, and this is a good thing. In general, you can expect to recognize three types of individuals or groups:

1. Those who could significantly influence the success of the initiative.
2. Those who provide a service or are connected with the service to be created by the initiative.
3. Those who have an interest in the sessions but would not benefit directly from them. These could be people in similar positions or company teams that want to learn how they too might have to change. They could also be people who want to know more about what is happening so they can transfer new habits to the rest of the company.

You can create a visual map of these three types of people to make them easier to identify. Feel free to change, personalize, and improve any of the techniques you see here.

At this stage, put aside conversations about role changes in the company, as this is an extensive topic and one of the biggest threats to the brain, producing unconscious fear and potentially hindering the initiative's traction. If necessary, plan future sessions where everyone can express their fears about role changes. You can also use virtual tools to make questions and answers visible to employees.

The next step is to focus on actions for achieving success: **How should behaviors change?** This also requires that you determine the minimum changes in behavior for creating the desired impact.

Here you will talk about the desired behaviors and barriers to the change of habits. There may be a lack of physical conditions (tools, offices, etc.) or there may be procedures, incongruous habits, or emotions related to past events.

Do not forget that these will be discovered as you carry out experiments. Once several points of view are shared, ask one last question to reinforce the previous ideas: **What experiment or simple task could be performed to confirm whether that minimum impact is viable?**

These answers can offer an initial perspective as to where to start, determine whether any of the participants have experiences in similar situations, or even change the initial draft of the change plan. It could also reveal barriers to be removed, new people to include in the conversation, or a Backlog to create with small experiments. In short, these are the questions you could use:

1. Identify the initiative's purpose and goal: **Why is it important that we head in this direction?**
2. Then focus on the people who need to change: **Who will be affected to achieve the goal?**
3. Next, focus on the minimum change in behaviors that would achieve that impact: **How should behaviors change?**
4. Finally, you should answer this question: **What experiment or simple task could be performed to confirm whether that minimum impact is viable?**

Once you have finished these sessions, everyone should have a shared understanding of the problem and the group commitment to take the first steps toward the transformation.

As you can see, *Impact Mapping* is a good way to start pre-liftoff work, because it produces quick results, identifies people and desired behaviors in a structured way, makes the strategy and value proposition visible, and specifies required capabilities or resources before taking the first steps. You will soon see how to connect the results obtained here with an A5 canvas so that the objectives of the first experiments can be understood, measured, and improved by all.

Making Boundaries and Interactions Visible

Because a Transformation Team has external members, the characteristics and abilities of its members should be visible at all times. The *limits and interactions map* is a simple and effective tool for identifying those who can help.

The map is usually constructed on a flipchart sheet and includes people's photos, characteristics, and personal skills. You can also add contact information such as email addresses and phone numbers. In addition to areas of expertise, it's important to mention both hard and soft skills that could benefit the team.

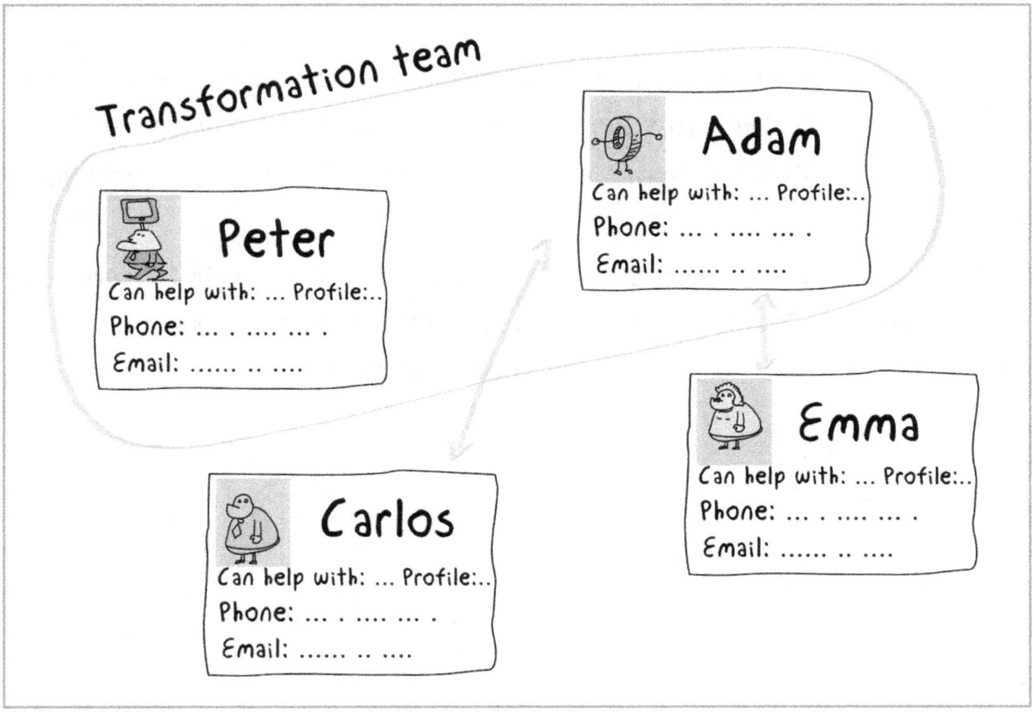

FIGURE 6.3: Limits and interactions map

Remind members to regularly update their profiles on the interaction map. New members must be familiar with the map and understand it within their first days at the office.

Establishing Explicit Working Agreements

For a Transformation Team to do its job well, its members should have solid foundations for their day-to-day behaviors, as well as positive interactions. They must know how to make difficult decisions, use techniques that increase transparency, and know how to behave in situations of high stress or uncertainty.

Each time you organize a session, prepare a clear agenda that informs participants of attendance requirements, duration, logistics, participants, roles, and expected results.

Explicit *working agreements* should be created during the first meetings of a Transformation Team, because they help core members and ambassadors to have a common starting point to begin collaborative work.

Table 6.1 shows examples of *working agreements* from teams I have helped:

Values	Working Agreements
Visibility	When something important changes, we will inform the rest of the group within 30 minutes.
Deliver powerful messages	We use powerful stories, descriptions, and analogies.
Support	We always support one another.
Speak from the heart	Instead of jargon, we use simple and clear language that everyone understands.
Ethical feedback	We are always open to feedback. If someone receives information regarding a team member, they should be informed ASAP.
Share knowledge	We regularly work in pairs within the team and with others outside our group.
Practice what we preach	We practice what we preach.

Table 6.1: Example of values and working agreements of Transformation Teams

As you can see, values are presented along with working agreements. While the former provides inspiration, the latter offers concrete attitudes. Working agreements are sometimes more specific and indicate actual daily habits.

Once in Mexico, a Transformation Team proposed that no one eat at the work table if their food had a strong smell and that mobile phones should be silent during meetings. If a phone rang at a meeting, its owner had to enter one dollar into a piggy bank, and the money was donated to charity at the end of the year.

To create explicit working agreements, you must start with one or more collaborative sessions with the core team to help determine the desired values and habits. Because the extended team will also be governed by the agreements, you should give them the opportunity to offer feedback.

Values and working agreements are not static, so it's necessary to establish techniques to amend and improve them. When a new member joins the team, the agreements must be updated, because each person brings something unique and usually alters the dynamics of the group.

Using a Roadmap and Objectives

At some point, the Transformation Team will have a vision of the change or product and a high-level roadmap. This will contain a timeline with information on the impact you want to achieve in each work cycle. Examples of these objectives are an increase in the quality of a service, a reduction in the number of after-hours emergencies, an increase in sales, and a specific impact on the client or employees.

But this roadmap won't help if we aren't fully aware of where we stand. Therefore, each work-cycle objective must have **objective tests** consisting of simple, quantifiable metrics that make it possible to assess the situation and know if the goal has been met. They allow us to align expectations and determine if we are on the right path or need to modify the approach.

During a work cycle, we must achieve small goals that contribute to the overall objective of the work cycle. It's here **missions** are required so we know what to achieve in the coming days, as opposed to one week, two weeks, or a month. Keep in mind that a single work-cycle objective is composed of several missions.

A **mission** is a small goal created by those who will perform the work. It allows them to know whether a step has been taken successfully—or not. A mission is always quantifiable and it helps keep people motivated and focused when it's impossible to see around the corner. A mission focuses on *what* to achieve but not on the *how*. This is so that people can discover the tasks to be completed *during* the work cycle, not before. A mission is not a detail of tasks to be performed but rather a set of small goals to be achieved.

The following are mission examples:

▶ Reduce process steps from ten to four.
▶ Provide team A with larger monitors within the next five days.
▶ Help team B move closer to team A.
▶ Ensure that the new micro-habit increases customer satisfaction from 4 to 4.2.

Once missions for the next few days have been created, establish their benefits.

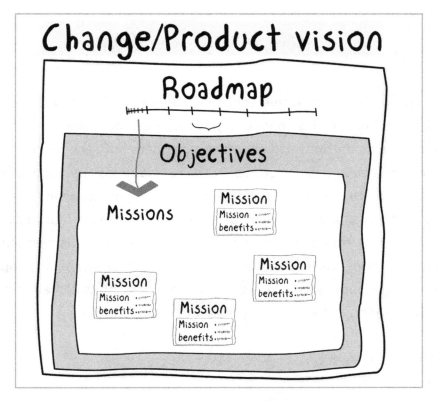

FIGURE 6.4: Missions and their benefits

Mission benefits consist of a list that indicates what you want to learn or what positive habits people want to acquire during a mission.

These are some examples:

- Learn how to place a logistics order.
- Learn how to install Jenkins in one morning.
- Learn two techniques for conducting user interviews.
- Reduce the time to fill applications from three days to two days.

When the benefits of a mission are mostly related to learning and self-development, people need time to reflect on the positive things that have been achieved as a group, as well as those areas yet to be improved.

Using an A5 Canvas

The *A5 canvas* is collaborative tool that can help a Transformation Team maximize the impact of a change initiative. The tool provides visibility so people can focus on the small experiments and identify the impact and the associated objective or mission. This canvas also helps the Transformation Team determine the need for such things as training and coaching.

I created this simple tool years ago, and I must confess that I have used it not only during transformations but also in almost any business situation that requires taking small steps and learning. The A5 canvas helps people see everything they undertake as a hypothesis that must be validated and result in specific learning. It focuses conversation on the following:

- Desired impact.
- Metrics.
- Needs and learning opportunities.
- Making it easy to focus on continuous improvement.

In the upper-left corner of Figure 6.5, participants should write down the current situation. Talking about it reinforces that sought-after initial shared alignment. In the upper-right corner, record the near-future desired impact or behavior. This must be specific and quantifiable.

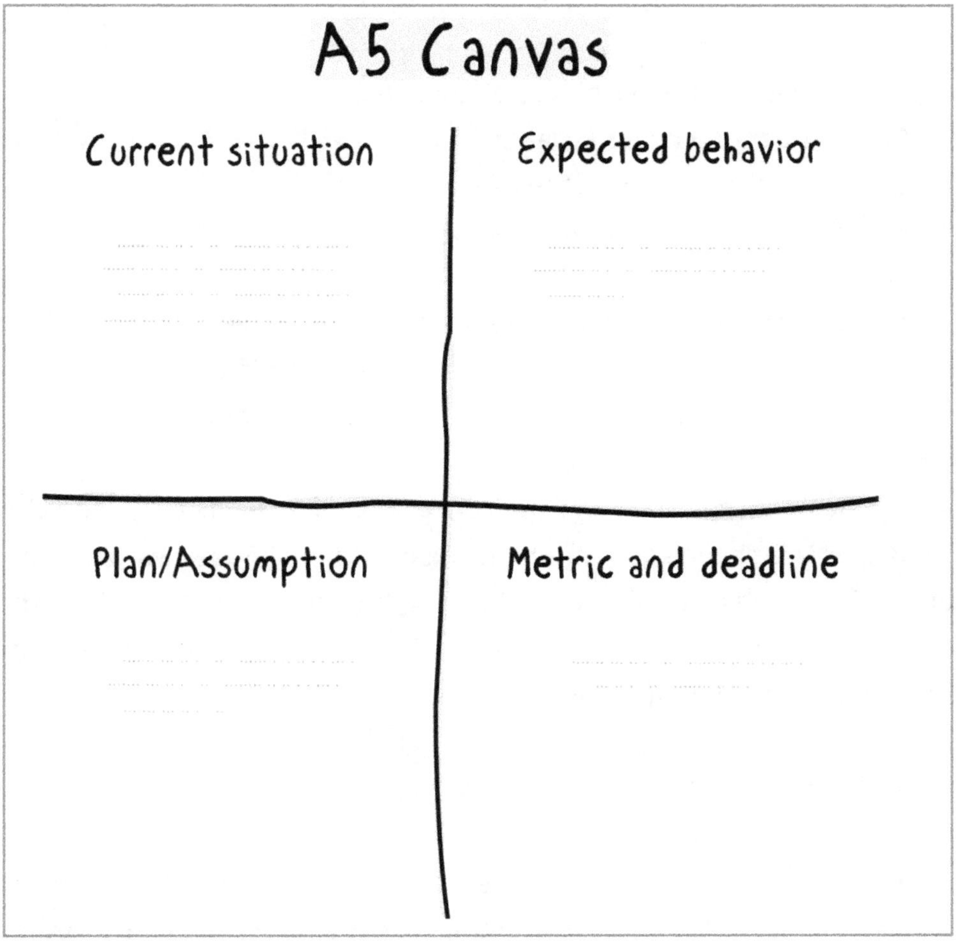

FIGURE 6.5: A5 canvas

In the lower-left section, indicate a small plan for a couple of days: a goal or hypothesis we want to demonstrate (for example: *Using technique X will increase the delivered business value to the client by 10%*).

Finally, in the lower-right section, indicate the deadline for the experiment and the evaluation of its success, as well as metrics for evaluation. The beauty of this visual tool is that it allows everyone to do the following:

▶ Talk about how they see the current situation.
▶ Focus on the impact.
▶ Determine needs (coaching, training, etc.).
▶ Create clear objectives (strategy).
▶ Set a common goal (hypothesis).
▶ Establish deadlines and metrics.

At the end of the work cycle, members can easily verify if the goal has been reached, the hypothesis has been checked, or if they require a new iteration. In case of the latter, you can use the same sheet to show the strategy improvement in each work cycle.

I have been successful using the A5 canvas with teams and people who see and evaluate change as something linear, with individuals who use more-traditional methods, and in moments of high uncertainty. In each of these situations, this tool has helped participants maintain focus and motivation while taking ownership of the work.

Creating Explicit Principles for Liftoff

A change plan isn't usually an isolated event but is more often part of an initiative that seeks to alter an existing service or create a new product. Preparing the liftoff agenda for an initiative is one of the activities that the Transformation Team should carry out with ease.

In general, it focuses on the following objectives:

▶ Understand the problem, the business context, and organizational constraints.

▶ Help create the product vision and understand the vision of change.

▶ Make it easier for everyone to use a common vocabulary.

▶ Develop a shared understanding of the scope.

▶ Ensure that teams have a clear definition of business value and of nonnegotiable minimum quality (Definition of Done), as well as a single work priority.

▶ Ensure that teams create values, principles, working agreements, and practices to carry out collaborative tasks.

▶ Confirm that the skills for the job are available.

▶ Have an initial strategy to help scarce resources or knowledge go from being linear to exponential.

▶ Be aware of any uncertainty and how it could affect people during personal development.

▶ Help people detach from anything they produced that will be discarded by the new plan.

▶ Offer guidance and techniques that increase self-organization in times of high uncertainty.

▶ Implement a credible plan.

▶ Create simple metrics that make progress visible.

▶ Provide techniques for understanding the economic cost of making one decision while delaying another.

The liftoff stage usually occupies the first weeks of the initiative. I do not include information on how to run this stage because there's already plenty of readily available material on the topic. Nevertheless, you will find a story about the liftoff stage at the end of this chapter.

You can learn more about running the liftoff stage in Diana Larsen's book "*Liftoff: Start and Sustain Successful Agile Teams.*"

Clear rules are necessary for establishing activity characteristics during liftoff meetings. The following are examples of principles for developing activities during liftoff meetings:

▶ Any person wishing to add an activity during liftoff should know and understand the vision of change.

▶ Whoever proposes a liftoff session must commit to delivering it—and comply (at least the first time).

▶ Over half the Transformation Team must agree with the activity.

▶ Only liftoff sessions with a practical purpose or that could positively influence people's attitudes should be included.

▶ Every activity must feed a sense of belonging and encourage the self-organization of teams.

▶ Every liftoff session must involve at least 50% practice, and each participant must know in advance the requirements and expected results.

▶ Remaining motionless while looking for perfection is not an option. The activities will be prepared in a short period and will be improved through repetition.

Explicit principles help to align expectations and develop effective planning in the early stages of the initiative. As with team values and work agreements, principles for a change initiative should also be checked and improved regularly.

Looking for the Right Physical Space

The Transformation Team requires space. In my experience, a closed office isn't a good option. Look for an open area close to the people, team, or department going through the change. The physical arrangement of the space can vary from one company to another, but a large table, separate from other desks, provides a substantial advantage. It's also a plus if the table is close to a wall, because this will allow for the display of work agreements, principles, and values.

In some companies, it isn't possible to stick anything on the walls. You can use flipcharts or magnetic sheets during the day and remove them at night, but the team must have the information available and be able to draw during conversations. In addition, the team should have plenty of sticky notes, pens, and blank sheets of paper. Extra chairs also help people feel that they're invited to informal talks and can stop by to ask questions.

Being close to a window is preferable, because natural light has a positive effect on interactions. You should also have a whiteboard and a projector for when you need to use the space as a learning room. The environment should grant everyone the opportunity to observe new forms of interaction, listen to transparent conversations, and promote learning within the company.

If you can't procure the adequate space and environment for the Transformation Team, start with something temporary. Even a corner can be a good alternative initially!

Measuring the Results of the Transformation Team

At some point, you'll inevitably be asked if there is concrete evidence that the business transformation effort will have a positive impact on the performance of the organization. You will have to ask powerful questions to help people discover what is to be measured and how they want to do this.

Using incorrect metrics often causes executives to lose sight of the purpose of the business, and they might begin to assess measurements related to changes in habits instead of what they should be measuring to accelerate the change. Corporate transformations are costly, and people become nervous about results in the short, medium, and long term. Large organizations often forget why the initiative is being implemented (purpose). To combat this, it's essential to have a point of view that covers the impact over the entire business.

If a technology department is affected, many will try to measure the relative improvement in the tools, increase in unit testing, time for product integration, and decrease of defects.

When the purpose for the change initiative is forgotten, executives will try to get their questions answered by requesting more performance measurements in the affected areas, or the exchange between those areas and the rest of the departments. The result could be data reflecting an increase in efficiency in the measured team while the rest of the company is negatively affected, increasing the complexity of the organization and *waste* in its processes.

The previously discussed metrics have an impact on the client, but they are not adequate for evaluating transformation from the business point of view. Seeing the question from different perspectives is essential, and focusing on the impact of the change is crucial. **How will this change help the business better serve its purpose?**

Answering this question requires an understanding that the change could have an indirect impact on external customers and a direct impact on internal departments. Measuring the transformation involves an awareness of the exchange between the impacted department and the rest of the company, as well as clearly establishing a cause-and-effect relationship.

You might think there's a relationship between the amount of ice cream sold and jellyfish stings, but this is far from being a true cause-and-effect relationship. For this reason, you'll have to facilitate workshops where people are exposed to different metrics and are able to experiment with them. This will allow them to feel comfortable experimenting with diverse metrics, challenging initial assumptions, and ensuring that they're measuring something useful.

There are three types of metrics you might find useful:

1. **Business performance metrics** (often called KPI or Key Performance Indicators).
2. **Organizational health metrics**.
3. **Habit-improvement indicators** or driver metrics.

Business performance metrics indicate what will matter to the clients or influence improvements in their lives. If consumers can't distinguish changes in the metrics, then they do not belong under business performance. It's common here to define a range and for executives to worry when the metrics fall below an established threshold. The number of updates of a product and a client's level of confidence could be an example of a direct cause-and-effect relationship.

Health indicators, on the other hand, are normally internal and refer to habits and aspects of the organization that will directly impact the interactions and mental health of employees. They affect performance metrics, but they aren't directly perceived by clients—although they could be indirectly noticed.

Habit-improvement indicators refer to actions that influence behaviors and help to achieve new and better conduct. Once the indexes have indicated that a goal has been achieved, they tend to disappear. Normally, these metrics are local (used only within teams) and help to visualize what teams should improve in their day-to-day work situation.

One of the risks of habit-improvement metrics is that they can lead to local optimizations, where improving a habit in one team can harm another.

In general, metrics on organizational health and habit-improvement indicators are used within the Transformation Team and help those groups to change, while business performance indicators help teams answer the following question from executives: **Is there concrete evidence that the effort will result in a positive and sustainable economic impact on the company?**

All managers and executives should understand the business performance metrics, as should others involved in the change. The transformation of traditional companies toward new ways of thinking and behaving usually implies a cultural change that requires an understanding of new values and principles.

Remember that face-to-face communication and feedback should always take precedence over the use of indicators, especially with executives and middle managers. This helps us to reason based on a collective understanding of objectives, practices, and processes. It also makes it possible to collectively think and encourage actions that improve reward systems, promote techniques that decrease resistance to transformation, and get everyone to reflect on how to replace scarce areas with exponentials.

Express Team Liftoff... Shaping a High-Performing Team in Record Time

By: Stefan Sohnchen, *Business Agility Coach*

A team messed up at its foundation cannot be fixed. Hence it is important to nail the culture right from the start. We know successful sports teams work hard on building their performance. We know that successful orchestras are similarly built on focused effort to build a well-arranged foundation. But in the workplace at the office we often assume that high performing teams just emerge because they have to. In reality it needs a lot of structured effort for people in office settings to become high-performing teams.

When looking back at working in a team setting, characterized by a well-formed foundation years later, you will realize that you will have forgotten what people said, you will have forgotten what people did, but you will remember how working in such a team made you feel.

Let me tell you about such an occasion from my own experience. A couple of years ago, I worked with **Joe Justice** and **Tim Myer**, both well-known Agile Coaches, on an Agile Transformation for Tait Communications in Christchurch, New Zealand. Back then Joe and Tim worked as consultants for SolutionsIQ in Seattle and they were members of Team Wikispeed.

A Team Wikispeed is a global team of enthusiastic agilists creating super-efficient commuter cars. You can read more about it here: *wikispeed.org*

While Joe has joined Scrum Inc. since, both he and Tim are still with Team Wikispeed.

The Tait Communications delivery team we worked with was cross-functional, using Agile project management techniques, Scrum, eXtreme Programming, and extreme manufacturing. There were software developers working with hardware developers, working with marketing, working with sales, etc. The close-knit setting that we managed to achieve produced a positive vibe that made people flow and get on with what needed to be done as traditional dividing lines between functional departments had become highly porous.

On day one, the team created a prioritized list of Tait's customers' wants. Four days later, the team had a working prototype of a new radio, a customer in the room with the team using that prototype, and a cross-functional team getting direct customer feedback faster than they ever had before.

In the previous *"phase gate"* model, the customer feedback loop would have never reached the engineers and the prototype would have taken at least 3 months.

How was this possible? It was possible because we started out with what is known as a Team Liftoff in the lead up to the week we worked with Joe and Tim.

Running a Team Liftoff is a golden opportunity to set ground rules and establish the structure—or lack of one—in which things get done. Think this through with a 2 x 2 matrix. On one axis you have highly trusted team members and less trusted team members. On the other axis you have a low alignment structure with poorly set rules, and then a high alignment structure where the rules are well set. The combination you want to aim for is 'high trust' people with a structure that provides a high degree of alignment.

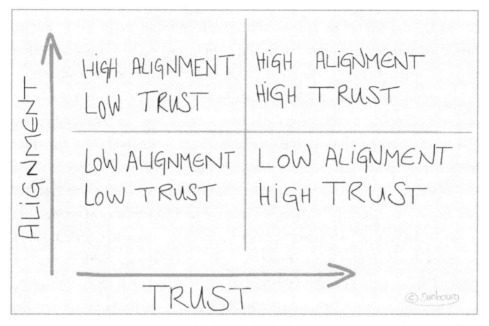

Trust and Alignment Table

As a result, people are rowing in the same direction, and not by accident. The team members are in sync, and henceforth, they can move on to the rest of the equation.

The one-day event of my express Team Liftoff starts with reiterating the purpose—*Why are we doing this?* This is tied in with the company's roadmap—*How and what will we do?*

Make it fun and invite people to come up with a name for their team. This is followed by the team creating their own Team Charter—a type of loose yet binding contract—to agree on the ground rules and factors that will make your team successful.

Once this is in place participants are given an overview on what it means to work in an agile way—or any other preferred way. Moreover, this is to align all team members in their understanding of the mindset required to succeed under the conditions of exponential growth opportunities.

As the facilitator or part of the Transformation Team, you want to quickly move on to team building and people getting to know each other through encouraging individuals to share interests and motivations.

Combine this with holding a *Skills Market* activity to see if the team has what it needs to succeed. Only then—and if you are planning to use the Scrum framework—should you suss out how you will work together in terms of *Sprint Cadence* and *Daily Scrums*.

While you can get through all the aforementioned during the first half of the day, focus on the *Backlog Refinement* and *Stakeholder Mapping* after lunch. Make sure you include the following people: customers, stakeholders, partners, the core and supporting teams. This will help you with identifying dependencies and agreeing on the best communication tools for your situation

You want to end the day with building a first version of your activity wall, or high-level view of a couple of Sprints out from where you are right now. Of course, don't forget to reflect back on the day by running a retrospective. At the end of this one-day express event, people will be exhausted as much as they will share the feeling of having accomplished important things together.

It is safe to say that without the express Team Liftoff at Tait Communications we would neither have been able to build the *Sprint Backlog* on day one nor deliver a working prototype on day five.

A Team Liftoff is not simply a technique for fixing a broken team. In fact, for any team—regardless of whether struggling to perform or high performing teams that leave everyone else behind them already—there is value in pausing to sharpening your axe.

A close cousin of the Team Liftoff is the *Team Reset*. Unlike the first, typically aimed at getting the team off the ground at the start of an initiative, the reset event aims at working with a team that lost its oomph while Sprinting for some time. The same structure applied for an express Liftoff can be tailored to re-energize a team at any time.

My experience with Liftoffs over the years is that you best work with a tailored approach rather than an off-the-shelf textbook structure.

Before running the liftoff it pays to invest time into understanding what really matters for the team, where they think they would get the biggest gain from pausing their day-to-day routine to reflect on their actions. An express liftoff well done will result in a return on the cost of losing one delivery day because the team will be enabled to collaborate more efficiently further into any project or initiative. Try it!

What You Have Learned

☑ How to establish alignment and common understanding.
☑ The characteristics of a Transformation Team.
☑ The reciprocity pattern.
☑ How to use Impact Mapping.
☑ How to establish values, working agreements, and principles for a change initiative.
☑ Three types of metrics.

1. Do you remember at least three characteristics of a Transformation Team?

2. What objectives could an experiment have in your company?

3. What questions does an impact map help answer, and in what situations could you use it in your company?

4. What are the three types of metrics you could use?

CHAPTER 7

Discover the Power within your Company with ESS

CHAPTER 7

> " Creative thinking inspires ideas.
> Ideas inspire change. "

Barbara Januszkiewicz, Artist

Chances are that your company has been looking for work styles that will allow it to quickly adjust to cultural changes and exponential market disruptions. If you add the effects of robotics, Big Data, cloud network, and always-connected consumers who provide constant feedback, then the result is constant pressure on every part of your organization.

In the previous chapters, you learned why change doesn't take place as fast as you might think. During the first months of a change initiative, executives mistakenly believe they can quickly deliver business value to customers without compromising the stability of the company. But the adjustments produced by an organizational transformation impact every department and can make processes ever-more complicated.

Many managers and executives have taken a step in the right direction by using the *Agile* and *Lean* mindsets, the Scrum framework, or Kanban techniques. But we must keep in mind that Agile originated in 2001 as a collection of values and principles for solving problems in software departments by adapting and learning faster and creating better applications that deliver more business value to the customer.

Today, you must go beyond Agile and Scrum if you want to transform the whole organization.

Differences Between Agile and Business Agility

Companies face the challenge of adapting *Agile* values and principles, as well as *Scrum* framework techniques (usually in the areas of IT), so that they fit with the rest of the organization.

You've probably also heard about *Business Agility*—techniques that can be used not only in IT departments but also throughout the company.

The Agile Manifesto for software development was created in 2001 to help companies create better software. Learn more here: *en.innova1st.com/70A*

Table 7.1 shows the differences between the Agile and Business Agility perspectives, so you can understand where to use each approach.

Agile	Business Agility
Focuses on making IT teams more flexible and adaptable to change.	Focuses on organizational design aimed at making the whole company more flexible (structures, forms of governance, budget, etc.).
Scrum, Kanban, etc.	Creates new ways of working throughout the organization.
Projects, products (fixed cost, variable cost, etc.).	Changes the way business value is created by modifying existing value streams.
Introduces a way of thinking.	Challenges every existing organizational belief.
Focuses on how the work is done (sequence, batches, etc.).	Provides ideas to alter people's patterns and behaviors throughout the company.
Establishes the foundation for forming excellent software teams.	Sets the foundation of a remarkable company.

Table 7.1: Differences between Agile and Business Agility

Successfully transforming a company, starting with IT teams and using Agile mindsets or the Scrum framework, requires that you do the following:

- Identify and adapt the practices and strategies from software departments so they can be used in non-IT areas of the company.
- Know which areas will offer greater or lesser resistance to change.
- Know which practices will not require any adaptation when used outside IT.

In my opinion, **Business Agility enables companies to adapt to new market conditions to create a competitive advantage without negatively affecting organizational health.**

Have in mind that changing or scaling an organization, scaling Agile, scaling Scrum, building new products or even developing new software, should never be your end goal. Your goal should always be to adapt as fast and effective as possible, to be able to deliver the most business value and greatest customer experience while looking after your employees.

The Seduction of Tools

During the steps before a business transformation, companies frequently focus on a particular methodology, tool, or software that will help accelerate cultural change and create a more flexible organization. I have seen large companies invest millions in software tools that promised to speed up transformation. You will need some of these tools as you become an exponential growth company, but for cultural change, you need to pay attention to other factors.

Many Transformation Teams, or sometimes even management, believe there are shortcuts to get employees to adapt more quickly. This often results in recommendations for team training, continuous improvement, process engineering, quality-control programs, cultural alignment, leadership development, and the like. I've even heard suggestions that the installation of a new software system (personnel management, tickets, defects, communication software, etc.) would solve most of the dysfunctions.

I have visited companies where it was believed that the more sophisticated or expensive the tool, the faster the cultural change would be. You have to ask: **Is your company using tools, or are the tools using your company?**

This is what we call the *seduction of tools*, a recurring trend you will find during the first months of the transformation of a business. But the real problem isn't the tools themselves.

> In the same way that music comes from the musician and not from the instrument, business adaptability comes from the people and not from the frameworks.
>
> Johnny Ordóñez, Agile Coach

For the company to evolve, we have to consider cultural factors, how these factors support people, how people relate to each other and learn, and how knowledge flows and evolves within the company.

Tools are important, but they must be an intelligent response to a correctly identified problem. Putting all your hopes in software tools as the remedy to your problems usually distracts people from what really matters—the cultural and human aspects—and keeps them from finding a sustainable solution.

The seduction of tools takes place for several reasons. It's often due to industrial-era mindsets that apply excessive control in areas where high creativity is needed, or in areas where people are already accustomed to solving problems with software.

There's no doubt that it's much easier to outsource a service or carry out a software update than to change mental processes. In my experience, except for the problems derived from limited resources (or even a complete lack of resources), most barriers are generally the result of human factors:

- Individual habits when interacting with others.
- How people process ideas or exchange knowledge.
- How individuals learn or assimilate learning.
- How they react to unexpected situations.
- How they accept feedback and resolve conflict.

As you can see, being a great facilitator during a business transformation requires knowledge about psychology, neuroscience, business rules, and organizational patterns. Therefore, the approaches you use should take into consideration both organizational complexity and the human condition.

As companies get larger and more complex, there's a tendency to manage to proxies. This comes in many shapes and sizes, and it's dangerous, subtle . . .

A common example is process as proxy. Good process serves you so you can serve customers. But if you're not watchful, the process can become the thing. This can happen very easily in large organizations. The process becomes the proxy for the result you want. You stop looking at outcomes and just make sure you're doing the process right. Gulp. It's not that rare to hear a junior leader defend a bad outcome with something like, 'Well, we followed the process.' A more experienced leader will use it as an opportunity to investigate and improve the process. The process is not the thing.

Letter to shareholders written by Jeff Bezos, founder of Amazon.

At this point you're probably wondering how you can finally achieve healthier habits during your business transformation. This is exactly what *Enterprise Social Systems* will help you with.

The First Steps in Enterprise Social Systems

Years ago, I was observing the operation of a small company and trying to understand what it had in common with larger corporations. I began to suspect that, regardless of the culture of the country or the size of the organization, employees might find it hard to support transformation initiatives.

By that time, I had witnessed several business transformations. One of the factors that caught my attention was people's resistance when attempts were made to change their habits or when they were encouraged to evolve their mindset.

I asked myself whether I could offer a set of simple concepts to help individuals from any area of a company change how they think. I reflected and established two initial rules to help me reach my goal:

▷ **Techniques should not be intrusive.**
   People should be able to use new concepts, different habits, or ways of reasoning without feeling intimidated.

▷ **Any individual in the organization must be able to use the new guidelines.**
   No specialization would be required to understand the foundations of sustainable change.

It was then that I began to experiment with organizational patterns, reframing techniques, System Thinking concepts, psychology, and neuroscience. Above all, I observed behaviors within Agile and digital companies. My goal was to increase the 5 types of agility in a sustainable way.

Little by little, I shaped what is now Enterprise Social Systems:

▶ An approach that makes it possible to observe the dynamics and functioning of a company from a different point of view.
▶ Five main components so that anyone, with or without specific abilities in change, can reason differently when facing a problem.
▶ Two change frameworks (*ELSA* and *DeLTA*) to facilitate the viralization of new ideas and habits.

Enterprise Social Systems was designed with digital companies in mind. **Its main objective is to help leaders, change agents, and coaches to create new frameworks, methodologies, or processes that accelerate change in the company, allowing it to turn exponential.**

To achieve this, Enterprise Social Systems employs techniques, organizational patterns, and concepts derived from psychology and neuroscience. With Enterprise Social Systems, five components are used to add new ideas and employ reasoning processes during the creation or execution of a change or improvement plan.

Enterprise Social Systems also helps teams and executives find innovative solutions and discover new practices to expand processes that increase the five types of Agility (Technical, Structural, Outcomes, Social, and Mental). Those who use Enterprise Social Systems can do the following:

▶ Plan a change in any type of company, regardless of whether traditional or modern ways of thinking are used.
▶ Create new and powerful processes, frameworks, or methodologies.
▶ Adapt existing practices or frameworks in software department so they can be used throughout the company.
▶ Use reframing techniques to analyze ideas from different perspectives and thus create powerful plans.

Enterprise Social Systems can also be used by any person in the company to improve what is being done, even if the person has no experience in organizational change.

Keep in mind that Enterprise Social Systems is not a scientific theory. I have great appreciation for those who dedicate their lives to the discovery of theories of this type, but my goal is to contribute to those who live every day with the complexity of the organization and urgently need better solutions.

The Four Layers of the Organization

In Enterprise Social Systems, a company is seen as a system based on four interdependent pillars:

- Social Systems
- Mindset
- Formal Organization
- Value Creation

Each of these pillars has specific characteristics and is altered by different situations. From the theoretical point of view, the main hypothesis of Enterprise Social Systems is that actions that increase the flow of relevant knowledge through these four pillars will have a positive impact on the company. But for this, you must first understand how the organization is viewed through the lens of Enterprise Social Systems.

Imagine that you want to take two weeks of vacation to visit cities you have never even heard of. You will first try to obtain a map to learn the location and proximity of each city. Then you will investigate its geography, the weather conditions, the most convenient ways to get from one place to another, the culture, and activities you could engage in during your visit. As you can see, the map not only shows the geographic location, but it also serves to organize your ideas so you know what to take and so you have an initial plan.

You'll agree that a change initiative is much less tangible than a trip, and sometimes you don't even know where to start. Enterprise Social Systems gives you a map to discover and sort those initial ideas, connect them, and create an initial change plan.

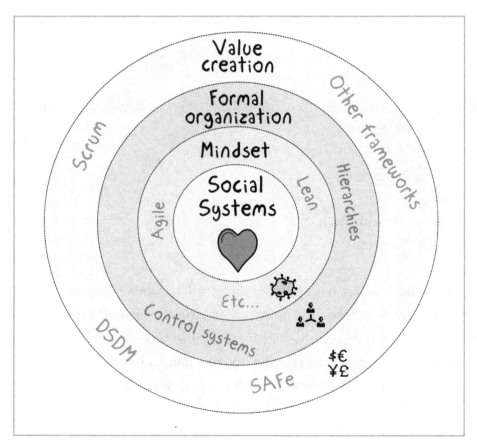

**FIGURE 7.1: The heart of Enterprise Social Systems
and the four pillars of the organization**

This map or conceptual model represents the dynamics of the organization and shows how they relate to each other. The four pillars are interconnected and are represented by concentric circles, with the center having the greatest impact on the rest. Its objective is to help build better strategies for change.

Social Systems

In the center of the map you find **social systems,** which **represents the forms of communication, interaction, and relationships between people.** These include their habits and micro-habits, the informal rules on how they make their work visible, and organizational patterns that you learned in the previous chapters. Any change in this pillar will strongly affect the rest, which is why it's found at the center of the organization.

These are external factors that can strongly impact social systems:

A Sense of Urgency

Urgency puts pressure on people and impacts their habits, behaviors, how they connect, and their mental state. For example, a deadline to deliver a product could make employees who had never communicated fluidly put aside their differences and begin to interact to achieve a common goal.

Number of People in the Organization

The size of the organization has repercussions on how people socialize. A company formed by a few people will have different habits from a corporation with thousands of employees. In a small organization, you are more likely to feel comfortable from day one and to act and speak freely with those around you. But in a corporation where there are hundreds of people around you, you will probably communicate more indirectly, through email or chat, and spend the first few days waiting for a superior to tell you what to do.

Organizational Health

These are the habits that directly impact emotional states and indirectly impact the results of the company. If people feel safe, they will communicate, move, and express themselves more openly. This increases shared knowledge and helps ideas evolve more quickly. If, on the other hand, a person feels insecure, communication will diminish, which may affect the company's learning, productivity, and innovation. In addition, if people multitask or have many pending tasks, this will also affect their emotional state, which in turn will affect results and the product's quality.

Remember that social systems are at the center of any organization, because any change here will strongly affect the other pillars.

Mindset

The circle that surrounds social systems is called *mindset,* and this represents the **beliefs, values, and abstract ideas that make up the company's culture.** When a consultant specializing in Agile or Lean mindsets teaches a new set of values or principles, the consultant is working directly in this area (mindset) and indirectly in the other areas.

This pillar represents a mixture of the company's culture, the values incorporated over the years, and the company's preferred reasoning style for solving problems.

Formal Organization

The third circle refers to formal organization. This is where the **structures that sustain work styles are *"allocated"* and give coherence to the information.** In this area we find the following:

Formal Structures

Formal structures hold the relationships of power and responsibilities within the company. If you ask someone to draw this area, they will usually draw an organizational chart.

Information Systems

These are the processes, areas, and tools that shape information coming from other layers of the organization or from outside the company. Their main goal is for information to make sense for people and be compatible with their beliefs and values. Artificial intelligence generally interacts with this pillar.

Control Systems

Control systems represent the processes, areas, and tools used to review the activities and outcomes produced by employees, resources, and time. The goal of control systems is to ensure that organizational structures can be maintained and function correctly, and that they do not change abruptly.

More-traditional companies, those that follow linear processes, mainly see a business change as an alteration to this layer. The objective of the formal organization layer is to ensure that information makes sense and to sustain and protect the company's structures so they do not change abruptly.

Value Creation

The external pillar focuses on the creation of value for the client and is where frameworks such as Scrum and DSDM, SAFe, Scrum at Scale, LeSS, etc. reside. Value creation is directly affected by the methodology, framework, or definition of business value. It is indirectly affected by changes in the markets or in the other pillars.

When you create a change initiative that contains small plans to impact each of these pillars, we say that you have created a **powerful plan**. This is the secret for having your transformation become exponential.

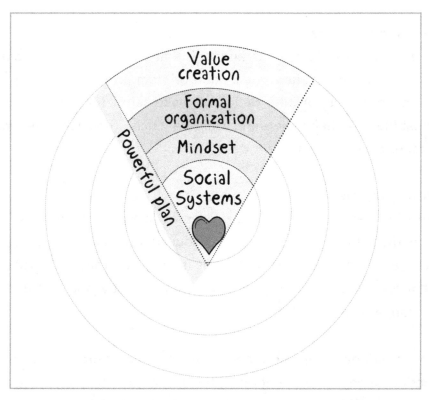

FIGURE 7.2: The four components of a powerful plan in Enterprise Social Systems

Remember that the conceptual model of an organization proposed by Enterprise Social Systems does not put artificial barriers between the company's dynamics. Instead, it shows what is needed to make a big impact.

Consider this question: *Upon which pillars do you put the most emphasis when creating a change plan?*

The Five Components of Enterprise Social Systems

In human activities, there are usually preferred forms of reasoning that guide people during the resolution of problems. These preferred forms of reasoning allow individuals to visualize how they will solve a problem by moving from an initial state **A** to a desired state **B**. The space between points **A** and **B** is the *challenge time*. This is when individuals invest their effort, trying to find solutions to a problem, establish processes and techniques, and create metrics to verify whether they are going in the right direction.

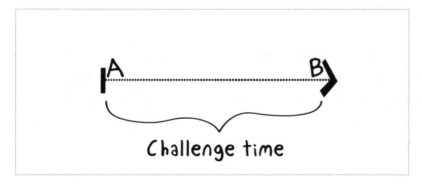

FIGURE 7.3: During the challenge time, people invest their energy to solve a problem.

During the challenge time, traditional companies often use forms of reasoning based on previous experiences, or they use structures and processes that are already in use in other areas of the organization. While this may work when dealing with well-known and relatively stable markets, we need to use different techniques when there is high variability and when creative solutions are required.

During the challenge time, Enterprise Social Systems offers five components so different forms of reasoning can be employed to maximize creativity and the impact of the change.

New ideas and mental processes change conclusions and help people establish new neuronal connections that will serve them well in future situations. Thinking differently makes it possible to develop new questions and points of view—and to move in a different direction. The following are the five components that help people during the challenge time:

1. **Enterprise Blocking Collaboration**
2. **Enterprise Social Density**
3. **Enterprise Social Visibility**
4. **Complexity and Complication pattern**
5. **Permission-to-learn pattern**

At the end of this chapter, you will learn how to use these five components to help others to create new plans or modify existing ones and to change processes, tactics, or habits. But first, let me explain what they are about.

Enterprise Blocking Collaboration

Many consultants focus on trying to increase collaboration between the company's employees. But this can be a trap. At the beginning of the book, I mentioned that a consulting firm for which I worked had a clause in its contract *"suggesting"* that we collaborate with another employee if requested by that employee . . . even if the tasks were of lower priority than what I was doing.

There are situations where cooperating benefits everyone, and I personally do so every day. But interrupting a task without taking into account the type of collaboration established between people can lead to less-than-positive consequences.

Imagine that your department improves its internal processes, but such improvement has a negative effect on the rest of the company. This is called *local optimization*. Would you consider this collaboration? Such situations are common and can be positive—as long as they are well planned, they are temporary, and the negative effects are limited.

Suppose someone asks you a favor when you are working at over 80% of your personal capacity and heavily multitasking. You accept the request and begin working on the new tasks. Obviously, you'll be under more pressure and your pending work will be delayed, which in turn will affect timeframes in the rest of the company. *Would you call this collaboration?*

Again, this type of behavior works better if the company has clear priorities for business value.

In the above case, it would mean that the request has a clear business priority and can be carried out without having to multitask. Unfortunately, in many of the companies I visit, people take on new activities that entail more multitasking. This increases the possibility of errors, complexity, and the cost of the product or service. Such a situation requires more energy and will usually reduce motivation. As you can see, there are two distinct types of collaboration:

- **Positive collaboration**
- **Blocking collaboration**

Positive collaboration favorably impacts the objectives of the organization, while *blocking collaboration* has negative effects on the workflow. It is healthy for people to understand, detect, and quantify the different types of collaboration.

Enterprise Blocking Collaboration refers to the cooperation between people or teams whose behaviors have a negative impact on the organization.

The executives of a company I visited asked me to help them find alternatives to reduce their fixed costs. They were concerned because they invested a million dollars every month in the salaries of their SAP department. The management team decided to make some employees redundant, thinking it was the only viable solution.

The managers wanted to ensure that no one had idle time, and they constantly checked that people were working at 100% capacity. You could often hear one of the middle-managers exclaiming, "*I do not want to see anyone working at less than 100%!*"

After speaking with the employees and analyzing the situation, I discovered that the levels of Enterprise Blocking Collaboration were really high: employees interrupted their work several times a day to perform unrelated tasks, in many cases, of lower priority. They also had high and variable workloads, already at nearly 95% of their capacity. Because of this, it was difficult for them to cooperate with others or to add additional work discovered during development.

Although employees working at 95% of capacity was considered positive by management, it created a vicious circle that led to less and less business value being delivered to customers.

Taking into account the multitasking, work capacity, and quality of the product, it allowed me to quantify the average cost of the employees' unhealthy habits. The analysis of the data showed that at least $0.78 of every dollar invested in the SAP department was lost in activities that did not provide business value for the client—all as a result of high Enterprise Blocking Collaboration. A more exhaustive investigation showed that such a situation did not occur only in that department, but throughout the organization.

I suggested adding explicit *working agreements* to change how work was done and set a nonnegotiable definition of minimum product quality.

I also made sure that every new procedure was supported by micro-habits. To achieve this, they had to modify processes, responsibilities, and expectations. We also had to set guidelines for people to feel safe.

Finally, we moved everyone belonging to the same value stream to the same physical location. This allowed them to achieve a more constant flow of work and knowledge.

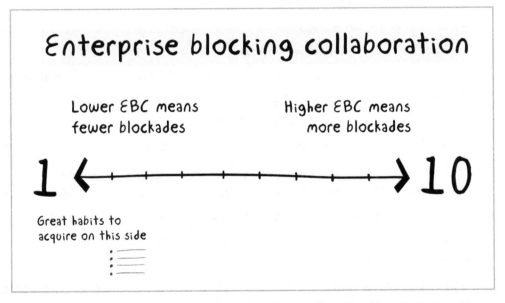

FIGURE 7.4: Initial ideas for measuring Enterprise Blocking Collaboration

It helps to have one or more individuals dedicated to explaining Enterprise Blocking Collaboration and removing the initial barriers produced by Enterprise Blocking Collaboration.

Below is a list of behaviors that can help you detect whether Enterprise Blocking Collaboration exists in your company:

▸ Employees take on new tasks even when they are already above 80% of their personal capacity or help is requested from individuals with limited availability.

▸ The answer to a new problem in the company is usually an increase of rules, bureaucracy, or a local optimization.

▸ People are stuck in an activity for more than fifteen minutes without asking for help from their teammates.

▸ Teams develop a product or service together and their communication is strictly by email.

▸ Cases of multitasking are widespread.

▸ Several reports are prepared for management, many of which would be unnecessary if replaced with face-to-face conversations.

▸ There is no clear definition of minimum, nonnegotiable quality of the product.

▸ There are teams where one or more of the key members are located in another office or geographical location.

▸ There is no clear definition of business value or there are contradictory definitions.

▸ People have high levels of psychological ownership of what they produce, and yet the product or service needs to be improved frequently.

▸ Reward and recognition systems don't explicitly focus on supporting healthy collaboration habits.

▸ Software development teams don't use tools for streamlining collaborative editing and debugging in real-time during development (Visual Studio Live Share, Codeshare, AtomPair, JustInMind, etc.).

Keep in mind that at times it isn't easy to identify if it's one type of collaboration or another.

Enterprise Social Density

In the traditional organization, many decisions and communications reach teams from the highest levels of the company. These groups, in turn, copy this form of communication, also relying on hierarchies to distribute knowledge.

But digital products require a high speed of adaptation, because everything can change from one moment to the next, which is why these more-traditional ways of managing people, information, and shared knowledge are generally not the most appropriate.

When was the last time you had a fluid conversation or acquired knowledge from someone inside the company? During a casual conversation, perhaps a colleague explained how to perform a task better, or perhaps you had coffee with someone you trust and you learned something relevant that weeks later would be formally announced by the company.

Formal communications flow through hierarchical structures, which generally employ formal steps, often require corporate decisions, and have little to do with how value is actually created for the client. Therefore, information travels much slower than when it is transmitted through informal or casual connections to people trusted by the *sender* of the information.

The more speed and the greater the amount of relevant information that flows through the networks of employees (or nodes), the higher the capacity for adaptation and the better the ability to make decisions in the company will be.

In the same manner, the more balanced or symmetrical the knowledge among the members of a group is, the better their results will be.

This is expressed in the economic theory of symmetric information, and you should take this into account when designing any process or framework.

Are you familiar with the economic *Asymmetric Information Theory*? It was proposed by the winners of the Nobel Prize in Economics for 2001: George Akerlof, Michael Spence, and Joseph Stiglitz. The theory explains how information imbalances between people can lead to inefficient results in the markets and in the company. Learn more about it at *en.innova1st.com/71B*

Communication, especially when transmitted informally, is a crucial component in the culture of exponential companies, and it is the basis for change that can multiply without limits throughout the organization. But for informal communication to be effective, the company must have a culture that supports these connections as part of its day-to-day life.

This informal flow of relevant knowledge among the employees of a company is called **Enterprise Social Density,** and it's an essential concept in accelerating a business change.

Enterprise Social Density can decrease because of psychological or logistical factors, or if the company employs rigid structures (processes and hierarchies) that do not allow employees to connect informally.

If the members of a team do not trust each other, they will communicate their experiences, opinions and knowledge through indirect means such as emails and virtual chats. This increases inefficiency and decreases business results.

This type of habit increases bureaucracy, dysfunction, and the final cost of the product, and decreases the number of experiments that the organization makes each month.

Enterprise Social Density consists of the flow of relevant, honest, informal, and effective information in an environment where people feel safe.

In general, a team that is geographically distant has a lower social density than a team whose members are all in the same location. Scrum Inc. states that there is a fall in social density even when people are over 30 meters (98 feet) away from each other.

There are cases when groups communicate only under extreme necessity, or where different cultures exist within the same company. This obviously affects the way knowledge flows.

I've witnessed teams that had to collaborate but were located in different buildings. When the managers and I looked into the reasons for this distance, I discovered that it was done with the explicit purpose of differentiating status between the teams.

Here's another example. At a corporation I helped, I decided to stop using email to get people used to talking to me in person when they needed help. At first, it took them by surprise, but eventually many copied the habit. This increased the flow of information and relevant knowledge throughout the organization.

If you want to delay a solution, your best option is to send an email or use an indirect means of communication instead of talking to the person directly.

Low social density can also occur when knowledge is scarce. In these cases, it's highly recommended that you increase employee rotation and that employees work in pairs so that the knowledge flows as uniformly as possible.

Some companies bombard employees with information, thinking this will help them make better decisions. It's common to hear people complaining about having to go to meetings over and over without understanding why. Enterprise Social Systems clearly defines "*necessary information*" in a company as information that is **relevant** to people; whereas "*relevant information*" is anything that gives a competitive advantage to people belonging to the same value stream.

It's essential that any practice, framework, technique, or new change initiative increases the social density among all people who create the product or service (value stream). For that to happen, you have to make it easy for everyone to use direct forms of communication as often as possible. You also need to reduce the levels of bureaucracy.

You can use the CD3 technique (Cost of Delay Divided by Duration) to calculate the economic impact of delays or impasses caused by a low social density in your company. Learn more about CD3 at *en.innova1st.com/72C*

You should also pay attention to how people are managed. In the most-traditional companies, decisions are made hierarchically (top-down); but creating a product or service today requires having employees from different areas and roles. Using strong hierarchical structures doesn't support good business value creation.

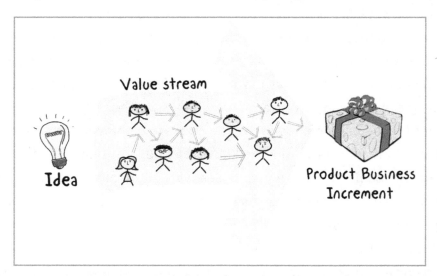

FIGURE 7.5: Change the way people are managed first to match the shape of the value stream. Then increase the ESD in the value stream.

To ensure a continuous flow of knowledge, decisions, and learning, it's essential that individuals can self-organize around their tasks and that obstacles blocking work are removed daily.

To increase the flow of knowledge, your company could define the minimum work unit as two people, indicating that there can never be a single person performing a task and that there should always be at least two.

Studies indicate that when you start working in pairs on activities that demand creativity, productivity falls during the first two months. The data also shows that growth is consolidated with a significant increase in the following months (The economics of software development by pair programmers, Hakan Erdogmus and Canada Laurie Williams).

Because collaboration *within* a team is usually continuous, but discontinuous *between* teams, it will often be necessary to create explicit between-team working agreements that clearly indicate how teams should collaborate and share knowledge.

Having implemented this paired-up working style, you will gradually see higher-quality results and more productivity compared to those working individually.

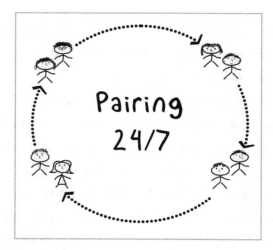

FIGURE 7.6: Pairing 24/7 means during working hours

Rotating people is also essential, allowing everyone to balance knowledge and appreciate different points of view. People may initially feel uncomfortable with this type of arrangement. For the new forms of work to be incorporated into the culture of the company, support from leadership is needed. My recommendation is that you create a metric to show how an increase in social density can impact business value and improve organizational health.

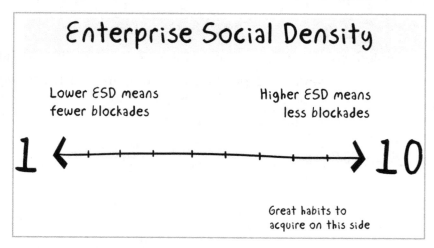

FIGURE 7.7: Social density metrics should account for the habits to be improved

The following are ten recommendations to support the increase of Enterprise Social Density. You should consider them when creating or implementing a process or framework:

1. Everyone in the *value stream* must be able to clearly identify the processes, activities, and individuals involved.
2. Face-to-face communication is used as much as possible.
3. Employees are given direct access to other employees who could help them, without bureaucracy or formal approvals.
4. Bureaucracy is actively simplified each time a new process is added.
5. Individuals teach each other using communities of practice or other informal sessions (*Lean Coffee* or another informal meeting).
6. Individuals can try new ways of working, feel safe if they fail, and identify the most-appropriate type of collaboration.
7. Informal structures that maximize relevant conversations are fostered.
8. A positive attitude is encouraged when the work to be done changes abruptly.
9. People are encouraged to work in pairs as much as possible.
10. Information provided by artificial intelligence or Big Data is available to all and is used in the same way as knowledge obtained by other means.

The Permission-to-learn Pattern

High Enterprise Social Density is key for the flow of relevant information. But without the right knowledge, techniques for quicker information flow are of little use.

Large corporations have explicit rules that regulate how people learn. This results in a flow of knowledge that isn't constant. In your organization, you might find that the following habits hinder continuous learning:

▷ Those around you have to ask for permission and wait weeks for the company to authorize training in new skills.

▷ There is no rotation within teams, or people do not frequently work in pairs.

▷ Employees can't self-organize around their tasks; it's usually the managers who assign the work.

▷ Skills are taught theoretically, with a person in front of the room explaining and showing examples.

▷ There are no communities of practice where individuals can acquire knowledge or provide feedback.

▷ When unable to perform a task, teams must turn to management to solve the problem.

▷ There are no informal structures to help employees teach each other. Remember that all who teach also learn!

In many places, long-term employees are told what and when they should learn. In such cases, it's common to require approvals and follow a long list of actions before the knowledge is acquired.

Waiting for knowledge increases workflow interruptions, which leads to an increase in blockades and in the final cost of the product. This also forces people to create techniques or processes to compensate for their shortcomings. I am not recommending that we eliminate all formal learning. But we do need to ensure that other means to gather knowledge are made available.

If your company lacks communities of practice, talk to those around you to learn the skills they require. Then involve those who have these skills and support them so that they can spread their knowledge.

In a company I visited, I suggested that communities of practice could be both a place to gain knowledge and a space where members could vote democratically on the strategies and technologies to be used in their products and services. A few weeks after my recommendation, the software architects worked hard to ensure that everyone better understood the options and that they had time to reflect before voting.

The Permission-to-learn pattern entails people waiting for a decision from the company before acquiring specific knowledge, instead of actively self-organizing around learning needs.

The higher the Permission-to-learn pattern index, the harder it will be for people to acquire knowledge or skills.

Understanding this pattern is important, as it helps employees focus on creative habits for maximizing their learning. I usually ask companies how long it takes to gain a skill after an employee requests a course. If the answer is over three weeks, you are likely witnessing an organization with a high Permission-to-learn index.

The company culture must support people teaching each other without formal approvals or unnecessary bureaucracy. Achieving this requires that you empower employees and give them the time they need.

A company where I offered coaching required that two of their software teams learn the Kanban techniques. The training course was approved after two months, and the members were thrilled. It was only at the end of this training that I discovered that the groups surrounding those members were all experts in Kanban.

Incredible! Why hadn't the groups shared this knowledge with each other?

The management team of another company that I helped was initiating an Agile transformation. They had created eight Scrum teams through a tortuous process, mainly because many of the skills were scarce or not available.

To overcome this situation, the three managers defined a formal procedure for team members to learn how to act if a new skill was needed. Despite this, the number of rules and exceptions to this procedure remained high, so I proposed an experimental activity called the *Farmers Market*.

About 100 people would have four hours to create new teams based on their personality and formal and informal skills. I proposed two simple rules:

1. Each new Scrum team must have all the skills to successfully implement a product.
2. Each team should have a maximum of eight core members.

During subsequent talks, the management team asked two interesting questions:

A. What would happen if one or more people were left out of the teams because others thought they had little knowledge or were not very skilled?
B. What would happen if the employees did not organize themselves and the game failed?

Clearly, this could cause the initiative to lose traction, and it was certainly a risk. But even though those situations could be problematic, I suggested moving forward and finding a solution for such cases if they arose. I even bet a month's salary that the dynamics would be successful!

In all honesty, I'm not sure that the bet influenced the management team's decision, but they finally gave the green light to my Farmers Market proposal. The following day, we asked each of the 100 participants for an informal resume that answered these questions:

▶ What's your name? Attach a photo for identification.
▶ What skills do you have?
▶ What are some recently learned skills that few people know about?
▶ What do you enjoy doing or have a passion for?
▶ What should others know to work comfortably with you?

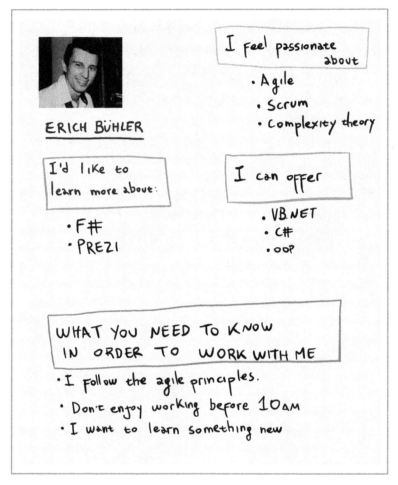

FIGURE 7.8: Sample resume created for the occasion

We asked everyone to temporarily forget about the already-existing teams and to give the new dynamic a chance to work. As they were all Scrum teams, there were already eight Product Owners and one Scrum Master per group.

The eight Scrum Masters and Product Owners were placed in the center of the room and told that the nearly 100 people would have half an hour to talk with them to learn more about the products to be implemented. It was also an opportunity for them to get to know the Product Owners' and Scrum Masters' personalities.

Shortly thereafter, the energy in the room was high and people were enjoying the dynamics. Everyone wanted to know more about the future tasks and discover each other's personality. When the time was up, we asked everyone to paste the previously prepared resumes on a wall, and we presented the two rules of the game. We started the timer and gave them four hours to form new teams.

People remained motionless during the first two or three minutes. The managers observed, worried, and asked themselves what was happening. They decided to stand back and give participants the space they needed to find their own solutions. A few minutes later, to the relief of the managers, everyone started speaking, asking questions and moving throughout the room to learn more about the available skills. Soon, individuals began to recruit and form new groups.

FIGURE 7.9: Participants looking for new team members

Not only did everyone want to know more about their partners' formal skills, but they also wanted to hear about their recent training and preferences. In addition, they sought out the personal and emotional connections that are key to success.

Without management intervening, the teams began to form, making offers to attract the talent they needed.

Forty-five minutes later, something important happened: they discovered that some necessary skills were scarce and that there weren't enough people with specific knowledge for the number of groups that needed to be created. Once again, the managers were concerned and considered intervening. I asked that they be patient. A short time later, they were surprised when explicit *working agreements* were created between teams, indicating how people would be shared and how some would act as coaches without being part of the groups.

Although we had planned the activity for four hours, it only took an hour and a half for the new *Scrum* teams to form. After this, we carried out the first work-cycle planning session (*Sprint Planning*).

Since this activity, the motivation and productivity of these self-organized teams has been surprisingly high. The activity was a success, and I felt confident I wouldn't be losing the month's salary I had waged.

When setting up new teams, the employees didn't consider only formal and informal skills. They also valued factors such as personality, learning approaches, and job expectations. This outcome freed management and saved the company thousands of dollars. It also established crucial habits for self-organization and group commitment. Reducing the Permission-to-learn pattern helped create self-managed teams, while the company learned exponential forms of work.

If your company trains in more-traditional ways, you'll want to learn about Sharon Bowman's six powerful, neuroscience-based principles. The following website will help you change your training habits and reduce the Permission-to-learn pattern: *bowperson.com*

To reiterate, create measurements so people can understand the areas to focus on and what has already improved.

When you create a new procedure, technique, change plan, or other transformation strategy, include informal structures that actively decrease the Permission-to-learn pattern. Below are ideas that could help:

1. Actively eliminate bureaucracy.
2. Support any additional activities, discovered while carrying out regular work, to be resolved collaboratively, without the need for prior authorizations.
3. Have communities of practice that, in addition to training, offer the opportunity for members to make decisions about the future of the products, both technically and strategically.
4. Provide an environment where teams can self-organize around scarce skills.
5. After teaching a new concept, ensure that everyone reflects on what they have learned.
6. Facilitate changes in the culture so people feel safe.
7. Focus on having employees learn while they are working (hands-on learning).

Teams need the autonomy to manage their budgets for formal (or external) courses and training. This could increase everyone's satisfaction and sense of fulfillment.

If you want to create an organization that can adapt quickly to markets, it's essential to decrease the Permission-to-learn pattern.

Enterprise Social Visibility

In the late 1980s, people began to realize that social changes in companies could not be explained without taking into account where their activities took place. In addition, certain behaviors couldn't be easily altered without changing the layout of the office.

Your company might not feel it's a priority to evaluate how physical space affects results, or how the layout of an office can impact the adoption of a change. If this is the case, it would be a good time to introduce ideas to help your company understand why evaluating this aspect is important.

Think about the software teams you consider successful. You'll see that they do not spend most of their time coding in front of a computer, but rather talking among themselves and working collaboratively on new ideas. They are confirming assumptions with clients and learning from each other. This is because activities that require creativity also need a high social component.

In 2001, the Agile mindset and Scrum framework suggested that those who contributed to increased business value for a product (the value stream) should be physically near each other and should communicate primarily face-to-face. Based on this, organizations began to give more importance to the interactions between individuals than to their processes.

But how do you get most of the information in your company? Those around you will likely say that their information comes from emails, chats, telephone conversations, or face-to-face talks. These standard channels have been used for years to communicate with employees and to get feedback from customers. We mustn't forget that people receive a lot of information by sharing space where they can see each other.

It is estimated that over 50% of your conscious information comes from what you see. Each optic cell has over a million nerve fibers. Ten million bits per second are transmitted to the retina and six million reach the brain. Of these, 10,000 are transmitted to the prefrontal cortex, and only 100 reach your conscious mind. It may seem like a small number, but this action is repeated several times per second. In addition, our amygdala can interpret between 2,000 and 4,000 subtle messages from our physical environment each day, without any of it perceived or interpreted by your conscious mind. Therefore, information from our physical environment greatly affects our learning and the decisions we make.

When visual information is scarce, creative activities aren't as productive. Individuals begin to create new behaviors or processes that replace the information they need and don´t have.

Many companies have employees in different geographical areas. In these cases, technology (video, chat, etc.) is used to replicate physical channels of communication. But experience tells us that groups who share the same space have much higher productivity than groups that are separated. Information from Scrum Inc. speaks of a loss of up to 50% of business value when the person acting as the Product Owner of a *Scrum* team is physically located at a separate site.

With distance, we lose channels where a great quantity of information flows. Individuals working remotely do not learn at the same speed, or they do not always fully understand what is happening. The result is diminished transparency and a need to add new processes or reports to make up for the lack of information.

To cultivate behaviors that favor the constant flow of knowledge, Enterprise Social Systems offers a specific component so that people understand what they must take into account when modifying a physical space or working remotely.

Enterprise Social Visibility refers to knowledge that supports the flow of work and is passively captured from the environment. It includes social interactions, information radiators, and the recognition of behaviors and facial expressions.

Enterprise Social Visibility focuses on educating people about where information comes from so they can create more effective plans, processes, or frameworks. Enterprise Social Visibility suggests five areas of action:

1. **Public Information radiators:** Use physical panels (paper, whiteboards, and screens) in public and visible areas, with relevant information for the people who do the work. As much as possible, information recipients should be aware that a board has been updated because of a social behavior. If you are dealing with electronic boards, for example, ensure that alerting others of the change requires a visible social interaction such as having to stand before the public touch screen to modify it.

2. **Visible social interactions:** People should be able to observe the standard social treatment or etiquette of other members; that is, recognize the social protocol of those around you (such as a handshake). This allows everyone to gain knowledge about different situations, even if they do not participate in them.

3. **Recognition of visible facial expressions:** Individuals should be able to observe the facial expressions of others to judge their emotional state, like when there is a conversation between two people at a distance but in the same space.

4. **Visualization of actions and movements for recognition and prediction:** Individuals should be able to observe others when they are performing other tasks (social movement within the office). This causes their brains to establish links (conscious or unconscious) with the people observed, and to store knowledge based on the results of the perceived interactions.

5. **Connection between the value stream and the physical space:** The physical space must represent how value is created for the client. If fifteen people are needed to do the work from the conception of a product to its availability, then the best way for that group to carry out tasks should align with points 1 to 4. If there's a change in how value is created, then the physical space must adapt as quickly as possible to the new value stream.

As you can see, interactions with the physical environment offer data that are constantly made visible, allowing individuals to reach different conclusions and decisions. For example, social knowledge creates links in your mind that can make you react in a certain way.

If you observe your task partner David meeting with a marketing expert who has a skill that's indispensable to your team, you will create a link in your memory that will relate the skills of that expert with David. In the future, if you need to know more about marketing, you would probably talk to David before looking for the expert.

The five key areas of Enterprise Social Visibility provide the foundation for maximizing the flow of knowledge from the environment, and this refers to any improvement process or new framework.

An idea to increase social visibility is to have all participants stand during talks or meetings. By doing this, people will move more and their minds will connect those actions with shared ideas and the environment.

Don't forget that information from the office is filtered by your brain. This means that it will only store what it considers **relevant**. A vision of the change, product, or definition of business value will therefore help minds prioritize what to pay attention to and what to discard.

Try This!

To keep everyone *"on the same page,"* visual facilitation activities can increase Enterprise Social Visibility. Use sticky notes or flipcharts to display drawings or notes, thereby capturing the essence of the ideas that arise during conversations.

Fixed-cadence meetings, or meetings that take place at the same time and place (*Scrum events*), also increase attention and have a positive impact on Enterprise Social Visibility . Here the brain is prepared in advance for what will come.

Tools can increase Enterprise Social Visibility in environments where teams are geographically distributed. Sococo (*www.sococo.com*) is a pioneer in virtually connecting social and spatial environments that produce a constant flow of information.

FIGURE 7.10: Sococo allows the creation of virtual spaces that provide rich social information

No matter where they are, this type of tool helps people observe who they are meeting, social movements and dynamics within the office, daily patterns of movement within the physical space, and cadence. It also allows face-to-face communication, when necessary. This will notably increase Enterprise Social Visibility.

It is worth pointing out that the Boston Consulting Group opted to take these concepts to the next level. In 2017, they opened offices in New York and set about maximizing the impact of the physical environment on the informal connections between people. They designed a workspace that increased interaction among the employees, ensuring these interactions were as unpredictable as possible. The goal was to increase the flow of random information and to ensure that knowledge flowed in all directions within the organization.

The design of the office forced employees to run into each other frequently, increasing the probability of exchanging knowledge informally (Enterprise Social Density) and thereby multiplying knowledge from the physical environment (Enterprise Social Visibility).

To achieve the latter, the firm Humanyze asked volunteer employees to wear sensors and work as normal for a few weeks while the Humanyze team recorded how and where they interacted.

Apart from when and where most of the communications occurred, they also monitored latency, that is, how long employees moved throughout the office without exchanging words with others.

The data collected allowed them to analyze all communication patterns and to know what areas of the office had higher or lower social density.

Next came the magic. Humanyze suggested modifying the layout of the offices to maximize the flow of relevant knowledge. As a result, their design ensured the constant flow of knowledge from the environment, enabling employees to adapt it to their existing ways of working.

The Humanyze design entailed the following:

▸ Flexible and open spaces that allow different uses and styles of work, and that maximize interactions between people.

▸ Large and fully equipped rooms for groups that work together for weeks or months.

▸ Multipurpose areas for social and community events that allow all office employees to get together.

▸ Spaces specifically designed for customers and employees to interact without physical barriers.

▸ Immersion rooms to facilitate the exchange of information in real-time among the participants, with giant screens and controls that enable virtual interaction.

▸ Hexagonal rooms with touch monitors to accelerate the design and incubation of new ideas.

▸ Technologies that allow you to work anywhere, at any time, and observe those who are in the office.

As you can see, Enterprise Social Visibility enables the flow of knowledge from social interactions and supports any change plan. The following are recommendations for increasing Enterprise Social Visibility:

1. Use information radiators (boards, *Kanban*, etc.) in public areas to share relevant data; alternatively, find other ways to share information—anything that attracts the attention of value network members.

2. Have employees who create value sit together as much as possible.

3. Ensure that the environment supports the product or change vision and how value is produced for the customer.

4. Organize events or meetings with fixed cadence, which prepares minds and increases predictability.

5. Ensure that physical space *forces* employees to walk by each other frequently but also allows them to maintain privacy, if preferred.
6. Promote a culture where people feel safe and can express themselves freely.
7. Keep in mind that bureaucracy and complication are increased if activities with high Enterprise Social Visibility are replaced with activities that generate less social information.

If a company executive wants to know how an organization with high Enterprise Social Visibility works, organize a visit to another company that excels in this area. This will provide the curious executive with more information than you could by explaining the concepts.

Remember to ensure that there's at least one simple way to measure the improvement of Enterprise Social Visibility in you company.

The Complexity and Complication Pattern

You have probably visited a place where everything seemed too complicated. If so, you're not alone.

It isn't only a company's processes or the steps for performing a task that are complicated. The techniques that our brain uses to solve a problem can also increase complication.

Say you face an unknown event. Your brain will instinctively want to control what is happening and simultaneously justify the actions or steps you use to solve the problem. It will attempt, by all means possible, to establish processes that order your surroundings, making what happens next more predictable. Consider how this human predisposition might condition the way your company works.

Suppose that abrupt changes are affecting your company. A new player has appeared in the market offering products with higher quality or more features than the ones you offer. Because of this unexpected disruption, you'll experience a period of uncertainty during which your company will face two new conditions, or *corporate requirements*, that must be met if your company wants to survive:

1. Your products must be of higher quality.
2. You must offer characteristics that are equal or superior to the competition.

Traditional organizations will usually respond to external changes by increasing levels of complication. You might be wondering, *What exactly is complication?*

Complication is the increase of processes, strategies, rules, coordination, approval forms, roles, and procedures to solve a problem. With such actions, these companies think they'll be able to control what happens around them and ensure that what happens next remains predictable. This is a *standard* response for which we are normally *wired*.

Going back over a century, many traditional organizational theories indicate that adding structures and processes will have a direct and predictable impact on the positive performance of a company.

If you look at how your brain works, you will see that it is biologically predisposed to seek comfort. When something changes abruptly, the brain tries to add steps, processes, or structures that give it comfort.

While this might seem sensible, experience tells us that the practice of adding processes in response to new corporate requirements can be counterproductive in the era of exponential market acceleration.

Logically, stacking one procedure over another, when many of these are contradictory, will only cause procedures to further multiply, adding more obstacles.

Don't confuse the complexity and complication concepts used to solve problems (you can refer back to Chapter 2). The definition used here represents the response to corporate requirements.

Here's an example I experienced firsthand. Albert was a Product Owner in a company that used Scrum. He wanted more time for executive tasks unrelated to the Scrum team. To reduce his workload, the company assigned Christian, a functional analyst. Every day, they would meet and decide who would be responsible for what tasks, and at the end of the day they would meet face-to-face for an update.

During the first weeks, everything seemed to work fine, and Albert had more free time. But then something happened. They gradually began increasing their interactions to clarify situations that occurred at different times of the day. When Albert was not available, Christian tried to make the decisions or communicate his personal perspective.

This led to misunderstandings, and both decided to add a couple of meetings each day as well as rules to dictate how to act in different cases. In addition to establishing new guidelines, they had intensified their interactions to meet the same number of needs they previously had. In the end, everyone was busier, and nobody knew why. They had fallen into the trap of complication!

As you can see, complication comes in different shapes and colors. More processes, more structures, or the unnecessary multiplication of interactions were required to respond to the same corporate requirements. This increased the complication index.

If things become more complicated, you will have less capacity for adaptation and innovation. With added complication, your product or service will also be more expensive to produce. In other words, the value you offer the customer will be lower.

But don't think that having structures isn't important! Keep in mind that **solutions should be based on keeping levels of complication low.** To achieve this, there are different recommendations at different levels of the organization.

The problem is not the corporate requirements but rather the way in which the company deals with them. It is impossible to have enough structures, plans, rules, or processes for solving the problems of an exponential company. For that reason, the answer lies in simplifying everything so that adapting becomes easier.

We previously covered implementing positive collaborations and increasing the flow of knowledge throughout the company. We also saw how to create work environments that radiate information. For all of this to work better, it's essential that the company reduces levels of complication.

The Boston Consulting Group has been investigating this for several years through its *complexity and complication index*. They have surveyed over one hundred Fortune 500 companies from the United States and Europe, their objective being to understand why many organizations have low productivity despite being well aligned and possessing excellent technology tools.

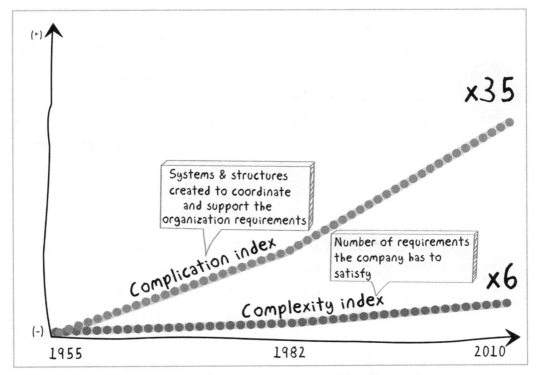

**FIGURE 7.11: The response to complexity according
to the Boston Consulting Group**

According to the Boston Consulting Group, complicatedness or complication entails the processes, structures, and approval chains for satisfying a corporate requirement (complexity). This has increased between 50% and 350% in the last fifteen years. When spread across the last five decades, the result is an annual increase of 6.7%.

If in 1955 you required one process to satisfy a corporate requirement, today you would have to establish 5.8 processes (35/6). The Boston Consulting Group indicates that a manager in an organization with high complication spends 40% of the time writing reports and 30% to 60% of the time coordinating jobs.

Such high complication attitudes can also exist in large corporations embarking on long business transformations. Levels of bureaucracy and processes are already extremely heavy, and trying to add a new methodology or framework will further increase levels of complication. In turn, this will make employees less happy, and they might choose to abandon the initiative and return to their previous forms of work.

Enterprise Social Systems clearly identifies the complication trap with the complexity and complication pattern so that people can be aware of this when creating a new plan, technique, or framework.

The **Complexity and Complication pattern** entails behaviors that increase complication (number of procedures, rules, bureaucracy, vertical layers, and coordination teams) to satisfy a corporate requirement (quality, price, performance, and time-to-market).

Here are some ideas for decreasing complication rates in your company:

1. Use face-to-face communication as much as possible. In addition, any technique that contributes to increasing Enterprise Social Density will generally help reduce complication.

2. Try not to create new roles or departments when you have a new organizational requirement. Use cloud tools to simplify your IT architecture, automate the need as much as possible or use artificial intelligence and robots. When the latter is not possible, have an existing team take care of the requirement instead of creating new structures or processes to solve the problem.

3. If a few employees regularly break a company standard, do not add new rules or processes to control them. Look for creative solutions that do not increase bureaucracy.

4. In any new plan or initiative, ensure that managers do not focus on managing people but focus instead on actively removing obstacles from the system (organization, team, etc.).

5. Keep in mind that products with low or fluctuating quality increase complication.

6. Ensure that people are not multitasking. How can you ensure that this does not happen during a new plan, process, or change initiative?

7. Have frontline employees, those in contact with the client, make their own decisions and bear the responsibility for their decisions. They should be able to make small adjustments to processes without having to ask management.

8. Keep in mind that complication increases in meetings that require a final decision but end without consensus. Begin to build group consensus before the meeting so you can arrive at a decision by the end of the meeting.

9. If you are scaling up a process, methodology, or framework, ensure that the teams involved have lower levels of complication (low bureaucracy, metrics, rules, etc.).

10. People who work over 80% or 90% of their ability increase blockades and the need for coordination. Therefore, they also increase complication.

11. Let teams self-organize instead of controlling and coordinating them. This will reduce complication to a minimum and stimulate collaborative intelligence.

12. At all levels of the company, ensure you have people who are exclusively responsible for removing obstacles. If you are creating a change plan, consider including this role from the very beginning.

13. Ensure that individuals feel safe in their work environment and that there is high visibility for where the organization is heading.

14. For any change plan, use frequent reflection sessions (retrospective) to improve processes and human interactions, remove blockades, and provide feedback to the company.

15. Reduce knowledge silos in teams. This can be done using techniques such as pairing sessions.

Now that you know about complexity and complication, go back to Chapter 3 and reread my friend Peter's story on decreasing complication.

Enterprise Social Systems in Action

The nature of complexity makes it difficult for a single person to find the best practice or technique to solve a problem. The best results are the product of collaborative work.

To maximize the impact on the four pillars of the organization, Enterprise Social Systems simultaneously uses the five components as part of a specific game. This adds new types of reasoning to your company and enhance the employees thinking skills. It also improves interpersonal and social skills.

When people are part of a game, they enter a *parallel* reality or *play time* maintained from the beginning to the end of the game. During this, people don't require permission and they can use different rules than those normally used in the organization.

To do this, you must clearly state the rules and establish the start and end of the game. This way, people will feel safe and be more receptive when they experience new concepts or ways of thinking.

To perform this game, you need several tables that can each comfortably accommodate five to six people. There should also be enough sticky notes and pens for all. The duration of the game will depend on the problems you wish to analyze. In my experience, you'll need at least ninety minutes.

At the beginning of the game, ask participants to use sticky notes to write the problems they want to solve or that they believe have not been solved properly. Explain to them that these problems should be as specific as possible, since the idea is to find specific actions that can be used when the game is over.

Provide three minutes for the teams to write one or two problems they are facing and place their notes in the center of the table. Then explain that each group will have fifteen minutes to select one of the problems and collectively create a plan with the necessary steps for solving the problem.

The steps for solving the problem should be as detailed as possible. The objective isn't to implement the solutions later but to compare the results of the current forms of reasoning to those that will be produced with the new techniques. Once time is up, give each team two minutes to share their solutions with the rest of the participants.

Next, deliver a different sheet of paper to each member of the team. On it will be the name of their new role, an explanation, and examples:

▶ An expert in reducing Enterprise Blocking Collaboration.
▶ An expert in increasing Enterprise Social Density.
▶ An expert in increasing Enterprise Social Visibility.
▶ An expert in reducing the complexity and complication pattern.
▶ An expert in decreasing the Permission-to-learn pattern.
▶ Optional: a facilitator to inspire and encourage conversations among members.

Each person will become an expert in a particular area, and any plan created from that point on should follow the recommendations of the experts at the table.

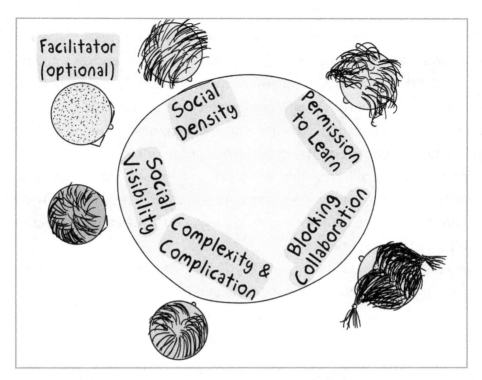

FIGURE 7.12: A team using Enterprise Social Systems roles

Ask each person to read the description of their role in three minutes. They should each then look for an individual from another team with the same role. They will have ten minutes to exchange ideas and clarify how experts in that area think. This will not only allow them to abandon doubts, but it will also enable them to help each other and establish a clear sense of community.

Use the Enterprise Social Systems game for people to safely experiment with new ways of thinking. You can download the description of each role at *Innova1st.com/ess*

Back to the teams, members will have thirty minutes to analyze the previously created plans using the new perspectives. For example, the person in charge of the Permission-to-learn pattern should make suggestions so the new plan improves in that area. If the person is an expert in Enterprise Social Visibility, the person should ensure that the execution of any plan includes specific recommendations about the layout of the office.

The new forms of interaction will result in different conclusions, and this will make it easier for everyone to compare the differences between the initial plan and the new one. The result should be powerful plans that impact on the four pillars of the organization.

Remember to modify the game as you consider necessary and thank the participants for their collaboration at the end of the game.

What You Have Learned

- ☑ The differences between Agile and Business Agility.
- ☑ The differences between the types of thinking of the traditional company (linear) and the exponential company.
- ☑ The effects of working in pairs.
- ☑ The meaning of the attraction of tools.
- ☑ The four pillars of the organization.
- ☑ The five components of Enterprise Social Systems and how they work.

1. Do you remember the differences between Agile and Business Agility?

2. Which pillar is considered most important when creating a change plan in your company?

3. How could you magnify the impact of a change using the four pillars?

4. In what specific way can the five components of Enterprise Social Systems help you change how people think in your company?

ESS (II): The ELSA and DeLTA Frameworks

CHAPTER 8

> "The limits of my language are the limits of my world."

Ludwig Wittgenstein, Philosopher

In Chapter 6, I explained how to make a change in the company using a transformation team. We will now embark in another direction and examine the ELSA and DeLTA change frameworks.

You can't always count on a transformation team or gain access to the leaders of the company, and you might not have a clear sponsor for the initiative. Many people prefer to postpone the implementation of a change plan until they are in a more favorable situation, but this isn't a suitable alternative in our fast-paced world.

Some choose to wait until the perfect leader can help initiate the change. In this case, I suggest that the following are the characteristics perfect leaders should have to be truly effective:

1. Leads by example and inspires.
2. Makes time for others.
3. Generates empathy and is transparent with their thoughts.
4. Maintains focus during difficult times.
5. Inspires confidence with their actions and words, and shows passion for their work.
6. Identifies logical connections between proposals.
7. Draws correct and well-informed conclusions about necessary actions (corrective and for the good of the company).

8. Distinguishes between what's complex and what's complicated.
9. Identifies relevant data and converts it into useful information.
10. Recognizes unproven assumptions, beliefs, and values, and challenges them when necessary.

Over the past thirty years of my career, I have NEVER seen anyone who meets all ten characteristics. And if this individual does exist, the person is probably not from this world. *Do you remember the* **six principles to start changing your world** *from Chapter 2?*

> *It is always a good time to make a change. (Another person's delay is not an excuse to wait!)*

You might ask how you can transform an idea into a tangible reality without having the necessary conditions in place. As will be explained, Enterprise Social Systems can help you achieve a great transformation using either of its two powerful change frameworks.

ELSA (Event, Language, Structures, Agency)

ELSA is a change framework that allows leaders of an initiative to amplify their message, helping the transformation become exponential. It allows people who are about to change to take ownership of new ideas to accelerate change and thereby support the transformation in becoming exponential. ELSA requires a sponsor and it also requires the leaders of the organization to support the initiative.

DeLTA (Double Loop for Transforming & Accelerating)

DeLTA is a change framework that allows *anyone* in the company to implement a change initiative that can become contagious. It's designed for situations in which the leaders of the company are not yet committed to the new plan or for situations when there is no sponsor.

As you'll see, each framework offers different possibilities. ELSA uses *shortcuts* in the brain to accelerate the speed of transformation, while DeLTA supports change and makes it contagious by using habits that already exist in traditional companies.

Although DeLTA does not accelerate the adoption of change as much as ELSA, it is a useful tool when key individuals are not yet involved in the initiative.

The ELSA Change Framework

Imagine your organization has decided to embark on a business transformation. The leaders are willing to do whatever is necessary, and the sponsor is eager to begin. The company is poised to make the biggest economic investment in its history. Both the leaders and the sponsor are aware that this is a big first step and that in a few months *changing* will be part of the day-to-day operation of the organization.

What are the first steps?

In a company that implements a change using traditional techniques, executive team members will often give a presentation informing their employees about the new plan, followed by training the employees and implementing the changes in their processes. But if you are starting an *Agile* transformation, you will probably start by teaching new values and principles, and then you will implement a framework that improves how everyone works and makes decisions.

Agile transformations don't always turn out as expected. In these cases, companies often want to *restart* the initiative after learning from past mistakes.

In your company, though, this is the first time that something like this has been attempted. Executives will want to increase the economic benefits and position of the company in the market in the medium term. They will also want to increase and improve the shared knowledge and well-being of employees. To achieve these goals, you will use the ELSA change framework.

You won't start by modifying processes or teaching new mindsets. ELSA believes that ways of conveying a message can alter employees' brain activation, which means that they could use different forms of reasoning and produce different outcomes. This, in turn, will also help evolve processes and interactions for the better.

There are a few questions to consider here:

1. Is there a connection between language and the way we think or behave? More specifically, is there a connection between language and the company's objectives?
2. Does the way you use language affect economic decisions?

Keith Chen, an associate professor of economics at UCLA, used a vast array of data and meticulous analysis to show that the grammatical structures of languages stimulate the brain differently, resulting in behaviors that support different economic decisions.

Languages that conjugate in the future tense, such as English and Spanish, distinguish between past, present, and future. But those that do not, such as Mandarin Chinese, use similar phrases to describe the events of yesterday, today, and tomorrow.

According to Chen, people who use languages without a future tense are 30% more likely to save money than those who use the future tense. This would obviously mean more money for retirement, less stress, and increased opportunities for undertaking new personal projects. When a future tense is used, ideas feel more distant and the motivation to save is diminished. Our brain focuses more on the short-term reward and less on the long term.

The way you use a language also has an impact on the skills you develop. The Pormpuraaw aboriginal community in Australia do not use the words *left* or *right* to refer to the position of an object. Instead, they use absolute directions such as north, south, or southeast to express location in their Kuuk Thaayorre language.

According to a study conducted by Lera Boroditsky, a cognitive scientist at Stanford University, and Caitlin M. Fausey, a professor of cognitive development at the University of Oregon, the Pormpuraaw community is remarkably good at staying focused and knowing where they are. On a research trip to Australia, Boroditsky and Fausey discovered that members of this community seem to instinctively know their spatial location and the direction they're facing. They can organize images of their trip, in chronological order, from east to west.

Boroditsky and Fausey also realized that there are differences in how guilt is felt in different languages. According to their research, if a person who speaks Spanish accidentally breaks something, the person will tend to say, "*Se me cayó <object>.*" This translates roughly to a passive expression such as, "*To me, it happened that <the object> fell.*"

But in English; the person who commits an action is generally named first: "*I dropped <the object>.*" According to the researchers, this grammatical usage points out why English speakers might more easily remember the person who commits an error (or who is to blame) than those who speak more "*passive*" languages, such as Spanish or Japanese. Additionally, when you hear a story from someone else, your neurons are fired in the same patterns as the speaker's brain. This is known as **neural coupling** and it creates a very strong connection between the speaker's brain and recipient's brain.

You can read about Caitlin M. Fausey and Lera Boroditsky's research at the following address: *en.innova1st.com/80A*

I'm not saying you should start making all important announcements using the present tense, or that you should refer to left and right as north or south, or use Chinese during meetings. We should simply understand that small changes in how we communicate can alter the way people reason and learn.

Remember how I suggested that you should change the term "*product requirement*" to "*product hypothesis*"? Since we are talking about how language can change the way we reason, it would be helpful to delve into the science behind this idea. Look at the following example:

Requirement: The sales cars screen in the SALESAPP should use a font 0.25 points larger so it is easier to read.

Hypothesis: If the sales cars screen in the SALESAPP used by the sales department uses a font 0.25 points larger, the fifteen members of that department should be able to read the data correctly.

In this example, the first sentence, the requirement, ensures that a specific action will solve the problem, while the second sentence forces us to get more information and to presume a result. This second approach increases learning, because people will know if the problem has been solved only after it is verified: that by increasing the font size, fifteen people can read the screen correctly.

Here a hypothesis means that you have a problem to be solved, and this will generally involve many people. In a perfect world, we would all understand each other at a glance and nothing could create confusion among us. But in the real world, we have to come up with ways to communicate our ideas so we are not misunderstood.

You can use many approaches and different notations to write better hypotheses and to ensure that everyone is *on the same page*. Although this topic is beyond the scope of this book, you'll be able to find many articles on it by searching for *"Acceptance Criteria," "ATDD," or "BDD."*

If you want to influence people's habits, you can convey a message in a way that makes this happen. I'll explain with a game a friend showed me in Europe.

Grab a pen and paper and write a number from 1 through 9, and then multiply it by 9. If your answer is a single digit, keep that number, but if your result is a two-digit number (for example, 24), add the two digits together (2 + 4) to get a single-digit number (6).

Next, subtract 5 from the number (<your number> - 5) and write down the result. Find the letter of the alphabet that corresponds to that number (for example, for 1 it would be A, for 3 it would be C).

Next, think of the name of a country that starts with that letter and write it down. Then choose the next letter of the alphabet (if you chose A before, you would now choose B) and think of an animal that begins with that letter. Write this down as well. Now go to the very end of the chapter (last review question) and see if I have guessed your answers.

How is this possible? I'm no fortune teller. I'm just using a phenomenon that in psychology is known as *priming*. Although there are more countries with the letter you chose, the fact that I mentioned Europe earlier made your brain choose what was most at hand, or what was more easily accessible in your memory.

Regarding the animal, you chose it because at school they taught it to you next to that letter, or because it's a very large animal that attracts a lot of attention. Clearly, this animal is foremost in your mind.

Do you remember how in previous chapters I mentioned that we use many thought processes we learned when we were children? Now you know it's true.

One way to activate the effects of priming is with language. Our brains react to priming even when we are unaware that someone is using it on us. If I ask you to think about the color yellow and then about a fruit, most likely a lemon or a banana will come to mind. Do you see how connections can help us get a particular outcome? Later I'll show you how to use this technique in your company.

Another curiosity is the so-called *Florida effect*, named after John A. Bargh's 1996 experiment. During a session, groups were shown random words and asked to form sentences with these words. One team was shown words related to old age: *wrinkles*, *baldness*, etc.

When the experiment was over, the pace at which participants walked was measured. To the researchers' surprise, participants primed with words related to the elderly were walking more slowly. This was true even though no word related to speed had been included.

The effects of priming can be long lasting, and they are reaffirmed when stimuli of the same sensory modality are used at the same time. That means that visual primacy works better with visual cues, and verbal primacy works better with verbal cues.

At one company, I suggested that a wall by the software development teams change color using a directed light that would vary based on how close they were to the end of their two-week work cycle. The first week, the wall was lit green. For part of the second week, it was yellow, and the last two days of that week it was red.

Like magic, the colors helped team members remember the tasks that had to be completed or had to be started immediately. If the wall was red, they'd automatically check if the product documentation was finished and they'd start the logistics for the Sprint Review meeting—all without realizing they were being primed.

But priming can also occur between different sensory modalities. In 2008, Yale University conducted an experiment in which subjects shared a room with a stranger. The participants were asked to hold their cup of hot or iced coffee and later read the profile of the stranger to assess their characteristics.

Even though every participant read an identical profile, those who held a cup of hot coffee defined the stranger as warm and open, while those who held the cup of iced coffee stated the person was cold, selfish, and competitive.

You can read more about the Yale University research here: *en.innova1st.com/81B*

As you can see, how a message is given and the environment in which it is given condition what is perceived by others as reality. We need to be aware of this as we prepare to use the ELSA change framework.

ELSA and the Perfect Event

Imagine a perfect day in your workplace, a day when that change you have in mind is already underway. People have fallen in love with your idea and they are inspired by what's happening.

What behaviors do you see in that vision? What's happening? What are people saying? What makes them happy? What inspires them? Now close your eyes and use your five senses to envision that scene again.

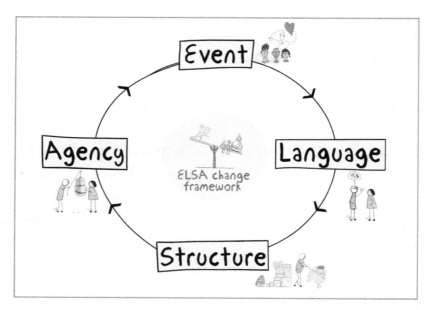

FIGURE 8.1: The four steps of the ELSA change framework

The ELSA change framework focuses on picturing that perfect day (**event**) before making any change in the organization. This crucial element distinguishes it from other change frameworks.

Many companies solve one problem after another until they gradually reach the ideal situation. But doing so prevents them from experiencing the entire **future event** in the present, because they are unable to visualize the change in its totality. This limits the solutions and the actions taken. Everyone's energy is focused on solving the next problem, impeding them from fully using their senses during the implementation of the plan.

Visualizing and feeling an **event** as **an ideal day** allows you to connect that experience with powerful and inspiring phrases, associate words with good memories (priming), and discover new emotions.

Many find it difficult to let their imagination fly to visualize that ideal day. Pixar Animation Studios, the creators of movies such as *Toy Story* and *Cars*, believes that we are all capable of using our imagination to find more creative solutions. It just takes a little practice.

As a sponsor or leader of the initiative, you and the others will be the main characters of the movie featuring that *perfect day*. You must be able to picture the future event as a series of short stories that connect emotions with what matters to those who should change.

Perhaps you feel that the first story that comes to mind isn't powerful enough to motivate those around you. It's true that imagining really good stories requires preparation and practice.

Pixar, for example, uses an iterative approach to its films. Stories and characters are reinvented several times before they reach the screen. This iterative approach not only supports creativity and imagination, but it also helps people improve how they transmit a message.

You should also imagine that perfect day in different ways, and you should use different perspectives. Movie creators at Pixar ask an initial question that might also help you imagine that perfect day. They simply ask, *What if?*

This question supports creativity and imagination, and it strengthens the desire to experience different types of stories and emotions.

Here are some examples:

▷ What if on that ideal day every team were multifunctional and everyone enjoyed their daily tasks?
▷ What if on that ideal day a change was seen as a learning opportunity?
▷ What if on that ideal day the customers enjoyed visiting and interacting with the new products or services?

This practice not only helps to create the initial story, but it also allows us to start looking for the right approach to connect people with the perfect day.

Once you can visualize and feel the event, you are ready to take the second step: to start creating the right **language** to support what you have envisioned.

It doesn't matter where you are—we are surrounded by things that inspire and make us dream: words, stories, and emotions that are impactful and that the people you want to change will enjoy hearing. Remember that powerful stories are conveyed with specific, relevant information (numbers, analogies, etc.) that inspire people and connect them with a shared positive purpose.

You can prime people by sharing stories about something pleasant that has happened in the company. You can also use near-present time and words that begin to shape that ideal situation. Now think about how you communicate your messages. *What changes should you make for your message to be more powerful?*

Visit the following address to learn more about how to tell powerful stories with Pixar's online course *"The Art of Storytelling"* at *en.Innova1st.com/82C*

Once comfortable, you can start sharing your message through **informal** channels so that it's received quickly.

Support yourself with people who are fully trusted by the recipients of the change or who are respected within the company. To do this, you'll have to ensure you have the right conditions (**structures**) so that communication flows informally among people. It may be necessary to create a more informal workplace so that people can meet face-to-face about the upcoming change. At some companies, it might be a matter of setting up an area for people to talk. At another, it could entail reducing the workload and giving workers some downtime.

You must identify the structures and small changes that are necessary in your company so that people want to talk informally and spread the new language and powerful stories. Every place is different, and you will need to reflect with others on what's most needed.

Finally, you'll have to make sure that changes in the company structures are not made solely by management, but that employees also have explicit permission (**Agency**) to take over and improve them. When trying out new ideas or ways of working to achieve that ideal day, employees should feel safe, even if they fail.

As you can see, ELSA works in a way that is contrary to other change frameworks: it starts by envisioning an **ideal day,** leading us to employ adequate language to provoke a change instead of first modifying processes or rules.

The language used must inspire and open the path for change. You may also need to make small changes in the office layout to encourage informal conversations. Keep in mind that ELSA is not only useful for applying small alterations in your company. It's also a powerful tool that enables any future states to be achieved progressively, little by little.

To this end, ELSA makes change plans collaborative and uses informal communication channels. ELSA positively stimulates minds, makes people take ownership of the change, allows for greater collective intelligence, and enables people to reach different conclusions and solutions. Following are ten initial recommendations for using the ELSA change framework. You and those around you should expand this list:

1. Always start by imagining that **ideal event**, and use your five senses (sight, hearing, touch, smell, and taste).
2. Use **words** that are **meaningful** (and inspire) from the point of view of those who must change, and include powerful stories that involve the five senses. Also use phrases or words that encourage learning.
3. **Prime** your audience during the message. If positive events took place and people associate certain words with those events, include them.
4. **Deliver** the **same message** in at least ten different ways, through stories and phrases, using different variations every day. Repeat the message as often as you can.
5. Make **discreet changes** to the physical environment so that it supports the informal exchange of messages.
6. Maintain **consistency** between what you say and what you do.
7. Ensure **high Enterprise Social Density** so that the message can reach all corners of the company, or wherever you want it to.
8. Spread the message among **people** who are **trusted** by those who are willing to change.
9. Ensure that everyone involved feels **safe** about **experimenting** with the new concepts, and that the company supports them at all times (even if they fail).
10. Once ELSA is used, **get feedback**, **improve**, and **repeat**.

The biggest difference between ELSA and other change frameworks is that you start here by making a change without making any physical alterations. ELSA focuses on modifying the way language is used and enabling the conditions for future change to happen. This is contrary to other frameworks, where you start altering behaviors, processes or roles. This makes the initial resistance lower, and that people more naturally want to change their ways of doing things.

The DeLTA Change Framework

You can't always count on the support of the company's leaders or have a sponsor for the change initiative from the beginning. In my experience, this is often the case in more-traditional companies, where the *simple loop decision* is normally used, or in places where there is little experience in running a business transformation.

If you face this type of situation, you could wait for the ideal moment, but your company could end up missing out on market opportunities. The DeLTA change framework offers a viable alternative to accelerate the adoption of change.

DeLTA's Eight Habits

More-traditional companies have many habits, structures, and processes in their DNA. These are meant to align people with clear objectives and to standardize actions.

Using these mechanisms in its favor, DeLTA focuses on gradually improving preexisting habits that help to make the change contagious.

The idea is to achieve a small improvement as quickly as possible in one of the eight DeLTA habits, and then move on to the next one. The progress in each area reaffirms the change, increasing its traction and impact.

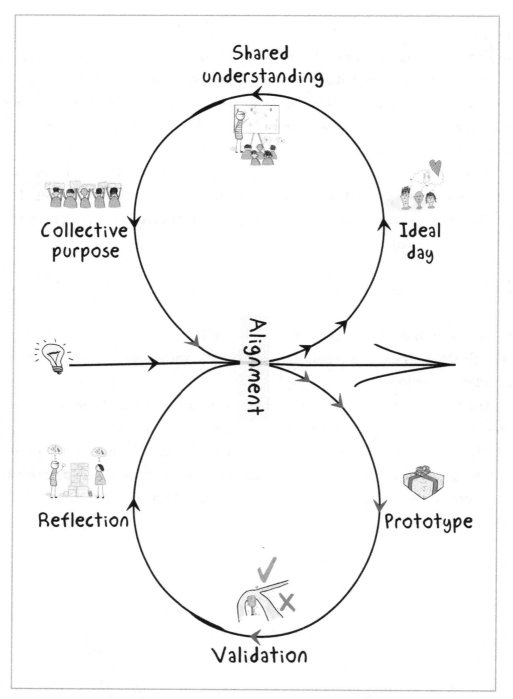

FIGURE 8.2: The DeLTA framework and the eight habits to improve

Keep in mind that DeLTA indicates only *WHAT* will have to be perfected, but not *HOW* to do it. Therefore, you and the others involved must choose how to improve the company using already-existing processes and forms of work.

DeLTA is not a prescriptive change framework, and it doesn't recommend a set of practices or processes for change. However, you can use many of the techniques you've learned in this book to achieve improvements, little by little, in each of the eight habits that DeLTA seeks to improve.

Habit	Expected improvement
Alignment	People ask more questions about problems they are experiencing and to reinforce habits that help them relate problems to those others are having.
Envisioning the ideal day	Individuals feel comfortable envisioning an *ideal day*. They can routinely use techniques to visualize that perfect day using their five senses.
Creating a shared understanding	People provide feedback to others in the company using the outputs from envisioning an ideal day, so they can easily share fears, barriers, or doubts.
Building a collective purpose	Collective behaviors help people feel they are part of a common good or initiative. This can include a collaborative creation of a vision of change, work agreements, or common goals.
Alignment (II)	People self-organize to create the conditions for the ideal day to become a reality. They should feel at ease with the new forms of work, new roles, necessary learning (decreasing the permission-to-learn pattern). They should feel comfortable making changes in the organization and establishing a start date for a change initiative.
Prototype (plan)	Employees develop habits that allow them to execute a plan without having to wait for others.

Habit	Expected improvement
Validation	People improve behaviors that help collectively understand the outcomes from a prototype. This can include positive conversations about what was meant to be achieved and what was finally achieved.
Reflection	People can share and reflect on what has been achieved and feel comfortable proposing changes in personal interactions, processes, the company, or anything else necessary for the success of the plan. And . . . start over again.

Table 8.1: The eight habits to improve with DeLTA

Imagine you want to make it easier for twenty-five people to use **three new practices** and to **automate a process** to replace a skill that is scarce in your company. The desired outcome is that the organization improves the quality of its products and number of releases to the market.

In a more-traditional company, management might set the date to start using new techniques or processes. While this is a quick and straightforward solution, it might result in people not feeling part of the initiative, showing little interest in improving the processes, lacking motivation to seek solutions, or pursuing habits that are not sustainable.

The DeLTA change framework suggests progressively improving eight specific habits and starting with better **alignment** habits.

Traditional companies already have structures and behaviors to support alignment (meetings and other activities). You can use these to your advantage. As a result, people will be exposed to situations they already know, and they will feel more comfortable and offer less resistance to change.

Going back to the previous example, with DeLTA you will provide twenty-five people from different teams with the time to **align** themselves with respect to the problem they are experiencing (everyone should understand the issue and any similarity it has with the difficulties experienced by others).

The expectation is that they will collectively discover the root cause of the problem. To achieve this improvement in alignment, you may need to organize one or several meetings, dynamics, and activities that are already common practice in your company.

As mentioned, your objective is to obtain a small improvement in this behavior and then move quickly to the next behavior of the change framework.

Once you've made progress in alignment habits, DeLTA suggests that you move to the next one, which is to encourage people to imagine what an **ideal day** would look like—you might have to remind the team that this means a day *without the problem in question*, and not a day of vacation.

Participants must let their imaginations fly so they can visualize how their team would work in an ideal situation, free of all obstacles. Imagining that perfect day makes it possible to use the senses, provide new ideas and points of view, and begin to feel its benefits. But it isn't yet time to present the final solution.

People should begin feeling comfortable incorporating habits of imagining that perfect day, and they should spontaneously provide their coworkers with feedback and points of view that weren't initially evaluated. As before, how you integrate this depends on the mechanisms that already exist in your company.

Next, DeLTA suggests that we focus on those habits related to creating a **shared understanding**, which is crucial to the success of the change initiative. The primary focus is on participants improving their habits when they provide feedback related to the company's ideal day. The goal is that they feel comfortable asking the organization to include their ideas in the initial plan, and that they can raise any doubts about barriers, their fears, uncertainty, or anything that will help them feel more comfortable.

As before, use tools and processes that are already present in your company to push this forward.

Once everyone is comfortable offering ideas on how to reach that ideal day, it's time to encourage habits to **build a collective purpose**, such as creating a vision of change, constructing explicit working agreements, defining common goals, and any other mechanism that helps set a shared goal.

At this point, people often start talking about specific metrics and common goals, as well as about removing initial obstacles.

The DeLTA loops back around to the center, **Alignment (II)**. This time, the objective is for participants to improve habits that allow them to quickly establish conditions for successfully executing a plan. Participants should usually be able to self-organize around the implementation of the change, deciding, for example, what learning is needed and the start date of the experiment or prototype.

Remember that every plan is only a hypothesis until it meets reality. The main premise here has been that the **three new practices** and the **automation** of a scarce resource will help improve the quality and speed of delivery of a product to the market.

Certainly, the initial plan could have been altered with employee feedback, but for simplicity, we'll consider that the plan remains unchanged.

You may have noticed that the **upper half** (Ideal Day, Shared Understanding, Collective Purpose) of the DeLTA loop focuses on **improving** habits or behaviors that prepare minds to maximize collaboration in preparation for a change. The **lower half** (prototype, validation, and reflection) focuses on improving the habits needed for its **execution**.

The first step of the lower loop, **prototype**, focuses on improving interactions or habits so that teams can comfortably start a short plan to test a hypothesis. The goal is for people to feel safe and at ease during the execution stage. To accomplish this, people need to implement the three practices and automate a process for a few days to examine the positive effects in the company.

I recommend that the execution of the pilot test last for a short, fixed timeframe, and that simple metrics be used to validate results.

At the end of the set time, those habits that help people **validate** and collectively understand the results of the plan's execution should be improved.

> It's so much easier to suggest solutions when you don't know too much about the problem.

Malcolm Forbes, Businessman

Finally, teams should focus on improving behaviors that help them **reflect** on their current ways of work. They should be able to progressively propose changes in their interactions, habits, processes, company structures, or anything else needed for the success of the plan.

The loop starts over again, at **alignment**. This means that you either continue in the direction initially intended, change course, or expand the solution to the rest of the company.

As you can see, DeLTA repeats itself over and over again and tries, with each complete cycle, to continuously make small improvements in habits, processes, and company structures to progress positively toward a better organization. DeLTA's main advantage is that it allows you to use preexisting forms of work and structures and to progressively modify areas so that the **change** becomes **contagious**.

What You Have Learned

☑   How language affects the way people reason.
☑   The effects of priming.
☑   How to imagine a perfect day can help you look for new solutions.
☑   The ELSA change framework.
☑   Ten recommendations for using ELSA.
☑   The DeLTA change framework and the eight habits to be improved.

1.   What techniques of the ELSA change framework could you use in your organization?

_____

_____

_____

2.   Is there any phrase or word that can positively alter the behaviors of those around you?

_____

_____

_____

3.   Is there any habit that DeLTA suggests and that needs to be improved in your organization?

_____

_____

_____

4.   Have you answered "Denmark" and "Elephant"?

_____

_____

_____

Thank You for Taking the Journey

I've always believed that leaders make themselves, and that they deliberately decide to become agents of change. We can all develop the skills to help others find the best solutions and offer clarity in times of turbulence. I hope you now have a better understanding of how human beings react to exponential change in companies. I also hope you feel that you have new tools to help individuals on their journey of self-improvement. I sincerely expect that you will begin to take the steps that give shape and meaning to your world, and that these steps lead you to new, positive experiences.

I invite you to share your experiences and success stories. Write me about the techniques you have learned by reading this book and how they have helped you and your company improve. I also welcome any suggestions on how to make this book better. Please, don't forget to rate this book on Amazon or Barnes and Noble.

If you have enjoyed and found value in reading *Leading Exponential Change*, please send me a photo of yourself holding your copy of the book and tell me what you found most interesting and most helpful in your day-to-day work.

I wish you the best in the forthcoming *exponential* months!

Erich R. Bühler
CEO Innova1st Consulting
Erichbuhler@innova1st.com
Twitter: @Erichbuhler

CPSIA information can be obtained
at www.ICGtesting.com
Printed in the USA
BVHW011159201220
596127BV00011B/218